THE ENCYCLOPEDIA OF THE WORLD'S MYSTICAL AND SACRED SITES

Also by John and Anne Spencer

Mysteries and Magic
Powers of the Mind
The Ghost Handbook
Alien Contact
Fifty Years of UFOs
The Poltergeist Phenomenon
The Encyclopedia of the World's Greatest Unsolved Mysteries
Spirit Within Her
The Encyclopedia of Ghosts and Spirits
The Encyclopedia of Ghosts and Spirits Volume II

Also by John Spencer

Ghostwatching (*with Tony Wells*)
Gifts of the Gods
The Paranormal: A Modern Perspective
UFOs: The Definitive Casebook
The UFO Encyclopedia
Perspectives

THE ENCYCLOPEDIA OF THE WORLD'S MYSTICAL AND SACRED SITES

John and Anne Spencer

headline

First published in 2002
by HEADLINE BOOK PUBLISHING

10 9 8 7 6 5 4 3 2 1

British Library Cataloguing in Publication Data

Spencer, John, 1954 –
  The encyclopedia of the world's mystical
  and sacred sites
  1.Sacred space – Encyclopedias
  I.Title II. Spencer, Anne
  291.3'5'03

ISBN 0 7472 7227 1

Typeset by
Letterpart Limited, Reigate, Surrey

Printed and bound in Great Britain by
Mackays of Chatham PLC, Chatham, Kent

HEADLINE BOOK PUBLISHING
A division of Hodder Headline
338 Euston Road
LONDON NW1 3BH

www.headline.co.uk
www.hodderheadline.com

This book is dedicated to
Rosina Violet Spencer (1929–2001)
A much loved, and much missed, source of inspiration,
guidance and fun

CONTENTS

MYSTICAL AND SACRED SITES IN EUROPE

MYSTICAL AND SACRED SITES IN THE MIDDLE-EAST

MYSTICAL AND SACRED SITES IN THE FAR-EAST

MYSTICAL AND SACRED SITES IN AFRICA

MYSTICAL AND SACRED SITES IN THE AMERICAS

MYSTICAL AND SACRED SITES IN AUSTRALASIA

ACKNOWLEDGEMENTS

Our thanks to many friends and colleagues who have assisted in the research, and supply of photographs, included in this book. Particular thanks to: Penny and Spencer James; Ian Mason; Adrian and Maureen Pruss; Claire Ruck Keene; and Jackie Watt.

Our long-standing thanks are overdue also for the invaluable support we have received for many years from Bob Tanner, Pat and Jill at International Scripts.

This book is the latest of several published by Hodder Headline and we owe thanks and appreciation to Lindsay Symons and her team there for their caring and careful handling of our work on this book and others.

INTRODUCTION

This book is a compilation of the sites around the world which people hold sacred: places on Earth which people revere or find holy, where they discover the mystical, either within the land or within themselves.

In selecting entries for this compilation it is worth bearing in mind that in Britain everyone is within ten miles of a sacred site; that there are nine hundred stone circles alone in the UK; and how many churches from the smallest parish church to St Paul's or Westminster Cathedral? Every country in the world can claim similar numbers of tributes to its beliefs. India, for example, has been described as one huge pilgrimage site, and many of the far-eastern countries have small roadside shrines at almost every turn of the road. So, there is no possibility of including every sacred site in the world in any compilation. In this encyclopedia we have selected those places which not only are special and of interest in their own right, but are also representative of a broader range of sites all over the globe. Ancient and modern sites are included, sites of living religions and sites of beliefs long lost to time. This selection shows the rich variety of worship over the centuries.

The book is divided into sections, each representing the most important sacred influences of the areas.

The section on the British Isles contains the ancient standing stones sites, the prehistoric burial areas, and those places which show the development of the Christian religion.

The European section includes the incredible artworks of the

1

ancients in cave paintings, the magnificent cathedrals and mosques of the great religions, the sites of holy visitations, and the places where saints meditated and found the meaning of their beliefs. The great pilgrimages of centuries past take their place alongside the mythologies of the Greeks and the overlay of conquering cultures on defeated peoples.

The sites of the Middle-East include the very birthplaces of some of the world's greatest religions; Islam, Christianity and the Jewish faith.

The Far-East is replete with temples, stupas and monasteries that are held sacred by Hindus, Buddhists, Jains, Taoists and Sikhs. Ancient cave temples and the influence of Catholicism are also included here, as is the reverence of some of the world's faiths for natural places, and mountains in particular such as Everest and Fuji.

In Africa there are the ancient rock-cut churches, the ruins of Great Zimbabwe and the monuments of ancient Egypt including the Pyramids – the only survivors of the Seven Wonders of the Ancient World.

In the Americas we see the sites of the ancient cultures of the Native Americans – their mounds and ancient cities – that once dominated what is now the United States, and the ruins of the great cultures of the Aztecs, Incas and others in the southern parts of the continent – huge pyramids the equal of those in Egypt, and temples and cities that still give testimony to the advanced state of these lost civilisations.

Australasia's ancient sites are mainly aboriginal, and show their reverence for the land itself. Australia's aborigines did not, and do not, build temples to their beliefs; rather their beliefs revere the land itself; their sacred sites are natural, and interwoven with their beliefs about the Dreamtime, that mystical period of the Creation itself.

But what makes a site sacred? Probably the answer lies in three aspects.

First, many people believe that certain points on the Earth's surface are inherently special, perhaps a focus of natural earth energy that can be sensed by people, a healing energy, or an energy that allows people to connect more easily with the forces of nature. Aboriginal 'Dreaming tracks' – the ancient paths that the Dreamtime ancestors walked – and the djang or thalu places may have parallels in leys and monolith-sites in Europe. Perhaps all of these are tapping into this source of energy. Consider the stone circles and monuments around Europe; their purpose is hotly debated. Some – or all – may have been designed as astronomical observatories or calculators, but many people, such as Guy Underwood and John Michell, believe they mark points of exceptional magnetic force which perhaps have natural healing energy. Colin Wilson, in *Mysteries*, comments that they may have been designed to tap the earth's natural energy in a way analogous to acupuncture.

Second, there are sites that seem to be chosen by the divinities. We include the homes of the Greek gods and the Indian deities, and sites seemingly chosen by God or the Virgin Mary for visionary appearances.

Third, there are places into which people have invested their belief and emotion. To some extent that must be true of all sites, including those of natural energy or divine visitation. Canon Carl Garner, whom we interviewed some years ago, suggested: 'The place may be "holy" because it is where [God] has been encountered in a deep way, or where He is praised and worshipped.' He added: 'The more the fire of faith burns, and God is worshipped and praised, the more "transparent" the place becomes to the presence of God.' Hindus refer to their sacred sites as "tirthas". This originally meant ford or bridge over water but has become a reference to any sacred site. It also means a site that is a spiritual bridge between this world and a heavenly realm: a place for the ascension of individuals to the realm of the gods, and a place where the gods may come down to earth. The fact that thousands, or millions, of people have gone to that site, invested in it their prayers, hopes, fears, and dreams, actually produces an energy all of its own at that point.

Some of the most impressive rock art in the world, at Altamira in Spain and Lascaux in France, could mean that these places are some of the world's earliest sacred sites. *The Times* of 19 October 2000 reported that Palaeolithic cave paintings from 35,000 years ago had been found in the Monti Lessini mountains above Verona, possibly making them the oldest such paintings in Europe. 'The cave paintings of Cro-Magnon Man led the Victorians to assume that he was artistically inclined,' pointed out Colin Wilson in his book *Mysteries*, 'but in this century it has become increasingly clear that the purpose of the paintings was basically "magical". The shamans sketched bison and other animals as part of some ritual to influence them, or to guide the hunters towards them. Nor would it be wise to dismiss such rituals as an expression of ignorance and superstition. Dozens of examples could be cited . . . to indicate that they often *do* work.'

The religious culture of Japan has been conditioned to some degree by the fact that it is a mountainous country; the gods were deemed to dwell in these hard to reach, remote locations that were so far removed from the flat and coastal areas where mortals lived and worked. As religions such as Buddhism were introduced into the country so monks sought reclusive sites away from people near their gods. They built their hermitages on the mountain slopes and some fought hard and weary battles to climb the mountains to commune with their gods. So were born both the traditions of religious observance on the mountains, and the concept of the pilgrimage, often deliberately a difficult and testing one.

Many of the sacred sites around the world relate to death, or at least to the passing of the spirit from this world to the next, because all cultures have a belief in some sort of life after death. In many cases the sites are an expression of the life to come rather than the death that has occurred. The tombs of Egypt are an obvious example of sites designed not just to honour the dead but to send them to the next life, with everything needed to sustain the person in that next existence. Perhaps there are similarities in the tomb complex at Knowth where Dr Philip Stooke has identified what he believes to be one of the oldest drawings of a map of the Moon, four thousand years old. The structure was so designed that moonlight would shine into the tomb, directly on to the Neolithic lunar map. Could it be that those who designed the tombs at Knowth and nearby Newgrange believed that their dead would be reborn on the Moon?

Western peoples seem, for the most part, to have lost their contact with these sacred sites. They seem estranged from the universe because they no longer believe in the myths that define and explain it. They have lost their sense of the divine, of the natural, and of their mythologies. Yet it is also true that many people are trying to reach back to those senses; the so-called 'New Age' was, and is, very much about trying to re-connect to those natural feelings, whether they come from within the earth or the people themselves.

In the phenomenon of psychometry we see the possibility that by touching an object something of its history can 'come through' to a sensitive person. Those who touch the ancient stone monuments often report a sense of wonder, or of history; perhaps they are genuinely connecting to the past. Many get a sense of divine from such contact − re-connecting them to their own mythologies.

That need on people's part is being met by official recognition. It is truly wonderful to see just how many of the ancient sites described in this book are now listed as World Heritage sites, with the intention to care for and maintain both their physical artefacts and their spiritual meaning. UNESCO now recognises 690 such sites around the world. And in Britain there is the Sacred Land Project to care for the thousands of sites, shrines, monuments, pilgrimage routes and more that have been allowed to fall into ruin and neglect.

The study of these ancient sites is also personal and internal. From studying our own roots, and understanding the roots of other cultures and faiths, we grow as individuals. We learn to empathise better with the needs and feelings of those of other races and religions. We discover emotional qualities within our-selves. The 'New Age' drive to re-connect ourselves with the Earth's past and our own heritage is a drive to re-connect the 'us' of the material world to the 'us' of the spiritual world. Our appreciation of sacred sites allows us to mature as individuals.

As Confucius said: 'Study the past, if you would divine the future.'

MYSTICAL AND SACRED SITES IN THE BRITISH ISLES

Arbor Low, Near Youlgreave, Derbyshire, England

Situated over three hundred metres up in the Derbyshire Moors, Arbor Low is sometimes known as the 'Stonehenge of the Peak District'.

It was once a collapsed Neolithic burial mound. Later a henge was added which itself has a burial mound built into it; it is likely that this happened sometime around 2500 BC. A stone circle was probably added sometime around 1700 to 1500 BC. The bank walls are over two metres tall and the circle is around seventy-six metres wide, with entrances to the north-west and south-east; the site was clearly ceremonial. The shape of the ditch and the walls were designed to contain people within a special place, rather than to keep intruders out.

The stone circle consists of over forty locally derived limestone blocks all lying face down, not unlike the face of a clock. It is possible that the stones were never upright and were intended to be in more or less their present position.

Over fifty leys are said to pass through the circle which Aubrey Burl describes in *A Guide to Stone Circles of Britain, Ireland and Brittany* as 'one of the wonders of megalithic Britain'.

Avebury Stone Circle, Wiltshire, England

In 1633 the author John Aubrey wrote to King Charles II and suggested the King visit Avebury because it '. . . does as much exceed in greatness the renowned Stonehenge as a cathedral does a parish church'.

Avebury was, at its peak of importance, a Sun Temple and a spiritual centre. It is known to have been in use between 2600 and 1600 BC, thus predating the Druids, and is older than Stonehenge. It is the largest prehistoric monument in Europe, arguably in the world, covering over twenty-eight acres. Perhaps its size can best be imagined from the statistic that a quarter of a million people could stand within its boundaries.

The site is basically a 450-metre diameter earth bank, eight metres high, containing an inner ditch some ten metres deep. Within this is the outer ring of stone sarsens, some weighing up to forty tons. Although only twenty-seven such stones now remain there were originally ninety-eight. Inside the outer circle were two smaller circles consisting of around thirty stones each. Many of the original stones were smashed down in the eighteenth century to provide building material which helped to create the village of Avebury, itself within the boundaries of this massive earthwork.

The exact design of the original structure is unknown. One avenue of stones runs south-east from the circle to a location known as The Sanctuary, at Overton Hill; this avenue is fifteen metres wide and five miles long. It is thought almost certain that a second avenue ran in the opposite direction, but no trace of this existed until recently. However, in May 1999 a previously undiscovered series of stone slabs was found under a farmer's field, by researchers Mark Gillings, Josh Pollard and Dave Wheatley. The stones probably formed part of this second, Beckhampton, avenue, supporting the contention of 'lost' avenues as first suggested by Stukeley; his 'Beckhampton Avenue', believed by many to have been only in his imagination, is now supported by archaeology. The whole configuration is believed to have represented a serpent design, the second avenue being designed in a double curve. Some authors have speculated that there might have been four avenues making up the shape of a Celtic cross.

The Sanctuary was a site of timber buildings and stone circles, and probably housed the image of the god or goddess worshipped by the builders, which would have been carried down the avenue to the main circle for religious rites, perhaps including sacrifices. The avenues were probably designed for processions, even dancing and racing, as part of religious or festival-day observances.

Burials and sacrifices are likely to have accompanied the setting up of the stones. The charter of King Athelstan, from the tenth century, states that burials were conducted there, and burial remains have been found at the base of four stones.

The arrangement of the stones, often alternating between phallic shapes and diamond shapes, suggests that the site may have been used for fertility rites. In local tradition girls seeking to be pregnant should sit on the Devil's Chair – one of the larger stones – and make an appropriate wish.

The most current theories suggest that the location was originally in use by the Bronze Age Beaker Folk as a burial site of great importance.

A Christian church was constructed outside the circle in AD 634, but the pre-Christian beliefs which Avebury symbolised continued to draw attention, and in the fourteenth century the Church authorities sought to solve this dilemma by trying to destroy the Avebury circle. Part of the ditch was levelled, and stones were overthrown or buried. The burial of stones, ironically, protected them from the later desecration in the search for building stone, and they were recovered and re-erected in more recent times. During the excavations of these stones one skeleton was found which is thought to be the remains of a man killed when a stone toppled over while he was helping to bury it.

Many believe that the site holds psychic energy which can be detected by either clairvoyance or dowsing. Theories to explain this include that the site was charged by ancient ritual, or that the stones and their arrangement 'capture' and 'focus' psychic energy. There are many reports of small figures seen dancing around the stones at night which some believe to be 'earth spirits'; more mundanely, they may be the product of a combination of natural luminous energy and wishful thinking.

The site lies on a major ley (the so-called Great Ley) which connects Land's End, Glastonbury Tor and Avebury, and goes across country to Bury St Edmunds in Suffolk. Some have theorised that the energies within Avebury can be used to make psychic communication between sacred sites on the ley.

The site was first investigated by Dr William Stukeley who documented it during the eighteenth century as it was being decimated. He was a scholar of ancient cultures and brought to his work knowledge of Egyptian, Hebrew and Greek history. It was Stukeley who recognised the layout of the Solar Serpent and the Sun Symbol in Avebury were similar to images used by the Egyptians to represent the highest truths and ideals, and the wisdom of inner truth. He wrote of the destruction of the site by locals: 'Thus, this stupendous fabric, which for some thousands of years has braved the continual assaults of the weather, and by the nature of it, when left to itself, would have lasted as long as the globe, has fallen a sacrifice to the wretched ignorance and avarice of a little village, unluckily placed within it.'

A lot of further research work was done by Alexander Keiller in the 1930s; his findings are displayed in the Avebury Museum which he founded.

In October 1916 Edith Olivier found herself near the huge stone megaliths at the end of the avenue on which they were sited and left her car to climb the earth mound. She could see that a fair was underway. She described in her book *Without knowing Mr Walkley*, published in 1938: 'The grand megaliths and the humble cottages alike were partly obscured by the failing light and the falling rain, but both were fitfully lit by flares and torches from booths and shows. Some rather primitive swing boats flew in and out of this dim circle of light: coconuts rolled hairily from the sticks upon which they had been planted . . . And all the time, the little casual crowd of villagers strayed with true Wiltshire indifference from one site to another. These great stones, the legacy of architects of an unknown race, had succeeded in adapting themselves completely to the village life of another day. I stood on the bank for a short time watching the scene . . .' She later discovered that the fair, which had been an annual event at Avebury, had not been held since 1850, more than sixty years prior to her vision of it. If her description is correct, then her vision even predates 1850 as she described megaliths in the avenue which had disappeared prior to the turn of the nineteenth century.

Nor was Edith Olivier's paranormal experience the only one known at that site. In August 1966 a Mrs Harris was at nearby Windmill Hill with her husband when they saw what they took to be a tramp, 'a heavy set man of medium height, dressed in a dark, heavy looking overcoat which hung well below his knees, and a dark hat with the brim turned down. My husband describes him as rather short and stocky, with the coat long and dark, too large for him and wrinkled looking, and a dark hat pulled down over his face.' They glanced away only momentarily and then found, on looking back, that he had disappeared.

In more recent years the area immediately around Avebury has been the focus of the most elaborate of the crop circles which have attracted great attention from all around the world.

Aylesford Priory, England

This place of pilgrimage and spiritual retreat is the home of the Carmelite Friars. The Priory was a place of rest and prayer on the pilgrimage journey to Canterbury and Becket's shrine; the Carmelites who lived there were referred to in the 'Summoner's Tale', part of Geoffrey Chaucer's *Canterbury Tales*.

The diarist Samuel Pepys visited Aylesford on 24 March 1669, describing it as: 'mightily finely placed by the river . . . the grounds about it and wall and the house were handsome. I was mightily pleased with the sight of it.'

The Carmelites originated on Mount Carmel in the Holy Land and settled in Aylesford in 1242 when Sir Richard Grey of Condor, one of the knights of the Crusades, donated his manor house to them. Because passage over the river at this point was free (most river crossings of the time involved paying a toll fee) the route became a popular one for the 'common people'. The Priory was also regarded as a place of sanctuary and protection for all.

The Priory was confiscated by Henry VIII in 1538, resulting in the Carmelites virtually disappearing from England soon afterwards. However, they returned in recent times and, in 1948, re-established Aylesford, which is to this day a place of pilgrimage.

Badbury Rings, Dorset, England

Badbury Rings is a hillfort dating from the Iron Age; that is, around 800 BC to the years of the Roman occupation in AD 43. It consists of three concentric circular ditches protecting a large inner sanctuary where people would have lived. Atop the hill are circular depressions which are thought to be evidence of wattle and daub dwellings constructed there. Chalk and soil excavated from the making of each ditch was used to create raised edges which effectively doubled the height of the fort and created a rampart. From the bottom of the ditch to the top of the rampart would have been approximately twelve metres, a formidable defence to overcome.

Furthermore, it is probable that above the rampart a timber construction would have been erected which would have provided defence similar to the battlements of a castle. Considering any invader would have to scale these three obstacles, this would have made the fort virtually impenetrable.

If the hillfort was only a defensive structure it would not qualify as a sacred site for inclusion in this book; however, there are only two entrances – positioned on the east and west sides – and this has led many researchers to believe that at least part of the purpose of Badbury was ceremonial rather than defensive.

It is also highly probable that the hillfort was constructed on a site of great significance in earlier times. There are four Bronze Age barrows in the immediate locality and several Roman roads converge at the site, these roads often following the lines of old tracks or leys. The fort has never been excavated.

Badbury is thought to have been one of several settlements belonging to the Dorset tribe, the Durotriges. It probably fell to the invading Roman armies under the Emperor Claudius.

A tenuous, and much challenged, Arthurian connection has been made with the Battle of Mount Badon. This was the last of the twelve battles listed by Mennius, a real battle fought early in the sixth century, where a fierce warrior, Arthur, repelled the invasions of Jutes, Angles and Saxons. The present day location of Mount Badon is unknown, but Badbury is thought to be one of the possible sites.

Of its earlier, and ceremonial, purpose Janet and Colin Bord, in *Mysterious Britain*, comment of the design that it is: 'like a coiled serpent, and when seen from the air they [the ditches and ramparts] are very reminiscent of the ritual mazes that are thought to have been part of the pre-Christian rites'.

Bevis Marks Synagogue, London

Bevis Marks Synagogue, situated in the City of London, was opened in 1701 and is today the oldest synagogue still in use in Britain.

Although followers of the Jewish faith first arrived in England with William the Conqueror, they were expelled in 1290 under an edict from Edward I. Jews were effectively denied an open presence in England for 350 years, though there is considerable evidence of Jewish presence in secret, while on the continent they were suffering the excesses of the Inquisition. During the seventeenth century the first Jews, known as Marranos, arrived in the City of London from Spain, though at the time they were forced to keep their worship a secret. They seem to have created a secret congregation headed by Antonio Fernandez Carvajal. In 1655 they laid a petition to Oliver Cromwell, who was known to be relatively liberal (for the times) in his attitude towards religions seeking freedom of worship. Their position as well-connected traders with the East, the West Indies, Holland, Spain and Portugal was also useful to Cromwell in furthering his own plans and he tacitly granted them their wish. In 1656 one floor of a house near Bevis Marks was opened as a place of Jewish worship.

In 1699 a synagogue was designed by Quaker Joseph Avis; it was completed in 1701 in The Plough Yard on Bevis Marks Street. It has stood relatively untroubled, apart from one fire in 1738, until recent times, but in the early 1990s it was severely damaged by terrorist bomb attacks on the City, after which it underwent extensive repair and renovation. Today it is back to its former glory, and looks virtually as it did when first completed 400 years ago. It houses the largest collection of original Cromwellian benches in the world.

Bryn Celli Ddu burial chamber, Ynys Môn, Isle of Anglesey

Bryn Celli Ddu (meaning 'the mound in the dark grove') is held by many to be the best passage grave in Wales. It started life during the late Neolithic as a henge with a stone circle, surrounded by a bank and inner ditch seventeen metres in diameter. Later, this structure was destroyed and a passage grave was constructed inside the ditch. The narrow passage is just over eight metres long and one metre wide, with a low shelf along one side, and is aligned north-east towards the rising midsummer sun. This passage leads into a higher, polygonal burial chamber, some 2.5 metres wide, covered by two capstones, and containing a free-standing pillar the purpose of which is still unknown.

The passage was once completely covered by a cairn, but the existing mound is a reconstruction which allows for certain features to be displayed: in particular a pit containing charcoal and a human ear-bone, and an upright carved stone.

The site was excavated in 1865 and again between 1927 and 1931. The researchers found both burnt and unburnt human bones, a stone bead, and two flint arrowheads, and outside the entrance and the ditch they made the rare find of an ox burial.

Cadbury Castle (South Cadbury Hillfort), Somerset

The huge Iron Age hillfort in Somerset at South Cadbury, known as Cadbury Castle, is speculated by some to be the site of King Arthur's Camelot. The summit rises over 150 metres above sea level, and from its top can be seen the Tor at Glastonbury, twelve miles away.

The link between Arthurian legend and Cadbury Castle dates back to 1542 when the historian John Leland noted: 'At the very south ende of the Chirch of South-Cadbyri standith Camellate, sumtyme a famose toun or castelle . . . The people can telle nothing ther but that they have hard say that Arture much resortid to Camalat.'

According to legend the hill is hollow and sleeping within a cavern there, behind gates of gold, are Arthur and his knights, occasionally rising, leaving the fort, and riding forth in full battle armour. It is said that when England is in need, with its back to the wall, then Arthur and his troops will ride out to protect the realm.

Whatever the truth of the legend, archaeological evidence has confirmed that in the sixth century – the Arthurian era – the site was the fortification of a warrior chieftain believed by many to be Arthur himself, or the inspiration for the legend. No equivalent fortification has been found dating from the Arthurian period anywhere else in Britain.

Local legend says that every seven years – on midsummer eve (or midsummer night, or Christmas Eve, according to the teller) – a door in the hillside opens and the troops take their horses down to Sutton Montis Church where they drink at a spring. In the 1930s a schoolteacher and a friend reported seeing just such an apparition, though perhaps what they saw was influenced by the legend. Driving past the hill late one night, the pair saw bright lights slowly moving down the hill. They stopped to inspect them, and saw that there were torches attached to the lances of a troop of armed warriors on horseback. The troop galloped into the darkness and then disappeared. In fact sightings have been rare, but there are reports of people hearing the hoofbeats of the Arthurian army on its way.

So persistent was the legend that when archaeological excavation was first undertaken there during Victorian times, a local villager asked anxiously if the excavators had come to remove the King.

Excavation did not remove any King, but interesting discoveries were made. The fort had been re-strengthened in post-Roman times; the ramparts had been strengthened with masonry taken from derelict Roman buildings. The remains of a large timber feasting hall, some nineteen metres by ten, were discovered, dated to the fifth or sixth centuries. Another fascinating discovery was that of an unfinished Saxon church from the fort's time as one of King Ethelred the Unready's defensive Burghs.

It is easy, and probably correct, to speculate that such a lavish construct of significant size is likely to indicate the work of an important chieftain or King. As Cadbury Castle is situated within the ancient Kingdom of Dumnonia, probably it was the capital of the Dumnonian Kings. A pointer to this may lie in the name of the fort; Cadbury may refer to Cado's Fort: Cado being the name of an early sixth-century Dumnonian King.

When Leland referred to Cadbury as Camelot he chose the one place in Britain that conformed to much of the legend, in its lavish size and the date of its use. It is unlikely to have been 'just' a lucky guess and suggests he was relating local legend of the time, a legend that may have had some basis in truth. Much of this was confirmed by the work of the Camelot Research Committee, which carried out excavations in the late 1960s under the direction of Leslie Alcock.

The only known written record of the fifth century describes a Britain divided into tribal kingdoms, and later Celtic accounts tell of a number of battles against invading Saxons, and of an army under the command of a leader called Arthur. It is speculated that Cadbury was well placed to defend south-west Britain and could have been the fortress from which he led his troops to the final battle of Mount Badon (see entry for **Badbury Rings**), which is accepted to have been a real battle but whose location is uncertain.

Cairnpapple Burial Mound, West Lothian, Scotland

Cairnpapple is an ancient burial mound and henge, a sacred site thought to be some four and a half thousand years old, displaying also a barrow and burial holes. This puts its construction in the same time-frame as both Silbury Hill and Stonehenge. It remained in use until around 1500 BC.

It was excavated and reconstructed during 1947 and 1948; the current mound is a reconstruction representing the original Bronze Age cairn. Analysis shows that Cairnpapple was probably built in five phases. The first constructions would have been created in the late Neolithic when an arc of seven holes was dug, into which cremated human remains were deposited. Later work would have been done in the Copper Age and middle Bronze Age. Excavation discovered the ritual holes and the remnants of the cremated human bones; other artefacts found include pottery, urns, a red deer antler pin, a bone pin, and flint axe heads and implements. The stone in two of the axes suggests that they originated from Langdale in the Lake District and from the Penmaenmawr Mountain in north Wales, indicating that there was communication and trade between the local tribes and groups more distant.

A rectangular grave containing fragments of a beaker was found within the henge; this grave had the hallmarks of having been that of a very important person. A second grave was marked by standing stones. Neither contained human bones, though it is likely they would have been decomposed long ago by the highly acid soil.

There are many similarities between Cairnpapple and Arbor Low in Derbyshire (see entry for **Arbor Low**). Their composition is very similar, though Arbor Low is somewhat larger.

One fact that makes Cairnpapple unique is that the site has, over time, been used by all religions pertaining to the indigenous people. It features in an ancient Celtic legend which describes it as an extremely important and holy site.

According to Jackie Queally in her booklet *The Lothians Unveiled*, part of a 'cup-marked' stone had been deliberately removed from Cairnpapple and local historian Jack Smith believed that it was the sanctuary stone at the settlement of Torphicen in the valley below. The speculation is that the locals removed the stone from Cairnpapple, which they regarded as magical or powerful, in the hope that they would be blessed by its presence where they re-set it.

The Callanish Stone Circle, Isle of Lewis, Outer Hebrides, Scotland

The Callanish Stone Circle, near the village of Callanish, has a huge central monolith, some five metres high, which forms the head-stone of a small, and partly destroyed, chambered tomb. It is surrounded by a ring of thirteen pillars. Three short rows radiate outwards from the circle more or less towards the east, west and south, and a broad avenue runs roughly towards the north; the overall impression created is similar to the spokes of a wheel. It is believed to have been erected during the late Neolithic era, around 1975 BC.

It is usually assumed, as with other stone circles, that the alignments are of astronomical significance, although there is doubt about how accurate any such readings at Callanish would have been, given the positioning of the stone monuments. The site was important in local customs until well into the nineteenth century; local people would gather at the stones on midsummer morning.

The site is believed by some to be linked to a range of hills on the island. The range is said to have the shape of a sleeping woman lying on her back: the Earth Mother, locally known as Sleeping Beauty. According to Margaret R. Curtis, a guide in the area and an expert on the stones, once a month for a few months every 18.61 years (the next due in 2006) the moon rises over the Earth Mother's breast and then passes through the stones a few hours later. While the moon is passing through the stones it appears to be 'reborn' from the Earth Mother. As Curtis described: 'For three minutes . . . the moon was captured in an artificial frame of megaliths, and the cold grey pillars of stone were bathed in a golden glow. Like a lighthouse beam, the moonlight stretched down along the avenue towards us and caught us in its light.'

There are three other smaller stone circles in the locale around the shores of Loch Roag. The stones are featured in many legends. In one, a white sea cow befriended a woman who had tried to commit suicide in the sea. She was told to go to the stones each night, and the sea cow would fetch milk for her. But one night a witch appeared and milked the cow into a sieve, and it disappeared. Another story, relatively common for stone circles, is that the stones represent people turned to stone, in this case for refusing to embrace Christianity.

Canterbury Cathedral, Canterbury, England

Canterbury Cathedral was, during the Middle Ages, a place of pilgrimage for Christians seeking to pay respect at the shrine of Thomas à Becket, Chancellor of England and Archbishop of Canterbury, who was murdered in the cathedral on the orders of Henry II on 29 December 1170.

The location was a sacred pagan site before the Roman invasion. A Celtic church was built there during the Roman occupation, but abandoned when the Romans left in the fifth century and the site reverted to pagan worship.

A Cathedral on the site was founded in AD 597, when St Augustine arrived from Rome to convert the Anglo-Saxon natives to Christianity, on the orders of Pope Gregory who sought to wipe out pagan worship. St Augustine was Canterbury's first archbishop. The original building was totally destroyed by fire in 1067; the present building was erected in stages over several centuries.

The murder of Becket was a pivotal moment in history; the passion of pilgrims visiting Becket's shrine seems to relate to the emotions released by the crime. There were miracles of healing reported at the site just after the murder, and for centuries thereafter. The shrine was reputed to have great spiritual power emanating from it. Henry II himself paid penance there just four years after Becket's death.

Pilgrimages to Canterbury were a major pursuit for three hundred years, and the surrounding area became virtually a 'tourist' town catering for their needs. The height of the pilgrimage era is best known through *The Canterbury Tales* by Geoffrey Chaucer, written at the end of the fourteenth century.

The pilgrimages were effectively ended by Henry VIII when he dissolved the monasteries in the sixteenth century. He also looted Canterbury, and it says something for the devotions to the shrine that he found it surrounded by the many crutches of the disabled who had been healed at the shrine, and that it took twenty-six carts to remove the gold and jewellery that had been left there as tribute to its healing and miraculous powers.

Henry ordered the destruction of the shrine of Thomas à Becket but the spot where he was murdered is still marked by a plaque.

Castlerigg Stone Circle, English Lake District

This is believed to be one of the first stone circles erected in Europe, possibly dating from as early as 3200 BC. There are thirty-eight slate stones remaining, each between 1 and 1.5 metres high, arranged in an elliptical ring nearly thirty metres in diameter. To the north is a wide entrance with two of the tallest stones either side of it. In the south-east of the circle is a rectangle of ten stones, an unusual arrangement not found in other such circles.

Within the circle there is also a mound suggestive of a burial site, though this has not been confirmed as there have been no excavations of this part of the site.

The circle is situated on a high moor in an open bowl of hills above Keswick, a spectacular setting that must have inspired the circle's builders.

The site probably had many purposes; religious, social and possibly as a trading post. Professor Alexander Thom has suggested that the Castlerigg circle was designed as an astronomical observatory, and there are clear astronomical alignments for some of the stones. For example, the tallest stone is in line with the Samhain (beginning of winter) sunrise. Professor Aubrey Burl suggested that one of Castlerigg's functions could have been to act as an emporium connected with the Neolithic stone axe industry in the Langdales. Stone axes found at the site support this theory.

Cerne Abbas Giant, Giant Hill, Cerne Abbas, Dorset, England

One of the most famous chalk-carved figures in Britain is the 60-metre 'giant' carved on a Dorset Hill; it possibly dates from over three thousand years ago. It has been a place of fertility rituals since early times and above the head of the figure can be seen the enclosure where maypoles were erected. May Day and maypole dancing have also been long associated with fertility rituals.

The general belief was that if a barren woman slept the night on the figure's erect penis she would be able to have children. Perhaps out of temerity, or perhaps harking back to that belief, many couples are found on the figure in present times. On May Day the sun rises over the hill directly in a line drawn through the penis.

The Cambridge archaeologist T.C. Lethbridge believed that the figure is the remnant of a group of figures that once adorned the hill. He believed it to be a representation of Hercules, or Gog.

Clava Cairns, Near Inverness, Scotland

In the New Stone Age, the dead were revered as important people; ancestor worship was a cornerstone of belief, and was reflected in magnificent tombs built as houses for the dead, such as the ones at Clava.

The three cairns are located to the east of the River Nairn. It is believed they date to approximately 2000 to 1500 BC; all three were built at the same time. Two are passage burial cairns and the third is a ring-type cairn. The north-eastern cairn, about eighteen metres across and three metres high, is a passage cairn surrounded by a ring of eleven standing stones, some thirty metres in diameter. The other passage cairn to the south-west is similar in size and structure. In each the entrance is pointing in the same direction, so that on midwinter's day, the rays of the setting sun are directed down the passage. The setting sun may have indicated 'death' to the builders, and strengthens the belief that the cairns were for burial. However, the lack of evidence of human remains at the site has left this interpretation open to challenge and others have suggested that the site was a focus for tribal, midwinter rituals of another, unknown, nature.

The ring cairn has an open, un-roofed, area where ceremonies could take place. Some of the stones in the ring have elaborate carvings on them which probably related to rituals performed there.

Many of the stones that composed the structures have been removed over the years for use as local building material, as has happened at many such sites, perhaps most famously at Avebury.

Dwarfie Stane, Hoy, Orkney Islands

The Dwarfie Stane on Hoy is the only example of a rock-cut tomb in Britain, and possibly in northern Europe. It dates from around 3000 BC.

It is a huge block of red sandstone some 8.5 metres long and 4 metres wide, hollowed out by Neolithic workers. The entrance is a square hole in the side with a short passage leading to two small chambers on either side. Lying near the entrance is a block of sandstone which once used to seal the opening.

The stone, and a nearby companion block of sandstone known as the Partick Stane, was probably carved off the nearby hill during the Ice Age and deposited by a retreating glacier; any other explanation for its appearance at the foot of the cliff would surely have resulted in the rocks being broken in their fall.

Originally it was thought that the stone had been hollowed out to create a hermit's retreat, particularly as there are bed-shaped surfaces cut into the interior, but that theory now seems unlikely. The general construction is not unlike rock-cut tombs in the Middle-East, the bed-like structure being where the bodies were laid to rest. The fact that the bed-surfaces are very small led to local folklore holding 'the little people' responsible, thus giving the Dwarfie Stane its name.

Other local folklore attributes the stone to the work of a giant and his wife who were later imprisoned in it by another giant who wanted to conquer their territory; the couple gnawed their way out through a hole in the roof.

Sir Walter Scott refers to the Dwarfie Stane in his novel *The Pirate*: 'this extraordinary dwelling which Trolld, a dwarf famous in the northern saga, is said to have framed for his favourite residence'.

Studies have shown that the tomb was sealed in the sixteenth century and it is believed that the hole in the roof, since repaired, was a crude attempt to break into the chamber within. No proper archaeological excavations have been undertaken at the Dwarfie Stane.

Gallarus Oratory, Co. Kerry, Eire

Gallarus Oratory, overlooking the harbour at Smerwick on the Dingle Peninsula, is regarded as one of the finest examples of an early Christian Church in Ireland. It dates from around AD 800.

This small structure, shaped like an upturned boat, was built without mortar and uses corbel vaulting, a technique used originally by Neolithic tomb-makers. The stones are laid at an angle which allows for rainwater run-off, and this has protected the structure over the centuries. Despite being in a notoriously wet place, there is no sign that it has ever let in the rain. Inside there are some signs of plaster that may have once covered the walls, though if so, it has largely disappeared now.

It is a simple structure, dimly lit, with a small doorway on the west side and one tiny window opposite. Inside the doorway are two projecting stones with holes which once supported the door.

Glastonbury, Somerset, England

If the New Age has a capital in Britain it is Glastonbury. Probably no other comparable town is surrounded by so many enduring legends. As Anthony Robert, editor of *Glastonbury: Ancient Avalon, New Jerusalem* writes: 'Glastonbury is one of those highly charged sacred focal points for the generation and transmission of cosmic energies. It is a planetary beacon and powerhouse of the spirit that enlightens all who approach its mysteries with a sense of humble participation and genuine love.'

Glastonbury has been described as the centre of pagan worship in Britain, as the first Christian settlement in Britain, and is held by some to be Avalon, the final resting place of King Arthur.

The main evidence of pagan worship at Glastonbury is two-fold. Excavations have found a quantity of animal bones, suggesting a community that ate meat, and meat-eating is not consistent with the diets of early Christians. Also, two graves were unearthed whose bodies point towards the south, generally a non-Christian alignment.

Glastonbury stands on the Great Ley which runs from St Michael's Mount in Cornwall, through Glastonbury and Avebury, and on to the Suffolk coast. It is an atmospheric site; a huge tor topped by the ruins of St Michael's Tower.

It is said that Joseph of Arimathea built the Old Church (the site now houses the ruined Abbey) which he dedicated to the Virgin Mary as the first Christian church in Britain. He is supposed to have brought with him – and deposited at Glastonbury – the Holy Grail, the cup used by Jesus at the Last Supper, and in which his blood was collected as he hung on the Cross. In another version of the story, Joseph was returning to Glastonbury, having visited it many years earlier with the boy Jesus. The connection of Joseph of Arimathea to Glastonbury appears towards the end of the twelfth century when the history of the Abbey was re-written by monks, following a fire that destroyed many of the records. Prior to that, for example in *The History of the Abbey*, written by William of Malmesbury in 1130, there is no mention of Joseph. The truth is that it is highly likely that Christianity came to Britain via Glastonbury, but that the local devotees wanted to strengthen the connection directly with Christ and so linked it with Joseph.

In about 1136 Geoffrey of Monmouth wrote *The History of the Kings of Britain*, in which he describes the death of King Arthur and his being carried off to the Isle of Avalon. Although he does not identify this location in this writing, in a later poem 'The Life of Merlin', he describes Avalon in a way comparable to Glastonbury and Somerset. Monmouth's writings are nowadays regarded as mostly fiction, but the writings of this period are certainly the major source of the legend of Glastonbury as Avalon.

The first direct reference to Glastonbury as Avalon arises around 1193 in *De Instructione Principis*, written by the cleric Giraldus Cambrensis who directly stated that Glastonbury had in ancient times been known as the Isle of Avalon. Probably the major claim for the identification of the site is that in 1191 a grave was exhumed which is alleged to have been that of Arthur. This is referred to by Giraldus who indicates that a Welsh soothsayer revealed the location of the grave to King Henry II. It was politically important for Henry to locate the grave in England, as such a find would demolish the Welsh hope that Arthur would return to fight the English and it would also support Henry's claim that he was a successor of Arthur. The grave was allegedly found to contain the bones of a large man – which fits the Arthurian legend – and beside him the skeleton of a woman. In the grave, it was said, was also a lead cross bearing an inscription confirming that Arthur and his wife Guinivere were buried there in the Isle of Avalon. Archaeologists in 1962 found what is likely to have been that grave, though the skeletons and artefacts must have been removed centuries earlier. Scholarly opinion is that the grave was not that of Arthur, which begs the question of why the monks would seemingly perpetrate a hoax. The answer is that in around 1194 there was a huge fire at Glastonbury and the monks were in severe financial difficulty. As Arthurian romance was, at the time, very popular, the discovery of Arthur's grave would have attracted 'tourists' and considerable income.

Another extraordinary claim for Glastonbury is that of the presence of the Glastonbury Zodiac, a rough circle some ten miles in diameter and thirty miles in circumference. Allegedly carved out in the Somerset landscape five hundred years before Christ, commented on by Queen Elizabeth I's astrologer John Dee, and rediscovered by Katharine Maltwood in the 1920s, the Glastonbury Zodiac is a representation of Arthurian legend. Towards the north is the sign of the Phoenix, representing rebirth. The Tor is within the head of the Phoenix which is facing Challis Hill; the hill within the body of the bird encompasses Challis Well, said to be the repository of the Holy Grail. Katharine Maltwood closely associated the zodiac signs with Arthurian legend so, for example, the Scorpion's sting is poised above Sagittarius (representing Arthur's horse). The Scorpion may be equated to Sir Mordred who, wounded by Arthur, dealt a fatal blow to the King. However, many researchers are doubtful about the reality of the Glastonbury Zodiac. Francis King, a researcher of the occult, comments: 'On a detailed map of any area, except perhaps a desert, it is perfectly possible to see zodiacs or grail carthals or anything else one wants to see.' Colin Wilson, similarly a writer on the occult, has stated: 'The mere demonstration that the configurations of the land could be the signs of the zodiac is no convincing proof. I would need to be told precisely how the worshippers used the configurations in their religious ceremonies.' Whatever the reality of an Arthurian Zodiac it is, like so much of Glastonbury, an enduring legend which has many modern followers.

Glendalough, Co. Wicklow, Eire

Glendalough is a monastic site that was founded by St Kevin in the sixth century.

Kevin was born near Rathdrum towards the end of the fifth

century, and lived to be 120 years old. He was tutored by St Petroc of Cornwall, who passed on his knowledge and passion for the Sacred Scriptures. Kevin went on to study under his uncle, St Eugenius, who was to become Bishop of Ardstraw.

The youthful Kevin was apparently a handsome young man who won the attention, and affections, of a beautiful girl, Kathleen. According to the story, she once followed him to the woods and Kevin, on realising she was there, threw himself into a bed of nettles, and then took up a handful with which he scourged the girl. The pain of the nettle 'fire' 'extinguished the fire within', and Kathleen repented her sins. (There is a later story, without historical foundation, that Kevin later flung the unhappy Kathleen from his cave in the hills into the lake.)

Kevin withdrew into the wilds of the Glendalough valley, where he spent many years in a cave, living alone in the practice of extreme asceticism. Over time he gathered around him a group of holy men who encouraged him to build the monastery, the ruins of which still remain today as a much visited site for tourists and pilgrims. Kevin's fame spread widely and he received many scholars and disciples, so that Glendalough became a great school of sacred learning, and a noviciate in which the clergy were trained in virtue and self-denial.

Probably the most famous pupil of Glendalough was St Laurence O'Toole, later Archbishop of Dublin. He is regarded as a great scholar, bishop, patriot, and saint, and owed his training in virtue entirely to the school. Even after taking up his office as Archbishop, he chose to retire from the city each Lent and spend the whole period in the cave above the lake where St Kevin had lived for so long alone.

The existing ruins at Glendalough are a striking, and tranquil, scene. Within the area of the original enclosure are: the great church; a cathedral probably built in the time of St Kevin; the Round Tower standing over thirty metres high; the building called St Kevin's Kitchen (his private oratory and sleeping cell); and the Church of the Blessed Virgin, for whom Kevin, like so many Irish saints, had a strong devotion.

Some twenty minutes' walk through the woods leads to the two lakes nearby from which the area gets its name (Glendalough means 'the valley of the two lakes'). Nearby the Caher, a stone-walled circular enclosure next to a simple cross, overlooks the upper lake, mountains and woods which contain crosses, temples, and St Kevin's cave.

Holy Island (Lindisfarne), England

Holy Island, just off the coast of Northumberland in north-east England, is connected to the mainland by a causeway at low tide.

The island was the site of an Anglo-Saxon settlement. The first person whose name we know who lived there was St Aidan, but he was not the first human being to settle there; Middle Stone Age Man was there from about 8000 BC and New Stone Age Man from 3000 BC. During the time of the Roman Empire, the Britons probably had a village on the island.

The exiled children of Aethelfrith, Anglo-Saxon king of Northumbria, who had died in battle, travelled to Iona in Scotland (see entry for **Iona**) to be educated by the Christian monks. One of the children was Prince Oswald and the result of his time there was to bring about the conversion of much of England to Christianity. When he fought to regain his father's kingdom it was under the shadow of a wooden cross to demonstrate his Christianity. As king, Oswald turned to the monks of Iona to seek a missionary to convert his people, and they sent Aidan in AD 635. Aidan was a missionary disciple of St Columba, and he was offered any land he wanted to set up his monastery; he chose Lindisfarne (the English name for Holy Island).

Aidan established a monastery, a small church, dwelling huts, and ancillary buildings. The monks of that monastery travelled from there to walk the lanes, talk to the people, and try to interest them in the faith; the method of contact Aidan himself had previously established. The monastery on the island was for men and boys only. Although this was far from universal, it had to be the way for Aidan's monks as walking the roads talking to people would not have been safe or socially acceptable for young women.

After sixteen years as bishop, Aidan died at nearby Bamburgh in AD 651.

Another notable figure on Lindisfarne was St Cuthbert. From AD 664 to 676 Cuthbert was prior of the Lindisfarne monastery; in 685 he was consecrated Bishop of Lindisfarne. When he was a young man, he had been tending sheep on the hills at night when he saw a light fall to Earth and then return upward along with, he believed, a human soul being carried to Heaven. It was 31 August 651; the night of Aidan's death. Cuthbert believed that he had seen St Aidan's soul making its glorious journey and it was a pivotal moment for him. He went to the monastery at Melrose, which had also been founded by Aidan, and asked to be admitted as a novice. For thirteen years he trained with the monks there. He helped set up a new monastery at Ripon, returned to Melrose to become prior, and later moved to Lindisfarne as prior.

Cuthbert was an active missionary, and he developed the gift of spiritual healing for which people visited him, even after he sought isolation in a hermitage on Inner Farne. There, in the company of Lindisfarne monks, he died on 20 March 687, and was buried on Lindisfarne.

The miracle of healing was claimed by visitors to his grave and the monks of Lindisfarne saw this as a sign that Cuthbert was now a saint in heaven. They sought the protection and blessing of his relics and so, after eleven years in his grave, his body was 'elevated' on the anniversary of his death. When his coffin was opened, it was found that his body had not corrupted; a further sign of sainthood. This produced the cult of St Cuthbert and a resurgence in pilgrimages to the island.

In AD 793 the monastery was destroyed by the Vikings, and evacuated by the monks, but in 1081 the Normans re-created a priory there.

After the Norman Conquest a Benedictine community sought to build a cathedral at Durham in which they planned to house St Cuthbert's body – which had been secreted away to protect it from the invasions – in a new shrine. They discovered at this time that the body was still uncorrupt. Throughout the Middle Ages huge numbers of pilgrims visited it. At the time of the Reformation, when the monastery was dissolved, St Cuthbert's body was buried in a plain grave behind the High Altar. His grave is still a site of pilgrimages today.

Iona, north-western Scotland

In Iona of my heart, Iona of my love, instead of the chanting of monks shall be the lowing of cattle. But Before the world comes to an end, Iona shall be as it was.

St Columba

Iona is a small island, barely three square miles, off the Scottish coast near Mull. The island exhibits evidence of Stone Age and Iron Age settlements.

Its most important claim to fame, however, is that it is where the Irish St Columba and twelve companions landed in AD 563 (at Port of the Coracle) and where he established a Christian monastery which brought Christianity to Scotland.

Columba had been born in Ireland in AD 521, and was descended from the kings of Ireland. He received a Christian education in monastic schools, Ireland having been Christianised through St Patrick (AD 389 to 461). He founded a monastery in Derry at the age of twenty-five and over the next fifteen years he toured Ireland founding hundreds of monasteries and churches. When Columba set out from Ireland on a mission for Christ he first landed on Oronsay, but left again as he was determined that his new home would be a place from where he could not see Ireland. This may have reflected the allegation that he exiled himself to Iona, to convert as many as he could to Christianity, as a penance for starting a dispute in which thousands of lives were lost; all because of a judgement that went against him in a disagreement with his former friend Finbar over the ownership of a copied manuscript.

Columba acquired a reputation as a strong and wise statesman, sought out by local chiefs and kings for sound advice. (He is also recorded as having what may have been the first claim of a sighting of the Loch Ness Monster; he allegedly defended a distressed fisherman by calling out to the creature: 'Touch not thou that man!') Columba had a marked love of animals, for example giving special instructions for the care of a crane which fell on the shore, exhausted by its flight from Ireland.

On a hill on the island, Cnoc an t-Sidhein, Columba had a vision of angels. According to his biographer, the monk Adamnan, '. . . holy angels, the citizens of the holy country, clad in white robes and flying with wonderful speed, began to stand around the saint while he prayed'. On another occasion, while Columba was at prayer in the church, a monk, Colga, saw the building 'filled with heavenly light'.

Columba died in AD 597 and was buried on the island. The site of the grave is accepted to be where a small chapel now stands beside the abbey's main door. During later Norse invasions the monastery was destroyed, but his remains were taken to Ireland for safe-keeping. The Norse invaders, having become Christians themselves, rebuilt the monastery.

A Benedictine community was set up on the island by the Lord of the Isles around 1200, establishing the presence of the Roman Catholic Church. The abbey church became the Isle's cathedral from 1507 until the Reformation, and in 1899 the abbey was given to the Church of Scotland.

The island houses the Iona Community, which is based on the teachings of St Columba, and was founded in 1938 by the Church of Scotland. The abbey was consecrated in 1951.

Iona became a sacred place of burial for the kings of Scotland, Ireland and Norway. Perhaps the most famous Scottish king buried there is Macbeth, later the subject of Shakespeare's play. More recently, special permission was given for the Labour Party leader John Smith, who died from a heart attack in 1994, to be buried in the abbey cemetery: considerable proof of his standing in Scotland.

Knock Parish Church, Knock, Co. Mayo, Eire

At a time of great upheaval in Ireland, including famine and economic distress, a Marian visitation brought hope to the people of County Mayo, one of the most depressed regions. During the late afternoon of 21 August 1879, in daylight but also in steadily pouring rain, Margaret Beirne went to the Knock Parish Church to lock up for the night, at the request of her brother. As she returned home she noticed a strange illumination covering the church, but at the time she did not mention it to anyone else.

At about the same time, though, another member of the Beirne family, Mary, had just finished a visit to the church with its housekeeper, Mary McLoughlin. At a point on the road from where they could clearly see the building Mary Beirne turned to McLoughlin and said, 'Oh look at the statues! Why didn't you tell me the priest had got new statues for the chapel?' McLoughlin said she knew nothing about new statues and the pair looked more closely at the church. When they got closer Mary Beirne commented: 'But they are not statues, they're moving. It's the Blessed Virgin.'

They and thirteen other witnesses were seeing a tableau on the south gable wall of the church. Central to this was the image of a beautiful woman dressed in white and wearing a large brilliant crown. Her hands were raised as if in prayer. Those who saw her were certain they were seeing the Blessed Virgin Mary, Mother of Jesus. To her right was standing a figure taken to be St Joseph, his head inclined towards the Virgin, and to her left St John the Evangelist, dressed as a bishop. To St John's left stood an altar supporting a lamb and a cross surrounded by angels. Since that time Our Lady of Knock has usually been celebrated under her ancient title of Queen of the Angels. The image was contained in a cloud of light, and lasted around two hours.

Even those of the village who did not see the tableau none the less reported seeing an area of brilliant illumination around the area of the church.

As the news of the Virgin's appearance spread, thousands of pilgrims began to arrive at Knock, many bringing with them sick friends and relatives. Many miraculous cures were soon reported, the first being ten days after the sighting: a young girl who had been born deaf suddenly found she could hear. Many who hobbled to the site on crutches and sticks left them there, no longer needed.

There were more apparitions of the Virgin in the same place, and with exactly the same appearance, in January and February of 1880. The Virgin Mary apparently said nothing during these visitations; the people of Ireland believe she simply came to be with them in their hour of need.

By the end of 1880 around three hundred claimed cures had been recorded in the diary of the parish priest. In that same year a statue of Our Lady of Knock was erected where she had been seen during the visions.

In the third year after the apparitions began, Archbishop Lynch from Toronto, in Canada, undertook a pilgrimage to Knock to give thanks for his own cure and for the cures of many in his diocese. He was obviously impressed by the priest and commented: 'This is another stroke of the providence of God to have such a priest in so celebrated a place that the pilgrims may carry away, besides other gifts, a great reverence for the priesthood of Ireland.'

The church undertook an official investigation of the events at Knock in 1879, and a further examination in 1936. They concluded that the witnesses were believable and that there was nothing in the visions which ran contrary to the faith.

Four recent Popes have all honoured Knock in different ways. Pius XII blessed the Banner of Knock at St Peter's and decorated it with a special medal on All Saints' Day, 1945: the Marian year. He also announced a new feast of the Queenship of Mary. John XXIII presented a special candle to Knock on Candlemas Day in 1960. Paul VI blessed the foundation stone for the Basilica of Our Lady, Queen of Ireland, on 6 June 1974. Lastly, Pope John Paul II travelled to Knock in person, as a pilgrim, to visit the shrine on 30 September 1979, the centenary year. While there, he also addressed the sick and the nursing staff, celebrated Mass, established the shrine church as a basilica, and knelt in prayer at the wall where the visions had occurred.

John Paul II's visit is seen as having given Knock papal approval, and has greatly increased the shrine's reputation as an internationally recognised Marian shrine. Today, around one and a half million pilgrims visit the church annually.

Knowth Megalithic Passage Tomb, County Meath, Eire

There has been human activity at Knowth for six thousand years, making it an important archaeological site. Certainly it has been both a place of burial and ceremony, but it has also been a social centre and place of political and military power in those thousands of years. It seems that the earliest structures were wood and wattle houses, with the tombs built around one thousand years later during the Neolithic Age. The people who built the complex were very advanced as both engineers and astronomers.

In the *Guardian* of 12 April 1999, Professor Eogan, engaged in research work at University College Dublin, said: 'No one can over-estimate the importance of Knowth. It was a massive operation and it shows how developed and educated society was. It demonstrates incredible architectural and artistic achievements and indicates how central to Atlantic European culture Ireland was.'

The passages at Knowth are aligned to the rising and setting sun of the Equinoxes in March and September (though a modern local building now cuts off the light at certain times of the day). Probably the reason for this is that the Neolithic builders were sun worshippers, believing that if the sun could enter the tombs then either it would give life back to those within, or take them to the realm of the gods.

There is evidence of a Beaker People (from the Bronze Age) burial at Knowth; the only known site of a Beaker burial in Ireland.

During the Iron Age the Celts settled at Knowth; and there are Celtic graffiti in the tomb passages. Celtic burial rituals included 'inhumation': the dead buried in pits in the ground in a crouched, sitting position. There are thirty-five such inhumation sites at Knowth.

Later Norman settlements turned the site into one of head-quarters for military conquest; though no permanent structures of note were built here.

Knowth is in the Boyne Valley which contains two-thirds of all the known megalithic art in Western Europe; half of this is in Knowth and the surrounding tomb structures, including Dowth and the more famous Newgrange.

A most fascinating aspect of the artworks found at Knowth was identified by Dr Philip Stooke of the University of Western Ontario. It is a finding that suggests the early people at Knowth might have worshipped not just the sun, but also the moon. His work involves making maps of asteroids and the moon; and he believes that one of the images at Knowth is a map of the moon drawn four thousand years ago. If so, then it is by far the oldest known such map; the previously oldest known was drawn by Leonardo da Vinci in 1505. In the *Guardian* of 22 April 1999 Stooke said: 'The people who carved this moon map were the first scientists. They knew a great deal about the motion of the moon. They were not primitive at all.' Investigation shows moonlight would shine into the eastern passage of the tomb, and would shine directly on to the Neolithic lunar map-drawing.

Melrose Abbey, Melrose, Scotland

The original site of Melrose Abbey was four miles from the present position, just below Scott's View. It was founded by St Aidan in about AD 660; an early prior was St Cuthbert who later became prior to Lindesfarne (see entry for **Holy Island**). In 1131 King David I of Scotland encouraged the Cistercian monks to found a new abbey on the present site below the Eildon Hills. It was dedicated to the Blessed Virgin on Sunday 28 July 1146, the earliest Cistercian monastery established in Scotland. It suffered at the hands of a succession of English monarchs: Edward II's army desecrated, pillaged, and burned down the church and Richard II set fire to the abbey. Thanks to the generosity of Robert the Bruce, a new church was begun in 1326. Countless benefactors, nobles and commoners, donated lands and possessions to Melrose making it a rich and notable abbey, a measure of the esteem in which it was held. An example of its wealth can be understood from twelfth-century records which show that during a time of famine four thousand starving people were fed by the monastery for three months.

In 1544 the army of Henry VIII burned Melrose Abbey down. The ruins were further destroyed by a fanatical mob in 1569, when statues and carvings were wrecked. The final humiliation was the stealing of its sacred stones to serve as building materials.

Some restoration of the abbey was carried out under the direction of Sir Walter Scott in 1822 and today it is in the care of Historic Scotland.

It is not only a sacred site for the Scots because of its religious associations but because it is also the burial place of the heart of Robert the Bruce.

Robert the Bruce was born in 1274 and was thirty-one years old when he became king. He married Isabella of Mar and then Elizabeth de Burgh; their son was to become David II. Robert the Bruce was regarded as a traitor by Edward I of England, who had appointed him his commander in Scotland, when he vowed to free Scotland from English rule. In a succession of battles he recaptured Scottish lands and castles from the English, and defeated them at Bannockburn in 1314, possibly aided by disguised soldiers of the Knights Templar.

He died in 1329 in Cardross, probably of leprosy. His body was buried at Dunfermline, but his heart was removed and taken on the Crusades by Sir James (the Black) Douglas who was killed in Moorish Spain and who, it is reputed, just before he died, hurled the heart at the enemy. The heart was recovered and taken to Melrose Abbey where David II asked for it to be buried.

In 1996 archaeological excavations within the abbey by a team from Historic Scotland investigated the lead container said to contain Robert the Bruce's heart. Fibre-optics were used to examine the interior of the casket which was then opened and a smaller casket found inside. There, an engraved copper plaque was found inscribed: 'The enclosed leaden casket containing a heart was found beneath Chapter House floor, March 1921, by His Majesty's Office of Works'. Though the casket contains a heart, Richard Welander, one of the investigating team, said that it was not possible to identify it as Robert the Bruce's, but added: 'We can say that it is reasonable to assume that it is.' No other heart is reputed to be buried there. This inner casket was not opened and was housed in Edinburgh until it was re-buried at Melrose Abbey on 22 June 1998. On the 24 June – the anniversary of Robert the Bruce's victory at Bannockburn – the Scottish Secretary of State, Donald Dewar, unveiled a plinth over the heart's new burial place in the abbey grounds.

Old Sarum, Wiltshire, England

The name Old Sarum is derived from Sorbiodonum (or Sorviodunum), meaning 'gentle river fortress'. It was clearly an Iron Age settlement, but was probably a significant site prior to that. It lies on the convergence of four Roman roads, which often followed leys, and is on the famous Stonehenge to Clearbury ley discovered by Sir Norman Lockyer.

The mound consists of a defensive wall and rampart rising at an angle of over 45 degrees and measuring twelve metres high. The site was subsequently occupied by the Saxons, and by the Normans. William the Conqueror chose this site to disband his army – suggesting some inherent significance – when he had subdued the country after four years of struggle following his invasion of 1066. A wooden Norman castle was built atop the site, later replaced by stone buildings. The original construction had been under the direction of Osmund, William's Chancellor.

A cathedral was also built on the hilltop. This was the consequence of the spiritual centre of the area being moved from Old Sherbourne to Old Sarum in 1075 following a direction from Lanfranc – the first Norman Archbishop of Canterbury – that spiritual centres be relocated to thriving centres of population, which Old Sarum had become after the King's royal castle had been constructed there. This first cathedral was destroyed in a thunderstorm, and was replaced by a second construction. By that time, however, the relationship between the Church and the army in the fort had deteriorated and the spiritual centre was moved in 1220, with the permission of the Pope, to a new site. Legend has it that an arrow was shot from the old site and the new cathedral built where the arrow landed, which is now Salisbury (New

Sarum) cathedral, on the same ley. Stone from the old site was used to build the new, perhaps just an economic necessity, but also perhaps a recognition of carrying the spirituality of the old stones to the new location.

Pentre Ifan, Wales

Pentre Ifan is a megalithic site dating from at least 4000 BC. Once known as Arthur's Quoit, Pentre Ifan means Ivan's Village. It is thought to be the finest Welsh hilltop megalith in existence. Originally it was probably constructed as a burial chamber, but over thousands of years the earth has been worn away, exposing the construction. The horizontal capstone, weighing many tons, is still in place, atop three uprights. The stones which make up the chamber are all of local igneous rock. On the portal stone there is a faint but clear trace of a decorative cupmark.

The site was probably built on a hilltop to be in keeping with the mythology of its builders. They believed that the souls of the dead would be closer to the spirit world if laid to rest on a hill, closer to the sun which was worshipped as the giver of light, warmth and life.

Excavations in 1936–7 and in 1958–9 showed that the burial chamber was originally in a shallow oval pit, covered by a mound of earth up to thirty-six metres long. The semi-circular façade was marked by upright stones on either side of the south-facing portal. However, no trace of burial has been found, and the number of artefacts discovered very few.

Local lore says that sometimes fairies are seen here, described as 'little children in clothes like soldiers' clothes and with red caps'.

The origin of the builders is subject to debate. Until recently it was thought that they were sophisticated tribes who derived from eastern Mediterranean regions and who, over time, gradually migrated westwards through Greece, Malta, Spain, Portugal, Brittany, and finally to the British Isles and Ireland. During their migration, they left in these countries examples of burial chambers, passage graves, dolmens and megalithic temples. However, carbon-dating has indicated that these sites in

Wales were constructed over a thousand years before their Mediterranean counterparts, challenging this theory.

Rock of Cashel, Cashel, County Tipperary, Eire

The town of Cashel (meaning fortress) is the home of one of Ireland's greatest sacred and historical sites – the Rock of Cashel. Set atop a dome of rock some sixty metres above the plain of the Golden Vale and the Suir Valley, this most famous Irish landmark, consisting of a ruined cathedral and surrounding buildings, imposing and mysterious, was once the seat of the kings of Munster.

Folklore says that the rock mound was formed when the devil bit a chunk of limestone from nearby mountains and spat it out on to the plain.

Legend also says that the Rock was used as a fortress by descendants of Eogan Mor, in particular Conal Corc who established the Cashel Kingship.

It was visited by St Patrick in AD 450 who found pagans worshipping idols there; the idols spontaneously crashed down when he arrived. He later performed baptisms there. (A seventh-century account of the life of the saints records that during the baptism of one of the clan's kings, Aenghus, St Patrick accidentally pierced him with his crozier; Aenghus believed the injury to be part of the ritual and suffered in silence.)

Brian Boru was crowned High King of Ireland at the Rock in the tenth century. It remained a seat of the Munster Kings until it was granted to the church in 1101 by King Murtagh O'Brien, at which time it became the seat of the archbishop.

The Rock was fortified in the Middle Ages. The cathedral was in use until 1749 – despite a fire in 1495 – when it was replaced by the present St John the Baptist cathedral. In 1647 the Rock was ransacked by Cromwellian forces under the leadership of Lord Inchiquin; this resulted in three thousand deaths, a high number because the townspeople of Cashel had fled to the apparent safety of the site.

Today the magnificent stone walls enclose the most impressive cluster of medieval buildings in Ireland, including the Round Tower, a Gothic cathedral dating back to the thirteenth century, a twelfth-century Romanesque chapel known as Cormac's Chapel, high crosses and other structures. St Patrick's Cross is a copy of the original which is now housed in the museum. It is said to have been erected in St Patrick's honour and his image is carved into it.

The Round Tower is the oldest surviving building on the site. It was probably built to commemorate the handing over of the Rock of Cashel to the Church in 1101.

Cormac's Chapel is Ireland's first and only genuine Romanesque building, with twin square towers in place of transepts. It is a building that inspires reflections of Ireland's Middle Ages. There is a stone sarcophagus in the chapel which was once thought to be that of King Cormac himself, but examination shows it to be from the eleventh century. Cormac's Chapel is also known as The Jewel of Cashel. Over the door is a tympanum featuring a centaur in a helmet with a bow and arrow aimed at a lion, perhaps intended as a symbol of good over evil.

Con Manning, a senior archaeologist commented of his work on the site: 'Cashel is always exciting. It's a dramatic place.'

Rollright Stones, Oxfordshire, England

The Rollright Stones are one of the most famous groupings in the British Isles. They are situated on a chalk ridge to the north of Chipping Norton, in Oxfordshire, and are believed to be older than Stonehenge. Despite the name seeming to imply that they might be able to re-balance themselves if pushed, they actually get their name from the nearby villages of Great and Little Rollright, itself a corruption of the Anglo-Saxon 'hrolla-landriht' – the land of Hrolla.

The site is made up of a stone circle known as The King's Men, a single stone known as The King Stone separated from the main group by a road, and a group of standing and fallen stones which are the remains of a once turf-clad megalithic tomb known as The Whispering Knights. The King's Men is a circle of seventy-seven stones about thirty-five metres in diameter. The Whispering

Knights is to the south-east of the main circle. Originally the site was probably an earthen henge, into which the stones were later set.

The most famous legend of the Rollright Stones describes a Danish King and his men who were crossing the Cotswolds when they encountered a witch. She promised the King that if he could take seven long strides and see Long Compton then he would become King of England. He thought this would be easy. He took the steps but found that a mound known as the Arch Druid's Barrow blocked his view of Long Compton. As a penalty the King and his men were turned to stone, and the witch turned herself into an elder tree. The King became the King Stone, his men the stone circle, and his knights the Whispering Knights stones.

The site was a favoured one for devotees on midsummer's eve, when the elder tree was cut and the sap (representing the witch's blood) was drained and placed on the head of the King Stone (the King) which was then said to move. The King Stone is also supposed to walk down to a nearby spring from which it would drink at midnight.

Common to many stone circles, legend says that the number of stones cannot be counted, that no matter how hard the viewer tries, he or she will get different results each time.

The stones are also associated with fertility rites; folklore suggests that a woman seeking pregnancy should, naked, embrace the stones.

Until the mid-twentieth century the Rollright stones were a prime place for witches' sabbats. However, in 1945 it is alleged that there was a sacrificial killing at the site and local pressure forced the witches to gather elsewhere.

Rosslyn Chapel, Roslin, Scotland

Some of the most elaborate and extraordinary carvings to be found in a church are in Rosslyn Chapel near Edinburgh, in Scotland.

This sacred place is also believed by many to be a mysterious site, and rumours abound as to its origins and present significance.

On the basis of atmosphere alone it deserves its reputation; it is a cramped and dark chapel, but one where a surprise lurks in every shadow. It has become a cause célèbre for those interested in the mystical, with themes involving Christianity, Freemasonry, the Knights Templar, Norse mythology, Hermeticism, and pagan beliefs all depicted in the imagery. There are carvings of plants from the Americas that pre-date by a century the discovery of those lands by Columbus. Amongst the chapel's many images are over two hundred carvings of Green Man images, more than in any other medieval building.

The chapel was built for William St Clair, Laird of Rosslyn and Prince of Orkney, in 1446; St Clair died in 1484 and is buried in the chapel. The foundations suggest that the original plan was to create a huge cruciform church, though the actual chapel is tiny by comparison. Probably the building was intended to be only the lady chapel of the huge church, the design of which is said to have been intended to replicate the Temple of Solomon in Jerusalem. The foundations of the nave of the intended church extend twenty-eight metres beyond the chapel's original west door, under the existing baptistery and churchyard. Both the workforce and the materials used in its construction were brought from afar, and the village of Roslin was originally created just to house the workforce.

By 1592 the altars of the chapel had been smashed and from then until the eighteenth century the building fell into decay. When Cromwell stationed his horses there while besieging the nearby castle he did little obvious damage; surprising since his troops had a tendency to destroy such sacred places. It suffered more at the hands of local anti-Catholics in later years. Sinclair's descendant, James, repaired some of the worst damage in 1736, but it was not until 1861 that extensive renovation took place when architect David Bryce undertook instruction from James Alexander, 3rd Earl of Roslin. The chapel was rededicated in 1862 and has been both under restoration, and in use as a place of worship, from then to the present day.

The Templar and Freemason connection is closely associated with Rosslyn Chapel. The St Clair family (later, Sinclair) were, from the outset, associated with the Templar traditions in Scotland, and became protectors of its derivative, Freemasonry, from the fifteenth century onwards. The founding Grand Master of the Templar order, Hughes de Payens, was married to Catherine St Clair. The first Templar commandery in Scotland was created close to Rosslyn. Further, there are rumours that the Templar fleet that left France during its Order's persecution eventually found port in Scotland, and that Templars were the 'alien' band of soldiers that assisted Robert the Bruce to defeat the English at Bannockburn. Templar signs and markings can be found in graveyards and churches all over Scotland.

The most famous tale about the chapel concerns the Apprentice Pillar. This ornately carved pillar is said to have been carved by an apprentice to the master Mason. The master had travelled to Rome to verify the details of a model of the pillar he was to undertake, and when he returned found that his apprentice had completed the masterpiece, based on a dream. Perhaps the apprentice expected praise, or even a bonus, but instead he was murdered on the spot by the jealous master who struck him in the head with his mallet. It is said that he was executed for his crime. This may be factual – it seems to be supported by carvings in the chapel alleged to depict the master and the apprentice – however, it may also be a story derived from the myths of the Masons, specifically the legends of Hiram Abif and the building of King Solomon's Temple in Jerusalem.

Some basis of fact may be suggested by the claims of Reverend Thompson, a minister of Rosslyn, that the bishop of St Andrews, which includes Rosslyn, was in Rome when the chapel was being constructed, and presumably at the time this murder took place. He apparently sought from the Pope a dispensation to cleanse Rosslyn Chapel from some unpleasant deed that had taken place within its walls.

Of the pillar itself, it is said that it represents the Yggdrasil tree of Norse mythology, which binds together heaven, hell and earth. The crown of the tree is made up of the constellations of the Zodiac and the branches symbolise the planets. At the base of the pillar the dragons of Neifelheim are attacking the roots, trying to draw off the lifeforce of the earth.

Most persistent of modern rumours is that the pillar was used to secrete away the Holy Grail, now contained within it. There is no scientific evidence for this belief, but some are trying to apply pressure to the chapel custodians for non-destructive examination of the interior of the pillar.

Royston Cave, Royston, England

Royston Cave is a bell-shaped chamber cut out of the chalk below Melbourn Street in the town of Royston, part of the ancient Icknield Way. Its origin is unknown, though the carvings on the walls are almost certainly medieval, and some have a clear religious significance. Some of the images have been characterised as St Catherine, St Lawrence and St Christopher. Other figures depicted are believed to include Mary Magdelene, Richard the Lion Heart, and King David, the author of the psalms.

The cave was discovered in 1742 when a millstone was lifted by workmen putting down posts to erect a bench. A small boy was lowered into the cave to see if treasure was hidden there. George Lettis and William Lilly, a tailor and a salesman who lived in a house over the entrance, directed work on the cave and supervised the removal of earth revealing the chamber. No treasure was found; instead were discovered the remains of a human skeleton, and fragments of a cup and a small piece of brass.

The cave may have been used by the Knights Templar before their proscription by Pope Clement V in 1312. Sylvia Beamon, a local researcher, believed it was connected with the Templars between 1199 and 1254 when they held a weekly market at Royston. The cave might have served as a cool-store for produce for the market, and also acted as a chapel for private devotions.

Some of the carvings seem to suggest a pagan origin. One of the most prominent is of a crowned woman holding aloft in her hand an eight-spoked wheel; Christian devotees have ascribed the name of St Catherine to the figure. The Templars held St Catherine in special regard as it was on St Catherine's day in 1177 that they won victory over the Saracen forces of Saladin. However, others believe the figure represents the Queen of the Underworld, Persephone.

The image of St Christopher may refer back to Hermes, patron of travellers. Hermits were his servants, guarding the roads and routes. One image, of two figures close together, has been suggested as the remains of a known Templar sign, that of two knights riding the same horse. Another wall carving in the cave has remained a puzzle, though recent suggestions again tie it to the Templars. The figure was thought to be a man standing in front of an altar, but it was pointed out that he appears to be wearing a heretic's hat. If so then Peter Houldcroft from the Royston and District History Society, who has spent years looking after the cave, believes the figure 'is likely [to be] the Grand Master of the Templars, Jacques de Molay, who was burned at the stake in 1314 in Paris. We originally dismissed ideas that the man was a Grand Master because he did not have a beard, but, of course, they were shaved off when you were executed. This is exciting because it dates the cave to around that time and also proves that it was used by the Knights Templar once they were forced to go into hiding. They used the cave as a place to meet in secret and swear in new members or pledge loyalty to one another.'

St Michael's Mount, Cornwall, England

Known as the 'jewel in Cornwall's crown', this is one of the most visited National Trust sites in Britain. From 1600 to the present day it has been the home of the St Aubyn family. It was given to the National Trust in 1954 by Lord St Levan.

It is essentially a huge granite rock rising from the water of Mount's Bay, topped by a striking and beautiful castle, which was originally a Benedictine Priory built in the twelfth century. It was a 'daughter house' of Mont St Michel in Normandy.

One legend of the Mount goes back to a time when it was a part of the mainland, and indeed when the whole of Mount's Bay was land covered in forest. It is said that in those times two giants lived there, Cormoran and his wife Cormelian. They were building a castle of white granite but Cormelian became lazy and tried to use some green rock from a nearer site. Cormoran caught her and she dropped the rock. A single chunk of greenstone known as the Chapel Rock can be seen today near the causeway. The concept of a forest in the bay is usually regarded as legend, and one that was derived from a parallel legend of Mont St Michel, but there is an account − possibly romanticised − by Robert Hunt in *Popular Romances of the West of England*, published in 1865, where he recalls travelling with other boys from Penzance to the Mount and, when the tide was out, seeing trees in the sand from which the children gathered leaves.

The Mount is thought to have been a well-known port for early traders and may be the island of Ictis from which Cornish tin was exported during the fourth century BC. The historian Diodorus Siculus described how Phoenicians from the eastern Mediterranean traded with the Cornish from an island that could only be reached by a causeway, dry at low tide. This would be a fair description of the link between the town of Marazion and St Michael's Mount, a causeway only passable for two to five hours a day depending on the prevailing tides.

The Mount is dedicated to the Archangel St Michael because of a vision of him according to Cornish legend, that appeared in 495. Some say this was seen by a hermit, some say by local fishermen, and others say it was by a group of monks.

Celtic saints are said to have dwelt there, and it is also said to be part of the legendary lost land of Lyonesse, submerged in a great catastrophe in prehistory.

From the twelfth century onwards the Mount has been a well-known place of pilgrimage.

Seahenge

During the winter storms of 1987−8, an egg-shaped 'circle' of timber posts was exposed within the intertidal zone off the coast of the Wash near Holme-next-the-Sea. This was examined by a Norfolk Sites and Monuments Record Officer on 13 August 1988 and the decision was taken to determine not only what could be learned from it but what was needed to be done to protect it.

The posts immediately attracted world-wide attention from various groups. Wooden structures from the Bronze Age are rare – indeed this is the first intact circle found in Britain – and this site had been especially well preserved because of the layer of peat that had covered it.

The structure consisted of fifty-five wooden posts in a tight circle some 7.5 metres across, with a central upside down oak stump wedged into the ground. It was probably built on marshy ground about a half-mile inland; but was covered by the sea as the coast eroded over time.

A combination of two processes were used to date the site. Firstly carbon-dating was used on samples of the wood. Secondly, tree ring growth was examined and compared to master chronologies of tree rings going back over seven thousand years which had been previously assembled and used as an effective benchmark in such comparisons. By cross-referencing the two results Alex Bayliss, of the Ancient Monuments Laboratory, was able to determine that the central oak had died between April and June of 2050 BC, and the surrounding timbers had died in the spring of the following year.

As to the purpose of Seahenge, several suggestions have been made. It may have been a site of religious sacrifice. Modern druids have speculated that the heads of important chieftains may have been placed there to protect the coastline from invasion. These druids have taken a considerable interest in Bronze Age sites, though it is unlikely that ancient druids did: it is thought that druids first came to England later, during the Iron Age, in around the third century BC. Nevertheless, such sites now form an important part of modern druidic belief.

Robinson Shaw, writing for the National Geographic Society, indicates that many archaeologists believe that it was a sky-burial site; that bodies were laid out on the central stump to decompose under the sky and allow the spirit to be freed.

The central oak seems to answer a long-standing question about such circular structures. In many excavations pits have been found in the centre, but it was unclear what the pits had been used for. Perhaps each pit housed a tree stump as a part of the overall structure. If so, why? Perhaps the stump represented an altar where the dead were laid out. Honeysuckle vines were found at the site, perhaps used to tie the body to the stump.

In the summer of 1999, the structure was excavated and removed to the Flag Fen (Bronze Age) Excavations site for analysis. It was removed mainly to protect it from further erosion, its protective peat layer having been worn away. In addition, the beach was subject to continuing erosion and sea-borers had got into the wood. Another reason was that Seahenge also happened to be in a Site of Special Scientific Interest (SSSI) and it was feared that the attention of tourists and New Age devotees would disrupt the wildlife in the area. It is a nature reserve with many endangered species of birds living there.

David Miles, chief archaeologist for English Heritage, commented: 'Lifting, recording, and analysing all the timbers will transform our knowledge of prehistoric religion and ceremonial sites. The structure stands at the boundary of earth, sky, and sea. To prehistoric people it probably represents a channel to the gods of the underworld and the heavens.' He also said: 'Never in twenty-five years of archaeology have I seen a site attract such a range of opinions and interests. It is amazingly evocative.'

The removal of the structure was controversial, not least with neo-pagans who protested during the removal of the artefacts. Rollo Maughfling, a modern druid, commented: 'It is no accident that the major axis of orientation of the Seahenge oak circle was found to be the line of the north-eastern summer sunrise and the south-western winter sunset, a feature it shared with the great stone circle of Stonehenge itself. More than this, the actual midsummer-midwinter leyline, on which Seahenge used to sit, is the very same one that passes through Stonehenge, and eventually through Maiden Castle in Dorset, making the Seahenge circle in Norfolk the coastal marker of the very first ray of light which enters the land on its way to the great sanctuary of Stonehenge itself.' The druids were of the belief that a better fate for Seahenge than total removal would have been repositioning the structure inland, on the same leyline.

Toby Fox, general manager of Flag Fen Excavations, where the timber circle was taken, suggested that Seahenge was a kind of mortuary constructed by the pre-Celtic Beaker people. He said: 'There's an amazing mysticism about this monument. When we reconstructed it after the excavation, everyone felt a peculiar power in its presence . . . Frankly, it's a bit spooky.'

Silbury Hill, nr Marlborough, Wiltshire, England

Silbury Hill is the largest man-made prehistoric mound in Europe. It is forty metres tall, thirty metres across its flattened top and covers five acres. The base circumference is five hundred metres. It consists of around 340,000 cubic metres of chalk and earth, and one estimate suggests that it would have taken eighteen million man-hours to build. Its construction has been variously dated from 2145 BC to 2750 BC, and appears to have been over two phases, an enlargement taking place shortly after work was commenced. Evidence from the remains of plants and insects suggests that the building of the structure began in the first week in August, perhaps at the time of a Celtic festival of Lammas. It consisted of steps, each filled with packed chalk, and then the whole mound was smoothed off.

The purpose of the hill has never been determined, though it is known to have been abandoned around 1000 BC. Michael Dames has suggested that it is a symbolic effigy of the ancient Mother Goddess and is associated with fertility rituals.

It appears to have been respected by the Romans. As Martin and Nigel Palmer, in their book, *Sacred Britain*, point out, it is one of the few times where the builders of famously straight roads introduced a dog-leg rather than cut through the ancient site. The road was following an ancient ley on which Silbury is positioned.

There have been three excavations of Silbury Hill. The first was in 1776, when a team of Cornish miners sank a shaft from the top through to the bottom. The second was in 1849, when a tunnel was dug horizontally to the centre. The third was in 1968–9, by a team under the direction of Professor Richard Atkinson, organised by BBC television. None of the examinations, though, has found anything particularly significant.

As to its uses, much is speculated yet nothing known with certainty. It has been suggested that it may have been designed to imitate a sacred mountain, or that it was intended as a burial mound for an important figure, though no trace of a burial has yet been uncovered, apart from a relatively recent one at the top of the hill (according to William Stukeley the top of the hill was dug into in 1723 when some bones were discovered together with an ancient bridle).

Legend has it that it is the final resting place of King Sil (or Zil), who is supposed to be buried there on horseback. Other versions of the stories suggest that he is buried on, or with, a fabled golden horse; or that the hill contains a man in golden armour on horseback; or a life-size figure of the King in solid gold; or the King himself buried in a solid gold coffin.

Another folklore story is that the Devil was carrying a huge mound of soil which he planned to deposit on the citizens of Marlborough, but he was seen by priests at nearby Avebury who forced him to drop it, forming the hill.

Late nineteenth-century researcher Moses B Cotsworth thought that Silbury represented a sundial determining the seasons of the year. Janet and Colin Bord in their book, *Mysterious Britain*, relate the impressions of psychometrist Olive Pixley who visited the hill. Her suggestion was that the mound had been used to cover a stone circle where black magic had been practised and the atmosphere of the place had become so evil that the circle had to be demolished and buried. The relatively small stones so far discovered by examination of the hill do not bear out such impressions.

In earlier centuries it was a custom for local villagers on Palm Sunday to make their way to the top of Silbury Hill and eat fig cakes and drink sugar and water.

In *The View Over Atlantis*, John Mitchell comments that: 'In view of the fact that in China mounds like that at Silbury were erected upon *Lung-Mei*, the paths of the Dragon, there is good reason to suspect that Silbury itself was sited by pre-Celtic Druids on a Dragon Line . . .'

On 31 May 2000, a Wiltshire resident reported to the police and local custodians that a hole some fifteen metres deep and three metres wide had opened up at the top of Silbury Hill. The suggestion is that the original hole created by the Duke of Northumberland, when he hired the Welsh miners to excavate in 1776, had collapsed due to settling.

Stanton Drew, Somerset, England

Just a few miles from the bustling city of Bristol are the three stone circles of Stanton Drew. The name Stanton is derived from the Anglo-Saxon 'stan' meaning 'stone' and 'tun' meaning 'farm'. The circles are believed to have been recorded first by John Aubrey in 1664, and the first plan of their layout published by William Stukeley in 1776. The media have dubbed the site Stonehenge II; indeed the site is actually bigger than Stonehenge.

There is a tradition, common to many standing stones around the British Isles, that the stones at Stanton Drew cannot be counted, and that death or illness are the rewards for those who try. The Great Circle is approximately 112 metres in diameter. A stone avenue enters the circle from the north-east, which is the approximate position of the Summer Solstice sunrise. Surrounding the great circle there is evidence of a ditch over seven metres wide. Next to the avenue is a smaller stone circle, also with its own avenue. To the south-west is a third circle; no avenue attached to this circle has yet been found, though that one existed is speculated. This third circle stands on slightly higher ground and may have been a sanctuary and a location from where activities taking place in the other two circles could be viewed. Most of the stones have fallen, although a few are still upright.

Just a few metres away, in the grounds of the Druids Arms Inn, there is also a small 'cove' made from three large stones, forming a box-like shape about three metres across. The 'box' is open to the south-east. It has been suggested that this is aligned to the rising of the moon; or perhaps represented the end of an avenue.

To the north, across the River Chew, is a standing stone known as Hautville's Quoit. Local legend is that it was thrown there by a crusading knight named Sir John Hautville, who was based at Maes Knoll, an Iron Age hillfort nearby.

Their proximity and relationship to each other, and the alignments between some of them, suggest that these various stones are part of one single complex. If so, given the size of the complex, it is reasonable to assume that in the late Stone Age Stanton Drew was one of the most important sacred places in Britain.

On 10 November 1997, the Ancient Monuments Laboratory of English Heritage confirmed that they had found traces of wooden posts at the site, though long since rotted away. Using a hand-held fluxgate gradiometer which measures variations in the local magnetic field caused by disturbances in the soil, the team was able to plot the former existence of a series of nine concentric rings of wooden posts in the henge below the stone circle. These range from twenty-three metres to ninety-five metres in diameter. Dr Andrew David, Head of Archeometry, believed this detection was possible either because of the burning of the original wooden posts, or because of bacterial activity in the wood. When the wooden posts rotted, they were probably replaced by the standing stones that are the visible part of the site today.

Stanton Drew was, therefore, possibly the site of a wooden temple in the Neolithic period. It is likely that such temples were the focal point for local tribes. There was a 'status race' involved; the size of a tribe's temple is believed to have represented their confidence and position in the locality. The tribe that worshipped at Stanton Drew can reasonably be assumed to have had high local standing. The temple would have drawn offerings from a wide area around, possibly making the tribe rich in resources; the pay back for those worshipping there would be that the bigger the temple, the more likely the gods would answer.

There have been similar finds at other sites such as Woodhenge and Durrington Walls but, as pointed out by Dr Wainwright, Chief

Archaeologist, 'The Stanton Drew find is by far the largest – twice as big as anything previously discovered.'

The henge spans in total over 120 metres and may have been up to eight metres high. This is thought to have made the site too large to be roofed, though it is believed that wooden posts found at other sites held up a roof. The evidence from Stanton Drew challenges that theory and the debate continues.

Sir Jocelyn Stephens, chairman of English Heritage, commented: 'In world heritage terms, wooden temples are one of the things that make Britain of international significance.' He added, 'The use of highly sensitive survey techniques has shown this site is of equal significance to its more famous contemporaries.'

There is a legend attached to the stone circles of Stanton Drew that is similar to one found all around the British Isles. It is that there was a wedding on a midsummer's eve which, in that year, also happened to be a Saturday. The bride, groom and guests were celebrating with much merry-making and dancing. At midnight all this should have ended as it was now the Sabbath Day, and the fiddler who was providing the music refused to play on. The bride, however, insisted that the dancing continue and said that she would go to hell to find a fiddler if she had to. At that moment a fiddler arrived at the party, ready to meet her wishes. He played, and the party danced on into the Sabbath. When asked to stop the fiddler refused, and the party could not stop dancing. The next day the fiddler – the Devil himself – was gone and the bride, groom and guests had been turned to stone; the stones of the circles. The circles are known as The Fiddler and the Maids, and the stones of the cove are sometimes called The Parson, The Bride and The Bridegroom.

Despite what is known about the site, there is a considerable mystery about one aspect of the location. There are no Bronze Age burial mounds in the area, unlike at similar sites such as Stonehenge and Avebury. It has been suggested that perhaps Stanton Drew was a failure, that the local tribes came to believe that it had ceased to attract the good attentions of the gods. This is not supported, however, by the fact that the site was clearly developed and renovated, such as when the wooden posts were replaced by stones. For a time at least it must have been regarded as 'operational'. The lack of burial sites is yet to be explained.

Stonehenge

Stonehenge is the product of successive phases of building. Phase 1, which has been carbon-dated to approximately 3100 BC, is a circular ditch and internal earth bank. The ditch is almost one hundred metres in diameter with a single entranceway. Around the perimeter are fifty-six holes, known as the Aubrey Holes, in which have been found the remains of human cremations. It is believed that in the centre was a wooden sanctuary.

Phase 2 is thought to date from around 2150 BC. The sanctuary was replaced by two circles of bluestones brought from the Preseli mountains in Wales, over two hundred miles away, and parallel ditches were constructed, forming an avenue aligned to the midsummer sunrise. Outside the circle was erected the 35-ton Heel stone.

The bluestones were taken down during Phase 3, around 2075 BC, and the sarsen stones erected, topped with lintels. The structure of two standing stones and a topping lintel is known as a trilithon. The sarsens appear to have come from the Marlborough Downs, relatively nearby.

In Phase 4, sometime between 1500 and 1100 BC, some sixty of the bluestones were re-erected in a circle within the sarsen circle, and another nineteen erected in a horseshoe pattern.

One estimate of the total construction effort says that over thirty million hours of labour were required throughout the phases of building. Only a sophisticated and organised society could have visualised and enacted so large a project, organised so large a workforce and possessed the design and construction skills necessary. With just very basic tools, the builders of Stonehenge shaped the stones and formed the mortices and tenons that linked the standing stones to their lintels. Using antlers and bones, they dug the pits to seat the stones.

The transport of stones from the Preseli mountains has been

the subject of much speculation. Almost certainly they were brought by sea, either up the Bristol Channel, or round Land's End, and then dragged across land to the Wiltshire site. For the journey by sea they were presumably either carried on large rafts or, as archaeologist T.C. Lethbridge suggested, slung in the water between two boats. This theory was put to the test in 2000 as a Millennium Project. A team of volunteers attempted to bring a bluestone – nick-named Elvis – from Preseli to Stonehenge slung between two light boats known as curachs, similar to those that would have been in use when Stonehenge was being assembled. The project was dogged with problems, not the least of which was the rope holding the stone snapping and Elvis sinking to the bottom of the River Avon. However, this proved that theories about the transport of the stones were probably right – Elvis turned out not to be the only such bluestone on the riverbed. Clearly our ancestors had had similar setbacks.

John Aubrey, in the mid-seventeenth century, suggested that Stonehenge was constructed by the druids. This has become a popular mythology, but it is unlikely that the druids had anything to do with the development of Stonehenge, as its construction significantly pre-dates the druids' arrival in England. Stonehenge had been completed, and may even have fallen into disuse, a millennium before their time.

No other monument has inspired so much speculation as to its purpose, and even today its use is uncertain. Archaeologists have generally assumed it to be a monument used in the rituals and rites of Neolithic peoples. In the 1950s, Oxford University engineer Alexander Thom and astronomer Gerald Hawkins suggested there were significant astronomical alignments within the structure. They proposed that Stonehenge was an astronomical observatory and believed it displayed exceptional mathematical sophistication pre-dating previous estimates of such knowledge in the British Isles. Thousands of years before the 'discovery' of Pi it seems that Stonehenge's designers had incorporated the concept into their structure. However, Thom and Hawkins' work has been challenged to some degree by

Benjamin Ray. In 1987, he suggested that much of the apparent astronomical significance is not as precise as earlier speculated and that wishful-thinking of the earlier researchers contributed to their findings.

The most current theories have therefore reverted to the belief that Stonehenge had, primarily, a ritual function for which its astronomical qualities were a tool rather than a main purpose. Ray has proposed that Stonehenge was intended to be a stone version of the wooden sanctuaries used in Neolithic times, one of which may have stood on the site in early times anyway. The fact that the area around Stonehenge has many ancient burial sites leads Ray to speculate that the monument had a function in burial rituals. In 1923 the skeleton of an executed man dating from around two thousand years ago, who appeared to have been beheaded by sword, was unearthed at Stonehenge. Scientists at first believed he had died of natural causes, and the skeleton was misplaced for some time. It was only with recent analysis, after the skeleton was rediscovered in May 1999 in the stores of the Natural History Museum in London, that the manner of his death was realised.

Popular amongst devotees of the New Age, and undoubtedly having some relevance, is that Stonehenge appears to be built on an ancient site of great power. It is on important leys, and may have been thought by its builders to be a site of natural energy. Perhaps this explains the use of specific stones in the construction of the monument – not least bringing hundreds of tons of bluestones from over two hundred miles away – if it was believed that the use of certain materials would channel the energies of the structure.

The attentions of new-agers, neo-druids and hippies finally made the authorities run scared and in the 1980s they roped off Stonehenge, preventing the public from getting near the stones. Police were used regularly during the summer solstices to regulate the hoards of hippies arriving at the scene. (One hippie said: 'They used helicopters, man. How high do they think we get!') It was not until June of 1999 that people were able to go in amongst the stones again and actually touch them. For many people that contact was important, and significant in their belief that the stones are a battery of natural energy.

Dowsers amongst the stones report high levels of such energy. Researcher Colin Wilson was amongst those who enjoyed the summer solstice at the stones in 1999 and took the opportunity to dowse. 'There was a strong tingling sensation, as if I had tuned in to an electrical force. I learned that afternoon that Stonehenge is the centre of a huge spiral of some kind of Earth-energy.' Wilson added, of the question why Stonehenge was positioned where it was: 'It was because the Earth in that particular spot was, in some sense, alive.'

That natural energy is indicated in the poet Layamon's tribute to Stonehenge dating from 1200:

> The stones are great
> And magic power they have
> Men that are sick
> Fare to that stone
> And they wash that stone
> And with that water bathe away their sickness.

The Temple Church, London

Temple Church was built by the Knights Templar, the soldier-monks of the crusades during the twelfth century. The church was constructed in two parts: the Round and the Chancel. The Round was designed to represent the holiest place in the Crusaders' world – the circular Church of the Holy Sepulchre in Jerusalem – and was consecrated in 1185 by the patriarch of Jerusalem, Heraclius, in the presence of King Henry II. It contains the life-size stone effigies of nine knights, the most famous of which was William, Earl of Pembroke, who acted as mediator between King John and the Barons in 1215. The Chancel was built in 1240.

This church was at the hub of Templar activity in London and therefore the whole of Britain and was built as part of an administrative and accommodation centre known as the New

Temple. The influence of the Templars was considerable: this preceptory was regularly used by Kings and legates of the Pope as a residence when visiting London. After the dissolution of the Templars, the London preceptory was taken over by King Edward II and eventually was rented to two colleges of lawyers in the city, which came to be known as the Inner and Middle Temples. On 13 August 1608 King James I granted a Royal Charter, giving these colleges use of the Temple in perpetuity, on condition that the Inns maintain the Church. Both the Temple and Church are governed by that charter to this day.

Although the church was undamaged by the Great Fire of London, Sir Christopher Wren decided to undertake some restoration work at that time. However, during the Second World War the church was greatly damaged and the restoration took many years to complete. The church was rededicated in March 1954.

Traprain Law, Scotland

Traprain Law is a well-known landmark of the East Lothians. Sometimes described as like a beached whale in appearance, it is a huge hilltop elevation with relatively flat farmlands, reminiscent of Uluru (Ayers Rock) in Australia. The name Traprain Law was applied relatively recently; its earlier names were Dunpender or Dunpelder meaning roughly The Fort of Stockades. It is the largest hillfort in Scotland and one of the most important prehistoric sacred sites in that country. A cairn there is thought to be the remains of a Bronze Age burial.

By the Iron Age, the whole hilltop was densely populated, as evidenced by the remains of buildings found there. Archaeological study of Traprain Law has also shown that it was a major centre of power during the Roman occupation, when the area was inhabited by the Votadini tribe who had good relations with the Romans. Excavations have located fragments of Roman pottery and glass. In 1919 a hoard of silver was discovered, thought to have been a payment by the Romans to the Votadini tribe for their loyalty. There is evidence of terraces which were part of substantial buildings, suggesting that the hill was occupied by wealthy or important people.

Even after the Roman period there is evidence of subsequent use. Fraser Hunter, Curator of Iron Age and Roman Collections at the National Museums of Scotland, said: 'We have found unexpected evidence for the later use of the hill, after its abandonment as a major settlement around the fifty century AD. A typical early Christian burial has been uncovered, providing evidence of some religious use . . . A sizeable medieval enclosure was also unearthed in the same area, right on the very summit. Although at this stage it cannot be proven, this could be connected with a church or shrine to St Mungo. These excavations have given us tantalising glimpses of this fascinating site. They show the importance of Traprain and the potential locked in to tell us about life in southern Scotland 2000 years ago.'

Nearby is the Loth Stone standing almost 2.5 metres high, and claimed to mark the grave of the mythical King Loth, from whom the Lothians are said to be named. However, excavations have revealed no human remains.

The hill is also a famous local site for UFO sightings, so much so that national and international teams of investigators have set up camp there in the hope of seeing such phenomena. The *Evening Mail* (Midlands) of 5 January 2000 reported that a 'UFO hunt takes to the hills.' It commented that a Japanese television company was to train a 24-hours-a-day camera on the sky at Traprain law, and at another local site, Berwick Law, for six months in an attempt to record a UFO. The camera was to be set up on the roof of a local hotel, the Templar Lodge. During a BBC television report, Stephen Prior, head of marketing at the Templar Lodge, said: 'We had heard various rumours locally that there were a lot of UFO sightings over Berwick Law and Traprain Law, some seeing them from as far away as Fife. I was sceptical – I believe people see things, but what they are on, heaven knows. There are Celtic stories about them being fairy hills, with fairy lights on them.' Although such reports are common at sacred sites Prior remained sceptical, adding: 'My own suspicion is that it may be tied in with coloured gas from the granite.'

Uffington White Horse, Oxfordshire

On the chalk hills of south-west Oxfordshire is a sacred area which contains probably the most famous of all hill carvings, the White Horse of Uffington. It has been dated to at least the Iron Age (approximately 500 BC) but may have originated earlier. A recent dating by the Oxford Archaeological Unit placed it at around three thousand years old. There have been several Iron Age coins found which depict a figure similar to the White Horse. White Horse Hill was first mentioned in records in the 1070s, and the Horse image itself was first referred to in 1190, in the records of Abingdon Abbey.

The figure is one hundred metres in length, thirty metres tall, and made up of ditches two to three metres wide and a metre deep. It has survived over the centuries by being regularly renewed by local villagers; it was an observed tradition to re-scour the image every seven years, restoring its integrity. The renewal was once part of a local festival, with villagers congregating on White Horse Hill for a weekend's partying. This tradition ended during the last century and the Horse is now in the care of the National Trust.

Although always described as a horse, its shape is more ambiguous and many observers have pointed out that it could well represent a dragon. It may therefore be part of a larger local tradition as the figure looks down on the mound known as Dragon Hill, where St George is said to have slain the dragon of mythology. Perhaps it is a portrait of St George's nemesis. It is said that no grass can grow where the dragon's blood spilled.

Alternatively, it may represent a Celtic god such as Epona, or it may have been a tribal symbol.

Above the White Horse, higher on the hill, is Uffington Camp, an earth enclosure surrounding nine acres of land with a single bank and ditch. Being in a good strategic position the Camp has been used by consecutive peoples over many thousands of years, probably beginning life in the Neolithic period.

Walsingham, England

In AD 1061 Lady Richeldis de Faverches, a widow living in a manor house in Walsingham, received visions of the Virgin Mary.

Mary showed her, in the visions, the house in Nazareth where she had been told by the Angel Gabriel that she would give birth to Jesus. She also asked Lady de Faverches to build a replica of this house at Walsingham, to be dedicated as a memorial to the Annunciation to Mary and the Incarnation of the Lord Jesus Christ. It was to be a place of prayer where Mary would be able to answer the calls of those who needed her. She had said: 'Let all who are in any way distressed or in need seek me there in that small house that you maintain for me at Walsingham. To all that seek me there shall be given succour.'

Lady de Faverches received the same vision three times, which convinced her that she must act, but she was at a loss to know where to construct the replica. She sought the answer in prayer, and it is said that Our Lady herself instructed angels to complete the construction exactly where she wanted it, just two hundred metres from where carpenters had begun work.

To protect the replica of the house a church was built around it. An Augustinian Priory was founded in 1153 to cater for the spiritual needs of the many pilgrims, and a Friary was also established. By the thirteenth century Walsingham had achieved status as a pilgrimage site on a par with Rome, Jerusalem and Santiago de Compostela. Many kings made the pilgrimage to the house: Henry III travelled there in 1248; so did Edward I and Edward III. Other famous pilgrims included Erasmus who visited in 1514.

The last king to visit was Henry VIII. He came in 1486 as a prince, and then later as king, but in 1534 he broke with the Catholic Church and Walsingham church, the house, and a statue of Mary, were destroyed on his orders as part of his general destruction of Catholic places of worship. As the Protestant movement gathered in strength, so Walsingham lost its status as a place of pilgrimage and worship.

In the nineteenth century an Anglican woman who later converted to Catholicism, Charlotte Boyd, began work to restore the shrine. On 20 August 1897, pilgrims from King's Lynn travelled to the Slipper Chapel to renew the site as one of public devotion to the Virgin. The Slipper Chapel, so-named for those who, particularly in the Middle Ages, removed their shoes to walk barefoot to the original Holy House, was a small Catholic chapel located nearby which had survived the destruction.

In the 1920s Walsingham's Holy House was rebuilt under the direction of Anglican priest Alfred Hope-Patten. The actual location of the original Holy House was the subject of much debate for years, but examinations in 1961 showed beyond all doubt where it had originally been situated, and this important sacred place is now clearly marked out for modern-day pilgrims. It is located near the ruins in the Priory grounds.

The Slipper Chapel became the focus of more modern pilgrimages; and indeed the site is now a very active place of pilgrimage once again. Known as England's Nazareth, it is a holy place highly regarded by Christians. Although once the Catholics and Anglicans had separated their interests at the site, and virtually ignored each other, the site is now under the joint care of both Churches. This reconciliation was brought about by Pope John Paul II who, when visiting England, celebrated Mass at Wembley with the image of Our Lady of Walsingham on the altar, an image that had been placed there by both the director of the Catholic shrine and the administrator of the Anglican shrine.

Our Lady of Walsingham is also known by her title of The Virgin by the Sea. It is said that she helps seamen in distress. The Anglican pilgrim hostel uses the name Stella Maris, meaning Star of the Sea, one of Mary's more ancient titles. Walsingham, being just a few miles from the sea, is regarded as a place of prayer for mariners.

Over the years there have been many miracles attributed to Our Lady of Walsingham, including one in which Edward I was saved from a falling piece of masonry.

The Sacred Land Project is creating a new section of pilgrimage route between the Slipper Chapel and the village.

West Kennet Long Barrow, Wiltshire, England
West Kennet Long Barrow is situated near the stone circle of Avebury, not far from Silbury Hill. It was first recorded by John

Aubrey in the seventeenth century and later by William Stukeley in the eighteenth century.

One of the longest chambered long barrows in Britain, it was originally a mound some 110 metres long formed from sarsen boulders and a capping of chalk from two local quarry ditches. The barrow is around 2.5 metres high; there are two burial chambers either side, and one at the end. The latest examinations show that the side chambers are positioned inside an isosceles triangle, the height being twice the length of the base. The entrance passage is through a semi-circular forecourt, and huge sarsen uprights are aligned along a north-south axis.

The barrow was first examined in 1859, and fully excavated between 1955 and 1956 during which time the sarsens were removed and replaced.

On excavation the remains of forty-six people of varying ages and both sexes, together with pottery fragments, flint tools, and beads were discovered. The burials apparently took place over a lengthy period of time. The studies showed that several bones, generally skull and thigh bones, had been removed, probably for ceremonial use. However, it is also thought that a local doctor in the seventeenth century took some of the bones for use in medicines.

West Kennet Long Barrow was probably begun around 3600 BC, and finally closed around 1600 BC.

There are ghost stories attached to the site. On midsummer's day a spectral black dog is said to appear, and there are also claims of a spectral white-dressed priest entering the tomb at sunrise on midsummer's day, accompanied by a white dog with red ears.

Wilmington Long Man, Sussex, England

The Long Man of Wilmington, sometimes known as the Wilmington Giant, is a 69-metre figure of a person, holding two stakes by his sides, carved into the slope of Windover Hill in Sussex. The figure is one of the largest images of a human anywhere on earth, second only to the 120-metre Giant Of Atacama, in Chile. The figure is slightly elongated, designed so as to appear to be of normal proportions when viewed from ground level.

Historical information about the Long Man is incomplete. Originally the image was carved into the chalk, and would have needed constant maintenance to keep it from disappearing under grass. In 1874, the figure was highlighted by the use of yellow bricks, a work undertaken by the Sussex Archaeological Society, and in 1891 these were replaced with white bricks. As a temporary measure they were painted green during the Second World War, to prevent the figure being used as a reference point by enemy aircraft. After the war they were whitewashed. Finally, in 1969 the image was re-created using 770 concrete blocks. However, the several re-linings of the figure have probably slightly altered its original shape.

A 1776 drawing shows the man holding a scythe and a rake, as is also mentioned in *Britania* by Richard Gough, published in 1806. However, the figure had not been holding such implements in 1710, when a drawing of the giant was done by John Rowley. So we know it has changed over the centuries; the feet, for example, which now point in the same direction, used to point away from each other. Possibly the figure was used to make current or political or social points at times in its long history. There are also accounts of it once having had facial features: eyes, nose and mouth.

The site is currently owned by the Sussex Archaeological Society, who were presented with it by the Duke of Devonshire in October, 1925.

The age of the figure is much debated. Traces of red Roman tile in the outline have led some to the speculation that the man is pre-Roman, and that possibly the Romans tried to defile or destroy the image in order to subdue a local cult not friendly to the invaders. Alternatively, perhaps the Romans tried to change the image to become an idol of their own. It is, however, almost certain that the Long Man is not originally Roman; there is no particular Roman influence in the immediate area.

Windover Hill itself is replete with archaeological sites dating from Neolithic times onwards. Flint axes and implements have been found on the hill during excavations. The area was an important route for travel and trade, for example for the transport of tin from Cornwall, and this has led to the suggestion that the Long Man was carved by Phoenician traders as an early advertising sign. It does resemble a Phoenician image of a figure holding two pillars of a temple.

Near the Long Man are also several prehistoric burial sites: barrows known as the Giants Grave and Hunters Burgh, and several bronze age round barrows. One such round barrow contains evidence of a high status burial, possibly of a late Neolithic or Bronze Age chieftain. Whether there is any direct connection to the Long Man is unknown. Perhaps the figure represented a magical protector of the Neolithic sites, or the flint mines, designed to keep away invaders. Other suggestions have been that: the figure was carved out by monks from Wilmington Priory to commemorate the visit of a pilgrim; that the Long Man represents Beowulf fighting Grendel with a spear in each hand; that the figure represents a deity or hero; or that the figure is a Green Man, thousands of images of which are found in various forms around the countryside.

The most likely probability is that the site, and the Long Man, had a religious significance, possibly representing an idol or fertility symbol. Alfred Watkins in his book *The Old Straight Track*, setting out the theory of leylines, suggested that the figure was a Dodman, a person who laid out the original leys. The Long Man is situated on a ley.

The most common local folklore is that the figure represents the burial site of, or memorial to, an actual giant, or it is the outline of the place he fell and died. In these legends it is said that he was killed by a shepherd throwing his food at him, or that he tripped and broke his neck, or was killed by pilgrims travelling to Wilmington Priory. Even more popular is the story that he was killed by another giant who lived on Firle Beacon.

Today the site is often used by pagans for worship or ritual. Childless couples have been known to sleep there in the hope that the figure, as a fertility symbol, might bring them a child. One Wiccan ritual which took place there in 1990, during the Gulf War, was apparently designed to oppose Saddam Hussein's influence.

The hill is one of several sites in the country with a strong legend of spectral black dogs, guardians of the graveyards, perhaps in this case the barrows on the hill. Visitors to the hill have reported the sound of paws padding along with them where no animal could be seen.

MYSTICAL AND SACRED SITES IN EUROPE

Altamira Cave, Spain

Situated near Santillana del Mar is the Altamira Cave, discovered by accident in 1869 by Marcelino de Santuola. It consists of a series of 'rooms' formed from erosion in limestone, and is some 270 metres in length. The first explorations were undertaken in 1875, though it would be four more years before the richness of the cave paintings, for which the cave is now so famous, would be discovered. Sadly for their discoverer, their condition was thought to be so good, and so well preserved, that they were first taken to be fakes, and it was not until after de Santuola's death that they were proved to be genuine.

The cave appears to have been inhabited during the Aurignacian period (around 32,000 years ago), to which the first figure-like images belong, and it was certainly occupied during the Solutrean and Magdalenian periods (that is, from around 19,000 to 11,000 BC), as carbon-dating of the organic remains found in the cave showed.

The 'main hall', including the ceiling, was decorated at the beginning of the Magdalenian period. The paintings consist of multi-coloured images of bison, horses, deer and boar. The images are large – a red deer is over two metres long, for example – and they are very detailed. In addition the artists appear to have used the contours of the walls to make the animals 'come alive', almost in 3-D. The overall effect is wondrous; the Altamiran Cave has been called the Sistine Chapel of Palaeolithic art.

It is strongly believed that such images were not mere depictions, but were magical paintings designed to attract the animals to the hunters; in effect they were visual prayers for a successful hunt. Such caves can therefore be argued to be amongst the earliest of sacred sites.

Assisi, Italy

The town of Assisi in central Italy is a place of Catholic pilgrimage and tourism, famous for being the birthplace of St Francis. The main focus of interest is the Basilica of San Francesco: two churches built one above the other between 1228 and 1253. The crypt houses the tomb of St Francis.

The town was, however, a sacred place before the Franciscan era. It is said to have been founded by Dardanus 865 years before the founding of Rome, and was then called Assisium. It was based around a holy spring.

St Francis was born in Assisi in 1182, and was originally named Giovanni Francesco Bernardone. He lived a relatively wild young life, but, after being held as a prisoner of war and suffering severe illness, he turned to helping the sick and to restoring churches as a response to religious visions. During Mass one day in 1208, he felt a calling to discard his possessions and go into the world to do good. That same year, he began preaching in Assisi and gathered around him twelve disciples who were the original brothers of his First Order of Franciscans. Along with a nun, Clare (later St Clare), he established the Order of the Poor Ladies, later the Second Order of Franciscans. He went to the Holy Land to continue his work, and on returning developed the Third Order of Franciscans – the Tertiaries.

St Francis rejected the hypocrisy of the church, effectively challenging a corrupt Papacy. He gathered a huge following by his simple life, his devotion to nature, and his quiet and serene character.

In September of 1224, after a fast lasting forty days, he was praying when he became the first person to receive the stigmata – the visible wounds of Christ's crucifixion manifest on his body. He spent the remainder of his life in Assisi, in pain with the stigmata, and almost blind, dying in 1226. He was canonised in 1228.

For over five hundred years pilgrims have flocked to the town; the Basilica of St Francis is one of the most visited shrines of the Christian faith.

Avila, Spain

Teresa Sanchez Cepeda Davila y Ahumada was born at Avila, Old Castle, on 28 March 1515. After her mother's death, when Teresa was fourteen years old, she was sent to be educated by Augustinian nuns at Avila, but had to leave them just after eighteen months due to illness. She returned to her father and was brought up by him, with occasional help from other relatives, in particular an uncle who educated her in the Letters of St Jerome. These helped to formulate her desire to adopt a religious life. Her father was not supportive of this decision and therefore she left his home in November 1535 and entered the Carmelite Convent of the Incarnation at Avila. In the following year she again became seriously ill; indeed she never fully recovered her health from that date.

In the year that followed she reported that God had visited her with 'intellectual visions and locutions'. These impressions troubled her as she did not believe herself worthy of them. Word of these visions got out, and became known to the whole population of Avila. She found guidance and support, both for her own inner turmoil and for her work, from St Francis Borgia and St Peter of Alcantara, and a number of Dominicans, Jesuits, and other priests. The account of her spiritual life, called *Life Written By Herself* was completed in 1565; she also penned additional material in *Relations* and *Interior Castle*.

During this period of her life, Teresa received the miraculous visitation for which she is most famous world-wide: the piercing of her heart, apparently by a mystical spear. She believed that this was done by an angel. She also suffered a vision of her destiny in hell should she waver from her course.

With this extraordinary background, and against considerable opposition, Teresa founded the convent of Discalced (Barefoot) Carmelite Nuns of the Primitive Rule of St Joseph at Avila on 24 August 1562.

In September 1582, old and in pain, she travelled to Alba de Torres where she passed away on 4 October in that year. After some years, her body was sent back to her home town of Avila, but later it was returned to Alba, where it is still preserved incorrupt. Her heart, showing the marks of the piercing, is on display there for pilgrims, a most important sacred relic for her faithful.

She was beatified in 1614, and canonised in 1622 by Pope Gregory XV.

Pilgrims honouring St Teresa often travel to Avila, her place of birth, which is a magnificent walled town, regarded as one of the finest remnants of Europe's medieval era. It has a mystical history, and was sacred to an ancient Celtiberian culture long before the arrival of the Romans or Christians. Its famous walls were built in the twelfth century, and extend for some 2,500 metres encircling the old town, punctuated by ninety, heavily fortified, stone towers. The church in the centre of the town was founded in 1091 and completed in the thirteenth century, and is where St Teresa had her visions and ecstatic experiences. Near the church is the house where St Teresa lived, also a major focus for pilgrims.

Carnac, France

Carnac – the name comes from the Breton 'Karn', meaning 'cluster of stones' – is a village in north-west France, on the south coast of Brittany, famous for its thousands of megalithic monuments consisting of menhirs, dolmens, and tumuli. It is estimated that there are three thousand such monuments, effectively arranged in three groups although it is generally believed that at one time they formed part of one elaborate group. The main group, the Menec system, to the north-west of the village, contains 1,099 granite monoliths, arranged in eleven almost parallel rows running over one thousand metres in length. They end in an arc which reaches around to the ends of the outer rows. The Kermario system consists of ten such lines, and 982 menhirs, and the third group is the Kerlescan system of thirteen lines, and 540 menhirs. The single menhirs and the multi-stone dolmens were cut from local granite; some of the stones are over six metres high. The Kermario lines point to the passage grave of Kercado which is covered by a barrow; this grave was explored in 1863.

The origins and purpose of these Neolithic monuments remain a mystery. They were worshipped by the Bretons until relatively recent times, and were also used by the Romans for religious purposes. Roman gods are depicted on some of the stones. The imposition of Christianity into the area is also depicted in carvings on the stones; there are examples of Christian crosses and other symbols.

The stone configurations are generally thought to be around five thousand years old, but it is clear that they were erected at very different times, including the early, middle, and late Neolithic periods.

A fence and security system was erected in 1990 to prevent damage from the increasing numbers of tourists to the site, and over the next ten years a programme of re-stabilisation of the stones was undertaken. The restrictions remained until late 1999, after which the work in some of the areas was completed and visitors were again allowed to roam freely within parts of the site. The remainder of the site is also being re-stabilised.

Cathedral Nuestra Señora del Pilar, Saragossa, Spain

Toward the end of the first century BC, the town then known as Salduba was made a Roman colony called Caesaraugusta (from which its Arabia name, Saraqustah, and its present name, were derived). It was later to become one of the first Spanish towns to be Christianised. In AD 714 it fell to the Moors, but in 1118 it came under the control of King Alfonso I and for 350 years was the capital of the region of Aragon.

Zaragoza (Saragossa) houses the Cathedral Nuestra Señora del Pilar, dedicated to the Virgin of the Pillar, patron of all Spain. It commemorates a visitation of the Virgin Mary on 2 January AD 40, when her apparition was seen by St James. This Marian appearance was unique as it was one of bi-location: Mary was alive at the time James saw her apparition. According to tradition, while in Zaragoza James had become disheartened at the lack of success of his mission and had prayed. The Virgin Mary appeared to him and gave him a small wooden statue of herself and a column of jasper wood, instructing him to build a church in her honour, saying: 'This place is to be my house, and this image and column shall be the title and altar of the temple that you shall build.'

Around a year later James had a small chapel built, dedicated to the Virgin Mary; it was the first church in the world dedicated to her honour. This early construct was enlarged over the centuries, and the present cathedral was completed in 1681. The two holy artefacts given to James by the Virgin are still displayed on special occasions.

For centuries there have been reports of mysterious apparitions here, a site which still attracts large numbers of pilgrims.

Church of Saints Geremia and Lucia (St Jeremy and St Lucy), Venice, Italy

This church contains the tomb of St Lucy, the patron saint of eyesight. It is said that rather than surrender her virginity, she tore out her eyes and presented them to her 'suitor'. It is the centre of pilgrimage for many who believe that touching her tomb can bring about cures to eye-ailments and blindness.

A recent study of the body within the tomb showed it to be that of a Sicilian woman, which matched the origins of St Lucy who was born in Syracuse. Her story – not all of which can be authenticated – is that she was born to a rich family in around AD 283. Her father was a Roman, her mother probably of Greek origin. Her mother was cured of medical problems by a miracle after visiting relics of the martyr Agatha, and Lucy later showed gratitude by distributing her money to the poor. Lucy's betrothed was angered by this and he denounced her to the governor of Sicily in AD 303. She was condemned to prostitution, but refused to submit and, it is said, tore out her own eyes. She was executed by the sword. Saint Aldheim in AD 709 is the first writer to offer an account of her life, by which time some distortion of the facts may have happened, and there is likely to have been some amalgamation of the stories of Lucy and Agatha.

However, mystery surrounds the remains of the martyr. The monk, Sigebert (1030–1112), in his 'sermo de Sancta Lucia', states that her body remained in Sicily for four hundred years before it was taken to Corfinium in Italy. Her arm was said to have been taken to the monastery of Luitburg. It is further said that when Constantinople (Istanbul) was captured in 1204, the relics of St Lucy were presented to the Doge of Venice and housed in the monastery of St George. In 1513 it is claimed by some that her head was given to Louis XII of France and secured in the cathedral at Bourges. Another account suggests that the head reached Bourges directly from Rome.

Brother Anthony (of the Franciscan Brothers of the Sacred Heart), who has visited the Church of Saints Geremia and Lucia in Venice, where her body is housed in a glass sarcophagus behind the altar, relates the story that in 1955, Cardinal Roncalli (later Pope John XXIII) requested that her face be covered with a silver death mask, which is clearly visible to pilgrims, but was himself perplexed at stories that the head was not in the sarcophagus, and at other mysteries concerning the relics. Brother Anthony says: 'I am finding conflicting accounts of not only the present location of the head, but I have also discovered that several other places claim to have her body as well. It would seem to me that her body at Venice has the most historical documentation.'

There is no doubt of the depth of respect in which St Lucy is held by many pilgrims, and perhaps the mystery of her remains only adds to the mystique for many of her followers.

Church of the Megolohari, Tinos Island, Greece

The island of Tinos has more than six hundred churches and monasteries, and is well known for its miraculous healing icon of the Virgin Mary. The island has always been a sacred place, once housing temples to Poseidon and Dionysos. An early Christian church was built on the site of the Temple of Dionysos, though it was later destroyed by invaders.

At the nunnery of Kehrovouniou, in June 1822, a nun, Sister Pelagia, reported several visions of the Virgin Mary who told her that the local people should search in a particular field where they would find an icon. On 30 January 1823 an icon was indeed unearthed there, and it was later found that the discovery was made on the very spot where the Temple of Dionysos and the Christian church had once stood, indeed in the crypt of the former church. The site is now known as the Chapel of Evresis (Discovery).

The icon is known as Our Lady of Good Tidings, and shows

Mary kneeling in prayer. It is presumed that it once belonged to the church; after it was found a new church was built on the site of the discovery. This was completed in 1830 and is known as the Church of the Megolohari (meaning Great Grace). During that time pilgrims were already visiting the island to see the icon which quickly attained a reputation for performing healing miracles. It is now regarded by many as the most sacred object of pilgrimage for the Greek peoples.

Every summer, thousands of people make their way to the island to celebrate The Assumption of the Virgin in a huge festival on 15 August. One reported stated: 'During the actual ceremonies, the spiritual emotion and the mystical atmosphere is apparent among the masses of believers . . . it is a moving experience.'

Cologne Cathedral (The Kolner Dom), Cologne, Germany

In the heart of the city, construction of the cathedral took place between AD 1248 and 1880. It is an imposing building: 144 metres long, 86 metres wide and sporting 157-metre tall spires. It stands on the site of a stone chapel built in the sixth century, on a flat-topped hill that had been a sacred site of worship for centuries. Excavations have also located the remains of a Roman temple.

The present, Gothic style, building is dedicated to the Three Kings (or wise men, or magi), Gasper, Melchior, and Balthazar, who are said to have visited the baby Jesus, and it is alleged to contain their remains. These remains were brought to Cologne, from Milan, in 1146 by Archbishop Reinald von Dassel, and have become a major subject of Christian pilgrimage. The shrine to the Three Kings and housing their remains, constructed between 1180 and 1230, can be seen today behind the high altar, heavily protected by security and kept somewhat distant from visitors. It is a gold, gem-encrusted, church-shaped receptacle.

The cathedral also houses a statue of the Virgin Mary and infant

Jesus, known as the Mailänder Madonna (The Milan Madonna) which was made around 1290.

During the Second World War, the cathedral was damaged, and was not returned to its former glory until 1956.

Cordoba, Andalucia, Spain

The most astonishing thing about the Mosque in Cordoba is that it contains a Christian church: Cordoba's cathedral. The building is an enormous, flat-roofed, low, square construction with a huge baroque church rising up in the middle.

The site has had a fascinating history. The Romans built a pagan temple there and, after the fall of the Roman Empire, the Visigoths replaced it with the Christian church of St Vincent. After the Arabs conquered the area in the eighth century, they razed the church to the ground and began building the mosque which, Cordoba being the centre of Muslim influence in Spain, was then the largest mosque in all of Islam outside Arabia. Then the Christians re-conquered Cordoba in 1236, and instead of building a new church they 'converted' the building to the Christian faith. During the sixteenth century, a cathedral was built within the walls, producing the present hybrid styles.

The original mosque was designed with open arches all around, to allow in sunlight which would represent the mystical journey to Allah. The Christians, however, blocked up most of the openings and converted them to chapels dedicated to various saints. The original minaret was encased with a belfry, which still stands.

The affection felt locally for the building by Christians is apparent in the seemingly contradictory statement many people make: that they 'went to Mass at the Mosque'. Most striking in the Mosque is the forest of columns which support the roof; these were taken from the Church of St Vincent, previously razed. Other columns came from homes in the city.

The story of the bells of Santiago de Compostela (see entry) is one that demonstrates a period of antagonism that arises from time to time between competing religions. The bells of that cathedral were stolen and taken to Cordoba by the Muslim warlord

Al-Mansur, where they were melted down to make lamps for the mosque. Then, two and a half centuries later, in 1236, the Castillian King Ferdinand III re-conquered Cordoba and, to avenge the humiliation caused by Al-Mansur, had the lamps carried back to Santiago de Compostela where they were melted down to make a new set of bells.

The Mosque was listed as a World Heritage site in 1984.

Cumae, Italy

Cumae was a fortified coastal city of south-west Italy. It was founded around 750 BC by Greek colonists: the earliest Greek colony, according to the Greek geographer Strabo. It became a powerful commercial centre with valuable maritime trading routes and an extensive trade with all of Italy. In 474 BC, when its strength became threatening, Cumae was attacked by a coalition of hostile tribes led by the Etruscans. The attack was defeated, but later the Samnites conquered Cumae in about 420 BC. The city came into Roman control about 340 BC. In AD 1205 Cumae was destroyed by the Neapolitans in retaliation against pirates who operated out of the city.

Fragmentary ruins of the ancient city are scattered over the site. By the early 1600s, archaeological activity had uncovered valuable treasures: statues, cremation tombs, beehive tombs, cellars and vaults. Below the ruins are several caverns, one of which was the seat of the oracular Cumaean Sibyl.

The story of the Sybil is a fascinating one. Centuries ago an old woman arrived in Rome to see King Tarquin (Tarquinius Superbus). She offered to sell him nine books that would reveal to him the future of the world. Her price was three hundred pieces of gold. The King thought this too high and refused. Several weeks later she came to him again and offered him six books for sale for the same price; then a third time she came and offered him three books for the same price. The King asked her what had happened to the other six books she had first offered him. She told him that she had burned them. He paid the three hundred pieces of gold for the remaining three books.

The old woman was the Cumaean Sibyl.

The King asked her to reconstruct the lost books, which she refused to do, so the information that might have prevented the eventual fall of the Roman Empire was lost. The existing books were supposedly kept in a vault, under guard, beneath the Temple of Jupiter in Rome, and were destroyed in a fire in 83 BC.

Virgil, in the *Aeneid*, describes the Sibyl when uttering her predictions: 'She changes her features and the colour of her countenance; her hair springs up erect, her bosom heaves and pants, her wild heart beats violently, the foam gathers on her lips, and her voice is terrible. She paces to and fro in her cave and gesticulates as if she would expel the gods from her breast.'

In Book 6 of the same work is a description of the descent into Hades which includes rowing across the River Styx. It was only in 1967 that the evidence was produced that this description might have related to visiting the Cumaean Sybil. An English engineer, Robert Paget, excavated the Baian Oracle near the cave of the Sybil. In this astonishing underground cave network, carved a fifth of a mile into the rock, is a canal, thought to have been built to represent the Styx, across which those seeking to consult the oracle were rowed in a small boat. It is presumed that those visiting the oracle were led to believe that they were genuinely journeying to the Underworld; and perhaps with the additional use of drugs they were even more inclined to believe so.

Delphi, Greece

The Town of Delphi is situated to the north of the Gulf of Corinth, on the slopes of Mount Parnassus, in Greece. It was once the most sacred site in the country, and housed the best-known and most widely respected Oracle in the ancient world. According to one legend Apollo expelled Gaea from her sanctuary after first defeating her guardian serpent, Python, and replaced her with his own priestess, Pythia. The gases, which entranced the Oracle were said to be emanating from the rotting body of the Python.

It is said that the properties of the area at Delphi were discovered by a shepherd named Kouretas who found his goats acting oddly near a fissure from which fumes were emanating, and when people got near to investigate it they too acted strangely, apparently in trance. A priestess of the Earth-goddess religion was appointed to serve as the official Oracle.

Delphi was known as the 'navel of the world'; it is said that Zeus commanded two eagles to find the centre of the world, and they met at Delphi. The site was once marked by a conical stone known as the omphalos which stood in front of the temple. Almost certainly Delphi was originally dedicated to Gaea, the Earth Mother, until it was rededicated to Apollo.

People from all over the ancient world would come to Delphi to seek guidance and insight from the Oracle; Apollo would speak through the priestess, the Pythia. So many people came to the site that it became a flourishing industry and a valuable part of the local economy. The donations offered allowed for the building of a theatre and a stadium. Delphi became a showcase of art and treasures; the Greek states would send rich gifts to encourage the Oracle to favour them.

In trance the Pythia would babble incoherently, and a priest would interpret the 'message' from the realm of the gods. For over six hundred years, until the shrine was destroyed by the Christian emperor Arcadius in AD 398, Delphi can rightly be said to have shaped a major part of the history of the world.

The Pythia seemed to have no limits to knowledge, understandably perhaps since 'her' babblings were supposed to be the wisdom of Apollo himself. Advice on religion, politics, philosophy, and more would be offered. The predictions were clever, and seemed wise. Scholars believe that the enigmatic and ambiguous utterings of the Oracles assisted in stimulating creative thought and as such they played their role in establishing the Greeks as free revolutionary thinkers. Such ambiguity could be dangerous, however. The classic story of this is the prediction given to Croesus, King of Lydia. In 550 BC he was making ready to invade the Persian Empire when he consulted the Oracle about his likelihood of success. The Pythia informed him that if he crossed a river 'Croesus will destroy a great empire.' He felt that the all-knowing Oracle had confirmed his likely success and he invaded Persia,

Arbor Low, Derbyshire, England: over fifty leys are said to pass through the circle which has been described as 'one of the wonders of megalithic Britain' (*Paranormal Picture Library/John and Anne Spencer*)

Avebury, Wiltshire, England: once a Sun Temple and a spiritual centre, it was in use between 2600 BC and 1600 BC and is older than Stonehenge (*Paranormal Picture Library/Jennifer Spencer*)

Iona, Scotland: the island where St Columba landed in AD 563 and established a Christian monastery (*Paranormal Picture Library/Martin and Chris Attridge*)

The Rock of Cashel, Eire: folklore says that the rock mound was formed when the devil bit off a chunk of limestone from nearby mountains and spat it out on to the plain (*Hulton Archive*)

Rosslyn Chapel, Scotland: the Apprentice Pillar is said to have been carved by an apprentice to the master Mason. It is rumoured to hide the Holy Grail (*Paranormal Picture Library/John and Anne Spencer*)

Silbury Hill, Wiltshire, England: the largest man-made prehistoric mound in Europe. It is thought to date from between 2145 BC and 2750 BC (*Paranormal Picture Library/Jennifer Spencer*)

Stonehenge, Wiltshire, England: the most famous stone circle in the world, and one that has generated great speculation for centuries (*Paranormal Picture Library/Jennifer Spencer*)

Carnac, France: there are believed to be three thousand megalithic monuments at this huge ancient site (*Paranormal Picture Library/Adrian and Maureen Pruss*)

A rock painting of a horse from Lascaux, France: cave paintings such as this may represent the first sacred sites of emerging mankind (*Bridgeman Art Library*)

The Grotto at Lourdes, France where in 1858 Bernadette Soubirous claimed she saw visions of the Virgin Mary. It has become a place of miracle healing (*PA Photos*)

These exhibits in Sardinia show the structures left by the Nuraghe people. The case on the left shows a tomb and the case on the right shows a section through one of the famous towers found around the island (*Paranormal Picture Library/John and Anne Spencer*)

St Peter's Basilica in the Vatican City is believed to be built directly over the tomb of St Peter. It is the largest church in the Christian world and draws visitors from around the world (*Paranormal Picture Library/John and Anne Spencer*)

The Ka'abah in Mecca, Saudi Arabia houses the Black Stone, supposedly given to Abraham by the angel Gabriel. All muslims seek to visit Mecca at least once (*Hulton Archive*)

El-Deir (the Monastery) at Petra in Jordan: a fine example of a building entirely hewn from the native rock and a place of worship since before the fourth century (*Paranormal Picture Library/Adrian and Maureen Pruss*)

The Wailing Wall (or Western Wall), Jerusalem: the closest point that can be reached to the Holy Temple that once stood on Temple Mount (*Hulton Archive*)

where he was roundly defeated; he believed the Oracle had been wrong and challenged her, but the Oracle confirmed that she had been correct – Croesus had indeed destroyed a great empire: his own.

For a time, during the Middle Ages, Delphi was lost, buried beneath a town called Kastri. Two scholars, Jacques Spon and George Wheler, worked out the location of the site in the seventeenth century, but it was not until 1892 that a French archaeological excavation dug out the ruins. To do it, they had to remove the modern town brick by brick to a site half a mile away – to the consternation of the inhabitants. The excavations uncovered temples, the Great Altar, a stadium, a theatre, the town walls, the treasury buildings inscribed with hymns to Apollo. The site contains more than four thousand inscriptions that provide valuable information about life in ancient Greece.

The centre of the site was the Temple of Apollo. During the 1892 excavations a pool, under the Temple and connected to an aqueduct, was found. It has been suggested that this is where the Oracle bathed, away from public gaze. Others have suggested that the aqueduct and pool were the symbolic representations of the River Styx, as found at Cumae.

Modern science had suggested an explanation for the Oracle. Two geological faults were recently discovered at Delphi, directly under the Temple, and geologists have detected hallucinogenic fumes emanating from a nearby spring. Jelle de Boer, a geophysicist at Wesleyan University in Middletown, Connecticut, commented: 'Everything fits with the ancient writers being correct. It shows again that many legends have some truth in them.' The site of Delphi is an area criss-crossed with geological faults, and often hit by earthquakes. Such a combination could easily have released trapped gases within the rocks. De Boer's team found deposits of travertine holding tiny bubbles of ancient methane and ethane gas, both of which can have slight narcotic effects. A nearby spring still releases small quantities of ethylene, a gas once used as an anaesthetic; it is likely that more concentrated doses could have acted as a narcotic, and possibly brought on a trance-like condition.

83

Delphi was not the only Oracle; there were several scattered around the Aegean Sea. It is possible that the original purpose of the Oracle sites was less for divination and more for mapping of the Earth's surface; the oracles were located at key points of latitude. For example, three main oracle sites in the west (Dedona, Delphi and Delos) were located at precisely the same latitudinal positions as three eastern such sites (Metsamor, Sardis, and Miletus). These layouts are believed by some to be evidence that they reflected a worship of the Mother Earth Goddess.

The Oracle at Delphi has been studied not just as a site of occult divination but as an intelligence centre, and it is apparent that many factors contributed to its reputation as a highly successful predictor of the future. It was located centrally and was very popular; therefore the priests working there had a good inflow of information from people all over that part of the Mediterranean and beyond, including leading political and religious figures, farmers, soldiers and sailors. In effect the Oracle was a clearing house for information and the priests were running an intelligence gathering network. The pronouncements of the Oracle were therefore based on a certain amount of information that probably was not readily available to all. It has even been suggested that a network of carrier pigeons was used to keep Delphi informed of the latest events, which could then be offered as prophecy since the information would reach Delphi probably long before any human could. It would not, however, be fair to suggest that this amounted to a fraud. It was in effect a political design to concentrate wealth and political power for the good of the empire.

There was probably a good deal of psychology at play. Most people consulting the Oracle were not looking for guidance but rather for support for their plans which they intended to undertake anyway (King Croesus mentioned above almost certainly comes into that category). No doubt this reinforcement actually did help certain people to feel more confident and do a better job, thus making the prediction come true. Where that was not the case the pronouncements were usually made sufficiently ambiguously to give the Oracle a get-out clause.

Although Oracles ceased to be used by the Greeks and Romans, who moved into astrology for divination, the technique certainly did not die out and indeed has been used up to the present day. The Azande people of Sudan consult Oracles before travelling or planting crops. The Dalai Lama was warned by an Oracle of the Chinese invasion in 1959 and was able to escape Lhasa in time; even in exile he has maintained contacts with an Oracle.

Einsiedeln, Switzerland

Einsiedeln is the site of a huge monastery, the most important pilgrimage site in Switzerland.

Einsiedeln means 'hermitage', and is so named for St Meginrat (or Meinrad) who, in about AD 828, withdrew into seclusion in what was then a wild forest where he lived and prayed, nourished by food brought to him by two wild ravens. On 21 January 861, he was murdered by two bandits, Richard the Aleman and Peter the Rhaetian, who set out to steal from him the treasures they believed he had hoarded. The two loyal ravens that had protected Meginrat pursued the criminals to Zurich and flew above their heads, making such a loud and piercing noise that attention was drawn to the pair who were arrested. They later confessed to their crime and were executed.

Other hermits followed in Meginrat's footsteps and sought to live in the forest as he had, and often used his abandoned cell. Over time this cell fell into ruin, though his little altar at which he had prayed was maintained. Eventually a small chapel was built to house the altar.

In 934, Eberhard, a visiting provost from Strasbourg cathedral, persuaded the hermits to form a Benedictine community, which they did. He became their first abbot and ordered the building of a church on the site, which was to be consecrated by Bishop Conrad of Konstanz. However, before the bishop was able to finish the ceremony, a voice was heard in the church crying out three times that Christ himself had already consecrated it. It is said that this was with the assistance of the four apostles, St Peter and St Gregory the Great. Pope Leo VIII announced that this was a miracle, and issued a Papal Bull, blessing the pilgrimage to Einsiedeln; this was ratified by his successors.

After that time the Benedictine monastery and church enjoyed special privileges, received substantial royal grants, and significant protection.

By 1286 the Chapel of Our Lady, which had been built over the ruins of St Meginrat's little cell, had become a focal point for pilgrims. It had housed a Romanesque figure of Mary which had been presented to Meginrat by Abbess Hildegard, Superior of a Zurich convent, but this was damaged in a fire in 1468, and was then replaced by a statue of Mary with the infant Christ, carved in wood. This latter figure, around 1.25 metres tall, blackened by smoke from centuries of candle-burning, became the main quest for pilgrims, and is today known as the Black Madonna.

The Abbey Library is astonishing, dating from 946 and containing almost fifty thousand volumes, including many irreplaceable manuscripts. It reflects the fascinating scope of the monastery's work, which included sending a colony of monks to America in 1854 to work with the native population.

Visitors have included three people who later became saints: Charles Borromeo; Benedict Joseph Labre; and Nicholas of Flue, the Patron Saint of Switzerland. Napoleon III made a pilgrimage there in 1865.

The site was a rival to Rome and Santiago de Compostela for some time, and was also a stopping point for pilgrims journeying to the latter. Currently, a quarter of a million pilgrims visit the site annually. The primary pilgrimage days are 14 September and 13 October, the former being the anniversary of the miraculous consecration, and the latter the anniversary of the translation of St Meginrat's relics from Reichenau to Einsiedeln in 1039. The highlight of any visit takes place each day at 4:30 pm when a procession of monks passes into the Lady Chapel, singing the Salve Regina, a tradition since the sixteenth century.

Epidaurus Sanctuary, Greece

According to Greek mythology, Asklepios, the son of Apollo, was raised by the Centaur Chiron and taught the skills of healing. He was very good at his art, but raised a mortal from death and was killed by Zeus for his temerity.

Temples dedicated to the cult of Asklepios became popular from the sixth century BC onwards. The sick would sleep in the temples, which often contained running water as it was believed that the healing energies of spirits were to be found in these waters. The most famous of these temples was at Epidaurus, built on the site of the original Sanctuary of Apollo Maleatas. Known as the Sanctuary or Asklepieion, in an area replete with running springs, it also included a theatre, gymnasium, and stadium as the Greeks believed that healing should be a holistic process of mind, body and spirit. Indeed, the theatre at Epidaurus is regarded as the largest and most impressive of those of the ancient Greeks and is in an excellent state of preservation. It was built in the fourth century BC by the architect Polyclitus, and could seat fourteen thousand people. It is still used today as part of the area's tourist attractions, with classical Greek tragedies and comedies performed there for local and foreign visitors.

The prominence of the cult of Asklepios brought to the Sanctuary significant financial prosperity, which, in the fourth and third centuries BC financed an ambitious building pro-gramme for the construction of monumental buildings of worship such as the temple and the altar of Asklepios, the Tholos, the Abaton, and others. It also paid for the construction of other buildings including the theatre and the baths.

Excavation on the site began in the late nineteenth century, and has been conducted under the eye of the Greek Archaeological Society. There has been continuous careful study of the site since then, most lately under the guidance of the Committee for the Preservation of the Epidaurus Monuments.

Restoration work at the Asklepieion started on the theatre in 1907 and has continued since. In 1988, the Asklepieion was included in the World Heritage List.

Fatima, Portugal

On 13 May 1917, at Fatima, the Virgin Mary appeared in a vision to three shepherd children: sister and brother Jacinta and Francisco Marta and their cousin Lucia dos Santos. They saw a bright flash of light at the Cave of St Irene – which was already known as a sacred location – and the light formed into the shape of a small woman. She told them only that she was 'from heaven'. The children described her as a 'young lady, dressed in white'. They were told there would be visions during the next six months – and were given a vision of hell that frightened them – and several warnings to pass on about how Mankind should stop offending God.

The children were accused of lying, were imprisoned, and even threatened with boiling oil, but they stuck to their story, and were eventually believed. The site of the vision became a focus of pilgrimage and in October of that year thousands of pilgrims visited to witness further visions. On the last day, 13 October 1917, it is estimated that up to seventy thousand pilgrims were present. Few people claimed to see the Virgin; most saw strange light phenomena, the most spectacular of which was the 'dance of the sun': the sun broke through clouds and seemed to rotate and dive towards the earth in a blast of multi-coloured light, and with much heat. The vision lasted approximately ten minutes and was believed to have been visible several miles away.

Witnesses described an extraordinary spectacle. 'I looked fixedly at the sun,' described one witness, 'which appeared pale and did not dazzle. It looked like a ball of snow turning on itself . . . Then suddenly it seemed to become detached from the side, and rolled right and left as if it were falling upon the Earth . . . After about ten minutes the sun climbed back into its place, as it had descended, still quite pale and without brilliance. When the people were convinced that the danger has passed, there was an outburst of joy.' Another described: 'To my surprise I saw clearly and distinctly a globe of light advancing from east to west, gliding slowly and majestically through the air . . . My friend looked also, and he had the good fortune to see the same unexpected vision. Suddenly the globe with the wonderful light dropped out from sight.'

The purpose of the visions, it was said, was to appeal for conversion to the Church and devotion to the Blessed Mother.

The children suffered for their new-found devotion to the Madonna. They drank dirty ditch-water, and beat themselves with nettles. Within three years the brother and sister were dead from pneumonia. Lucia however lived on and is, at the time of writing, a Carmelite nun in Portugal.

In 1943 Lucia wrote down the three prophecies that the Virgin had given, and sent the document to the Vatican. Two of the prophecies were soon made public. The first was that Russia would turn to communism, the second was a prophecy of the end of the World War that had at the time of the visions been raging, together with a prediction for a Second World War. Sceptics pointed out that by the time these two prophecies were revealed both had already come to pass. The third secret, however, became a long-standing mystery.

Theories abounded; the third secret was of the end of the world, was the apocalypse, told of a Muslim Second Coming, predicted the end of Christianity, foresaw nuclear meltdown, even that the secret was so frightening that it would never be revealed. Pope Pius XII is said to have swooned with horror when he read the prophecy. In 1997 a series of earthquakes in Umbria forced the Vatican to confirm that the third secret did not predict the end of civilisation as we know it. Pope John Paul I apparently blanched white in the face after he met with Lucia, six months before his election to the Papacy.

Then came Pope John Paul II, and as it turns out the prophecy had such special meaning for him, he chose to reveal it to the world on the anniversary of the original visions, on 13 May 2000. On that day he visited the tombs of the brother and sister and said Mass to beatify the two children. Beatification is the last formal step towards sainthood and the two became the first children who had not died as martyrs to receive such an honour. He also attended the Virgin's statue at Fatima and laid there a gold ring that had been given to him by his mentor, Polish primate Cardinal Stefan Wyszynski. The ring was, said a spokesman, 'one of the most precious possessions the Pope had'.

For the significance of the prophecy to the Pope we must go to 13 May 1981, again an anniversary of the visions. On that day John Paul II was shot and wounded in an assassination attempt in St Peter's Square, in Rome. It is said that at the moment of the gunshot he glimpsed a poster of Our Lady of Fatima, and was convinced that she saved his life. The bullet that struck him is now in the crown worn by the Virgin's statue in Fatima. And the third prophecy, it turns out, was the prediction of an assassination attempt on the life of a Pope.

On 8 October 2000, in a ceremony involving fifteen hundred bishops and a 'sea of people', John Paul II entrusted humanity and the third millennium to the protection of the Virgin Mary. He did so in front of the original image of the Virgin of Fatima, which had been brought to St Peter's Square for the occasion. The Pope spoke for the world's pastors when he prayed to Mary for her protection. 'Today we wish to entrust to you the future that awaits us, and we ask you to be with us on our way,' he said. 'We are the men and women of an extraordinary time, exhilarating yet full of contradictions. Humanity now has instruments of unprecedented power. We can turn this world into a garden, or reduce it to a pile of rubble. We have devised the astounding capacity to intervene in the very wellsprings of life. Man can use this power for good, within the bounds of the moral law, or he can succumb to the short-sighted pride of a science that accepts no limits, but tramples on the respect due to every human being. Today, as never before in the past, humanity stands at a crossroads. And, once again, O Virgin Most Holy, salvation lies fully and uniquely in Jesus, your Son.'

After the ceremony the statue was taken to St Peter's Basilica before being returned to Fatima.

The Field of the Burned, Pyrenees, France

In the thirteenth century there was an upsurge of religious revolution, a reaction against what were seen as excesses of the Catholic Church, which would lead to a most cruel event in French history.

This upsurge was the emergence of the Albigensians, or Cathari, meaning the 'pure ones'. Their faith was simple, seeking to bring religion to the poor in a way they perceived the Catholic Church was not doing. Cathar doctrines, based largely on the Gospel according to John, offered an alternative to the existing Church hierarchy.

The central core of Cathar following is the concept of Duality, the battle between the spiritual and the material. This may be interprepted as the battle between Good, represented by God, and Evil, represented by the Devil. To the Cathari, each person was created of three components; the body, the soul and the divine spirit within. By leading a pure life the spirit can be liberated to live in the Light, so the Cathari worshipped in forests and on mountains, held ceremonies in caves, and renounced worldly riches. They created vibrant, ordered co-operative communities throughout the region.

They believed that Christ was a Holy Ghost in spirit form moving amongst people; they did not believe him to be a material being, and therefore they rejected many of the rituals associated with his earthly body such as communion. Because of their belief in the spirit they did not fear death – as 16 March 1244 was to prove.

The Catholic Church grew alarmed at the popularity of this rival Christian belief system: a challenge to its domination. In 1208 Pope Innocent III demanded a crusade against the Cathari; it was to become known as the Albigensian Crusade, and the Cathari were hunted down throughout France, often tortured and massacred in an attempt to destroy the sect forever.

When it first became apparent that they were to be victims of persecution on a scale rarely seen before, they created a central base and headquarters at Montsegur Castle. It was a ruin, used by the Cathari as a meditation site; now it would be a stronghold, fortified with a garrison. Perched high on a hill, almost atop a needle-like peak, it would be easy to defend. Many believe that Montsegur held the most sacred treasures of the Cathari – perhaps the Holy Grail itself.

Attacks on the Cathari throughout southern France were led by the brutal Simon de Montfort, whole towns and villages being wiped out in the most vicious manner. However, de Montfort's attempts to bring down Montsegur castle during 1209 were unsuccessful and the fortress became a symbol of hope. The establishment at this time of the Inquisition added to the religious pressure brought to bear, and by the early 1240s the Cathars were largely destroyed, bar a few strongholds. Montsegur was one such stronghold, and it stood firm.

In May 1243 a total of 205 Cathars, and three hundred soldiers, were besieged in Montsegur by a force of some ten thousand men. After around ten months of siege, on 1 March 1244, Pierre-Roger de Mirepox left the castle under the flag of truce to negotiate a surrender. He was told that the soldiers would be allowed to go free, but the Cathari had to renounce their faith and come back to the Catholic Church to seek forgiveness for their heresy. If they did not they would be burned alive. Huge bonfires were lit at the foot of the mountain as a clear indication of their fate if they did not surrender. The soldiers left, except for a few who converted to the Cathar belief, and then, on the morning of 16 March, 216 Cathars, singing together, marched straight-backed down the mountainside and into the flames below.

The site where they went to their deaths is known as the Field of the Burned and is marked by a simple memorial cross. Many people have reported feeling the intense strange energy of the area, and a white ghostly mist has often been reported rising from the Field of the Burned and up to the castle ruins. Of the 'Perfecti' – the most devout of the order – it is said that their ghostly forms are seen at their various strongholds, perhaps still trying to protect their secret treasure.

And the treasure? Some say that it was a spiritual treasure, not a materialistic one. Others say that a small number of Cathari escaped prior to the massacre by lowering themselves down the steepest side of the mountain on ropes, taking it – whatever 'it' was – with them. There are many who believe that 'it' was taken to nearby Rennes-le-Chateau and hidden there. Two of the escapees were said to have been seen in Italy afterwards. However, treasure was never found.

Lascaux Caves, Dordogne, France

On 12 September 1940, four teenage companions, Marcel, George, Jim and Simon, and a dog called Robot, were walking in the forest south of their home village of Montignac, in the Dordogne in France, and went up Lascaux Hill to play. During the day they realised that they had lost Robot, and set off to search for him.

The dog had fallen into a hole in the ground, one that was already known to Marcel. H. Baumann, in his book *The Caves of Great Hunters*, quotes Marcel as saying: 'I know already what it is. It's a cave, but there's no way of telling how big it is or how far down it goes.' The boys decided to get some equipment rather than venture into the dark cave. So they returned the following morning with ropes and torches and lowered themselves into the cave, searching for Robot.

What they descended into was one of the most important and extraordinary sacred sites of prehistoric man. Lascaux is one of the largest such caves, and its art is amongst the best preserved. It consists of a main cavern twenty metres wide and five metres high, now known as The Hall of the Bulls, and many steep galleries. Painted, drawn and engraved images of animals cover the walls: a diary of Palaeolithic times.

Carbon-dating indicates that the cave was in use from about 15,000 BC when most of the artwork was probably created, to as late as 9000 BC.

The cave was first studied in depth by French archaeologist Henri-Edouard-Prosper Breuil, known as the Father of Prehistory. There were difficulties in studying the paintings, many of which were in difficult to get at places. Breuil and his team believed that the ground had sunk deeper over the years, seemingly placing the paintings higher than they originally were, and that the artworks would have been easier to reach in those days. That said, however, there is the suggestion that ladders and scaffolding must have been used; in fact what seem to be sockets for scaffolding beams were found in the cave.

News of the discovery became internationally known and people travelled from all around the world to see it after it was opened to the public in 1948. It received probably one hundred thousand visitors annually. Sadly, within a short time the exposure of the cave to the pressures of tourism, to the lighting introduced, and to the huge increase of nearby traffic, caused the colours and details of the artworks to fade. Fungus grew on the paintings. As a result, the cave was closed to the public in 1963.

The animal artwork in the caves depicts many species: bulls, bison, and horses. There are some six hundred animal paintings and almost fifteen hundred engravings. The paintings are on a light background in shades of yellow, red, brown, and black. Perhaps the most remarkable pictures are of four large bulls five metres long, and a mysterious two-horned animal that is perhaps intended as a mythical creature.

There are also many images of human forms. Interestingly the animal images are much more elaborate and detailed than the human ones which are little more than stick figures; the suggestion being that it was the animals that were important to the artists. It is believed that the tribes would have used magic to assist them, and that the cave paintings were a manifestation of that magic. By drawing the images, perhaps the tribe hoped to encourage the real animal to come to them, which would supply them with food and other provisions. The paintings would have been an aid to the hunters of the tribe. Breuil commented (as recorded in P.M. Grand's *Prehistoric Art; Palaeolithic Painting and Sculpture*): 'That only those peoples who lived by hunting and, collaterally, by fishing, had practised this [hunting magic] art'. The caves were not therefore homes for people; they were, in effect, the first temples where prayers to their deities could be made, prayers to make the hunt a success. If not actually in prayer in the way we understand today, these early people would have spent time in front of the images creating in their minds what a successful hunt would be like, in the hopes that the gods would make the real thing equally successful. Caves like Lascaux were sacred sites, housing sacred images. Grand described them as 'places [that] could have served only as specially chosen repositories for the secrets of a civilisation'.

The cave was added to UNESCO's World Heritage List in 1979.

To meet the demand for tourism, in 1983 a partial replica painstakingly re-creating the original, known as 'Lascaux II', was opened to the public nearby; by the mid-1990s it was receiving some three hundred thousand visitors annually.

In August 2000 an interesting speculation was put forward about the images in the Lascaux caves. According to Dr Michael Rappenglueck, a researcher at the University of Munich, some of the images may be representations of parts of the night sky. Lascaux's artists may have had a fascination for the realm of the gods. One such prehistoric map was found in a part of the cave known as The Shaft of the Dead Man. On the wall is painted a bull, a bird on a stick and the figure of a half-man, half-bird. Rappenglueck believes that the outline of the three images forms a map, with the eyes of the bull, birdman figure and bird representing the stars Deneb, Vega and Altair. These are the stars of the Summer Triangle, prominent stars in the summer night sky. Another image lies close to the entrance: an elaborate painting of a bull which appears to include an indication of the Pleiades, stars known as the Seven Sisters. The Pleiades have featured more recently in many New Age accounts and in the proclamations of so-called 'UFO contactees': those who claim to have been in contact with aliens. Rappenglueck believes these paintings are evidence of early man's interest in the stars. 'It is a map of the prehistoric cosmos,' he says. 'It was their sky, full of animals and spirit guides.'

Lindholm Hoje, nr Aalborg, Denmark

Nothing exhibits the sacredness of a site to a people so much as its use for commemorating the dead. Many of the sacred sites in this compilation relate to burial or cremation, or are monuments to the dead. The seven hundred or more graves in the Viking graveyard at Lindholm Hoje, near present-day Aalborg, are just such a tribute. Lindholm Hoje is one of the most significant ancient monuments of the late prehistoric period in Denmark.

The graveyard is built on the chalk hills rising above the north side of the Limfjord. This is a very significant strategic spot, where the fjord is at its narrowest and the hill rises forty-two metres above sea level, giving its former inhabitants command over the fjord and restricting enemy approaches.

The site is known to have been both a settlement and a burial ground since around AD 450. Two villages from later periods of occupation, one to the south and one to the north of the burial site, have been excavated at Lindholm Hoje. The northern village dates from between 700 and 900, and seems to have supported six families of ten to fifteen members each. The southern settlement dates from between 1000 and 1150, and was the last settlement on Lindholm Hoje.

The graveyard is an impressive sight. The seven hundred or so graves are marked by stones laid out in the shape of an oval, a triangle or a ship. Women were buried in the oval-shaped graves and men in those marked by the triangular or boat shapes. As most of the dead were cremated – the Vikings did this in order to speed the deceased's journey to the next world – the sex of the graves' occupants has been identified from the objects buried with them, perhaps for use in the after life. Pearls and combs were found in the female graves; weapons, buckles and rivets in the male graves.

The hill was abandoned in 1200, probably when accumulating sand, resulting from the erosion of tree-cover, made the soil incapable of supporting the communities that lived there.

Lourdes, France

Probably the most famous location where visions of the Virgin Mary have been reported is Lourdes, on the Gave-de-Pau River at the base of the Pyrenees.

Once a famous fortress town, Lourdes became a pilgrimage centre for Christians after a fourteen year-old peasant girl, Bernadette Soubirous, claimed she saw eighteen visions of the Virgin there in 1858.

Her first vision was on 11 February 1858 when Bernadette was with her sister, Toinette, and a friend, Jeanne Abadie, gathering firewood. The other two girls waded across the River Gave, but Bernadette stayed in the cave known locally as the pigsty. Bernadette described what then happened: 'I looked up and saw a cluster of branches and brambles underneath the highest opening of the grotto, tossing and swinging to and fro, although nothing else stirred. Behind these branches and inside the opening, I saw at that moment a girl in white, no bigger than myself, who greeted me with a slight bow of her head.' Bernadette went on to describe the figure: 'She was wearing a white dress right down to her feet and only the tips of her toes were showing. The dress was gathered high at the neck from which there hung a white cord. A white veil covered her head and came down over her shoulders and arms almost to the bottom of her dress. On each foot I saw a yellow rose. The sash of her dress was blue and hung down below her knees. The chain of the rosary was yellow, the beads white and big, and widely spaced. The girl was alive, very young and surrounded with light.' No verbal communication took place at that time. Bernadette described only: 'When I had finished my rosary she bowed to me smilingly. She retired within the niche, and suddenly disappeared.' Bernadette certainly did not at this stage identify the figure as the Virgin, but used the expression 'aquero' meaning 'this thing'.

Bernadette described her experience to her mother, Louise Casterot, for which she and her sister received both a beating and a warning never to visit the grotto again. However, Bernadette did return, and between this first sighting on 11 February and the 16 July she had a total of eighteen visions. During the sixteenth sighting, on 25 March, the figure described herself as The Immaculate Conception. This was a reference to the Virgin Mary that had first been used by the Pope just four years earlier. During the time of her experiences Bernadette also had contact with a priest who was a believer in the visions of the Virgin Mary that had been reported at La Salette twelve years earlier. It is possible that Bernadette was eventually influenced by the beliefs of others to identify her 'aquero' as the Virgin Mary.

During the communications between the figure and Bernadette, the Virgin Mary asked for a chapel to be built, and for processions to be held in her honour. She pointed out the site of a previously unknown bubbling spring which, Bernadette was told, was bringing forth healing waters.

In 1876 a basilica was completed, and there is today a large underground church at the grotto. The visions were declared authentic by the Catholic Church, and the site became a shrine for pilgrims; the first formal visits taking place in 1877.

In 1866, Bernadette joined the Sisters of Charity, a group of women bound by annual vows to religious and charitable work. In 1877 she became a nun, and died two years later when aged thirty-four, in the Convent of St Gildard at Nevers, from cancer in the knee. In 1909 her body was exhumed and, according to an eye witness, 'not the least trace of corruption nor any bad odour could be perceived'. She was beatified in 1925, and canonised in 1933. Her feast day is 16 April.

Lourdes today is a site of pilgrimage, but has also become immersed in tourism, to the extent that it has become almost the Disneyland of Catholic religion. The town sells hundreds of thousands of models of the Virgin Mary, of various sizes and quality; trinkets with the Lourdes logo; and pastilles made from Holy Water. The town consumes more candles than any other place on Earth, seven hundred tonnes a year. It has more hotels than any other town in France, apart from Paris. In the first year of pilgrimage, 1877, 366 people visited the shrine; in the year 2000 an estimated six million passed through the town.

Despite this, most visitors still regard Lourdes as having genuine curative powers, and value regular visits to it as a deeply spiritual place. Many of those queuing to see the grotto, or to obtain quantities of the Holy Water, claim they are not seeking a miracle, rather that the atmosphere of Lourdes generates a way of making the best of things. People with disabilities, illnesses and grief claim that by sharing with other pilgrims they can better accept their lot.

Miracles though are not unknown; the Catholic Church has officially recognised sixty-six such claims, an impressive number from one location. For example, in 1976, twelve-year-old Delizia Cirolli had inoperable bone cancer and her parents ignored the advice to have her leg amputated, taking the child to Lourdes, where she bathed in the baths there. One morning they found the tumour had disappeared. This was recognised as a miracle by the Medical Bureau of Lourdes, a body set up by the church which includes amongst its members non-religious doctors.

Medjugorje, Bosnia–Hercegovina

Since 1981 this small village in war-torn Bosnia–Hercegovina has been the site of many Marian visitations. The Virgin Mary first appeared to six children, now adults.

At around 6:45 pm on 2 June 1981 the children had a vision of the Virgin. They were initially scared by what they saw; one of the children, Ivan, found sleeping that night difficult. Over the next day the children told their parents and word of the encounter spread locally.

That next day four of the children went to the same place, with two others, Marija and Jakov, and again the Virgin was seen. On the third day the children took holy water which they sprinkled on the Virgin; she just smiled at them. That evening she told them she was the Queen of Peace.

On 2 August 1981 150 witnesses claimed to have seen a 'miracle of the sun' similar to the vision seen at Fatima (see entry) decades before; the sun or some luminous phenomenon apparently moving strangely above them. At the same time it was said that the horizontal bar of a cross on Cross Mountain disappeared and left only the upright which turned white.

The children have explained that they pray to the Virgin and she comes to them. Vica was told the story of the Virgin's life which she finished receiving in April 1985; Marija was given messages every Thursday for the people; her apparitions ended at Christmas 1992; Ivanca's visions ended in May 1985. Over time Mary has confided ten secrets to the children which are to be revealed at a later time; but it is known they are designed to bring people back to the path of Christianity. To the remaining visionaries Mary appears daily, and gives a message each month for the world.

In her message of 29 November 1984 the Virgin said: 'Be aware, loved ones, that I am your Mother and that I come to earth so that

I can teach you to listen with love to God and to pray with love . . .'

Mary has also said: 'Do not think about wars, punishments, evil, because if you do you are on the road toward them. Your task is accept divine peace, to live it, and to spread it.'

Our Lady has told the visionaries that these are her last appearances on earth and it is for this reason her visits are so long and frequent. She has come to tell us 'God exists'. Before her last appearance she has promised to leave a visible sign on the mountain where the first apparition occurred, so that all will believe.

There has been debate about the spiritual authenticity of the phenomenon. The first bishop to investigate the claims believed they could be explained by natural means. Local political consid-erations created argument over this, the findings were set aside and a new study set up. The next study was inconclusive. Despite this the site has been visited by millions of pilgrims, and even after the outbreak of war in the country, there were still many who braved snipers and difficult terrain to visit the location.

Formal church approval for the visions has not been forthcom-ing and local church leaders are cautious in their public comments. There has been relatively low-key support from the Vatican, presumably because they do not want to pre-empt their own investigations. Another obvious reason is that most visionary experiences are approved after they have concluded and it seems that Medjugorje's are still ongoing. Even at the time of writing, in 2001, the messages are still being received. For example, the message of 25 January 2001 was: 'Dear children! Today I call you to renew prayer and fasting with even greater enthusiasm until prayer becomes a joy for you. Little children, the one who prays is not afraid of the future and the one who fasts is not afraid of evil. Once again, I repeat to you: only through prayer and fasting also wars can be stopped. – wars of your unbelief and fear for the future. I am with you and am teaching you little children: your peace and hope are in God.'

In 1986, the Pope said, 'Let the people go to Medjugorje if they convert, pray, confess, do penance and fast.' Some thirty million laity and clergy have visited and returned home spiritually renewed.

Priests have been keeping a record of claimed miraculous healings at Medjugorje, in the hopes that a scientific study will confirm the truth of the visions.

Mount Athos, Greece

Mount Athos is located in the peninsula of Halkidiki, also known as the peninsula of Athos. It is the only place in Greece totally dedicated to prayer and worship of God, and is therefore known as the Holy Mount. It covers an area of about 135 square miles.

The history of the mount is shrouded in mythology. Athos was a Thracian giant, and during a conflict between the giants and the gods he threw a huge rock at the god Poseidon, but he fumbled and the rock dropped to the ground, forming what is now Mount Athos. (In a different version of the story Poseidon threw the rock which crushed Athos beneath it.) Mount Athos is also said to have been the first home of the gods Apollo and Zeus, before they went to Mount Olympus.

The history of Christianity at Mount Athos is no less dramatic. According to the local traditions, in AD 49 the Virgin Mary and John the Evangelist were sailing towards Cyprus, to visit Lazarus, when a stormy sea forced them to land at what is now the Holy Monastery of Ivira. Mary instantly loved the area and asked God to let her have the mountain as a gift. God said to her: 'Let this place be your lot, your garden and your paradise, as well as a salvation, a haven for those who seek salvation.' Mount Athos is sometimes known as The Garden of the Virgin Mary.

In the fifth century AD, the first monks came to Mount Athos, and found the wild beauty of the location perfect for their worship of God. The first monasteries were built there in the ninth century. The Holy Mount is divided into twenty self-governing territories; each territory contains a principal monastery and various other monastic establishments such as cloisters, cells, hermitages, etc. There are seventeen Greek monasteries, one Russian, one Bulgarian, and one Serbian. The area was recognised as an autonomous district by the Greek constitution of 1975. It is presently home to around three thousand monks.

Since the eleventh century, no female – human or animal – has been permitted on the peninsula.

Almost every visitor to Athos reports a sense of great mysticism, great tranquillity, and a harmony of nature. It is a place where spirituality comes easily.

Mount Olympus, Greece

Mount Olympus was the home of the Greek gods, the twelve main deities that ruled Greece, according to ancient mythology. These were Zeus and his wife Hera; his brothers Poseidon, god of the sea, and Hades, god of the underworld; his sister Hestia, goddess of the hearth; and his children: Athena, goddess of wisdom; Aries, god of war; Apollo, god of the sun; Artemis, goddess of the moon and of the hunt; Aphroditc, goddess of love; Hermes, messenger of the gods; and Hephaestus, god of fire and blacksmiths.

On Olympus the gods feasted on ambrosia, a food which was supposed to keep them immortal, and were entertained by Apollo's lyre, and by the Graces and the Muses.

The palaces on Olympus were built by the giant Titans known as the Cyclopes. This race was freed from Tartarus by Zeus, and in return they gave him his thunderbolts. Hephaestus created the furnishings and artwork on Olympus in his forges. The entrance was through a gate of clouds, which was guarded by the lesser goddesses known as the Seasons.

Zeus and Hera's private apartments overlooked Athens, Thebes, Sparta, Corinth, Argos and Mycanae. At the other end of the palace were the servants' quarters, and around a square in between were the homes of the other deities. Homer declared that no wind ever blows on Olympus; no rain or snow ever falls there, and it is bathed in a glorious light. In *The Odyssey* he writes:

> . . . *Olympus, the reputed seat*
> *Eternal of the gods, which never storms*
> *Disturb, rains drench, or snow invades, but calm*

The expanse and cloudless shines with purest day.
There the inhabitants divine rejoice
For ever.

Although originally regarded as an elusive place far above the earth, it was only much later that it became associated with a mountain-top site. Later still, it became associated with specific mountains. What is now known as Mount Olympus is a massif of four peaks on the boundary between Thessaly and Macedonia, near the Aegean Sea. The highest of these peaks, and the highest point in Greece at 2,917 metres, is Mount Mytikas. It overlooks the deep chasm called Kazania (the cauldron). The other peaks surrounding the chasm are Stefani, Skala, and Skolio. Stefani is also known as Thronos tou Dia (the Throne of Zeus), and from some angles does indeed look like the back of a gigantic armchair or throne.

Mycenae, Greece

Mycenae is an ancient city, now within the modern town of Minaiki, occupying a natural citadel in the mountains. It was founded in the sixteenth century BC, during the early Bronze Age (though little is left of those early structures), and reached its height of influence during the thirteenth century BC, when it was a heavily fortified city defended by walls made of huge blocks of stone. The Mycenaean culture replaced the Minoan culture as the most powerful civilisation of the Aegean at the time. Its navy would have controlled the surrounding seas, and colonised the Cyclades, Crete, Cyprus, the Dodecanese, northern Greece and Macedonia, western Asia Minor, Sicily, and parts of Italy. Legend has it that the city was founded by Perseus.

The Mycenaeans, called Achaeans by Homer in the *Iliad* and the *Odyssey*, originated from tribes that arrived in Greece around 2000 BC. In the *Iliad*, Homer describes the Mycenaeans, led by Agamemnon, as the main participants in the Trojan War. According to legend, Agamemnon, King of Mycenae, had a brother named Menelaus, King of Sparta. Agamemnon married Clytemnestra, and Menelaus married Helen (later popularly known as Helen of Troy).

103

Helen was offered to the Trojan prince, Paris, by Aphrodite, and went with him, apparently willingly, thus enraging the two brothers. Agamemnon devised an expedition to bring Helen back from Troy, resulting in the ten years of the Trojan War. However, during those ten years of Agamemnon's absence Clytemnestra took a lover, Aigisthos (who was Agamemnon's cousin), and together the couple ruled Mycenae, after having driven Agamemnon's son Orestes and daughter, Electra, into exile. When Agamemnon returned, Clytemnestra and Aigisthos murdered him. The god Apollo told Orestes that to avenge his father's murder he should kill both his mother and her lover; which he did, encouraged by Electra.

It is almost certain that there is some historical basis to this story, although romanticised by Homer and other poets and writers.

Based on these stories, and taking them as literally as possible, German archaeologist Heinrich Schliemann set out in 1876 to hunt for Agamemnon's palace and tomb. His quest was successful, not perhaps in finding Agamemnon's actual tomb, though he believed he had, but certainly in discovering the valuable and informative lost treasurers of Mycenae.

The citadel, entered through the famous Lion Gate, contained a royal palace and around thirty royal graves, most of them being what is known as shaft graves, arranged in two circles. The Lion Gate is a powerful sacred emblem; the two lions' forepaws are resting on what seems to be an altar, and although the heads are now missing they were almost certainly of gold. From the Lion Gate a road, 3.5 metres wide, leads to a ramp supported by a multi-terraced wall and then on to the south-west entrance of the palace. Almost certainly the palace housed an important shrine, as evidenced by the discovery of magnificent ivory carvings consisting of two goddesses and an infant god.

Various houses within the citadel have interest for archaeologists, such as the House of the Columns which was three storeys in height. South of the grave circle lies the ruins of the Ramp House, the South House, and the House of Tsountas.

Other houses stood outside the citadel, including the famous

Ivory Houses set out in Iphiyenia Tournavitou's book, *The Ivory Houses at Mycenae*. Examination of these four structures (the West House; the House of Shields; the House of the Oil Merchant; and the House of Sphinxes) was undertaken between 1950 and 1959, directed by A.J.B. Wace and N.M. Verdelis. Their work revealed a number of Linear B texts (the Greek language of the time, which confirmed that the Mycenaeans spoke Greek) and a quantity of over eighteen thousand ivory goods. It is likely that the houses were not so much a place of working ivory, but a storehouse and a place of using ivory, in, for example, adorning wooden furniture.

The Grave Circle contained the bodies of nineteen prominent people from the city, with later burials in different tomb structures, known as beehive tombs, or 'tholoi', of which there are nine at Mycenae. During excavation into the graves a huge quantity of objects, mostly in gold and silver, were discovered. The most famous is the so-called Mask of Agamemnon which Schliemann believed was the death mask of the ancient king; in fact the Mask and the other discoveries almost certainly predate Agamemnon by about three hundred years. When discovering the largest of the beehive tombs Schliemann believed it had been used as a Treasury, which is why it has its present, wrong, name of Treasury of Atreus.

The Mycenaeans' belief in the afterlife is difficult to determine. The Greek scholar G.E. Mylonas speculates that they believed that the decay of the flesh represented the freeing of the spirit, and that as the body rotted away so the spirit was free to complete the journey to Hades, and would no longer haunt the material world. This, he believes, explains the apparent disregard for the previous bodies in the shaft graves when new bodies were interred.

Sometime after 1200 BC, the Aegean civilisations along with the Mycenaeans, lost regional supremacy, though the reasons for this are unclear. It seems to have been mainly a factor of the arrival of the Dorians, but political insurgence and famine may have played a part. The city remained functional, but non-influential, for several centuries, and in around 468 BC was besieged and destroyed by the inhabitants of nearby Argos, and left to ruin and decay.

Notre Dame, Le Puy, France

The Angelic Cathedral of Notre Dame on Mount Corneille acquired the title 'Angelic' because St Vosy was allegedly told in a vision that the angels themselves had dedicated the cathedral to the Blessed Virgin Mary. Among the bishops of Le Puy was Guy Foulques (1257–9), who became Pope Clement IV.

No French place of pilgrimage was more visited in the Middle Ages, and many leading figures chose to make Le Puy a place of their own devotions. Charlemagne visited in 772 and 800, establishing a foundation for 'the ten poor canons' there. Louis IX and the King of Aragon met there in 1245. In 1254 Louis visited Le Puy on his return from the Holy Land and presented the cathedral with an ebony image of the Virgin Mary (a Black Madonna) clothed in gold brocade. The mother of Joan of Arc went there in 1429. Four popes visited Le Puy to pray, and Pope Leo IX stated in a Bull that: 'Nowhere does the Blessed Virgin receive a more special and more filial worship.' The Catholic Church's website states that: 'The Church of Le Puy assumed a sort of primacy in respect to most of the Churches of France, and even of Christendom.' The Cathedral was one of the most important stopping places for pilgrims on the way to Santiago de Compostela (see entry).

The site was originally sacred in prehistoric times. A huge standing stone, or perhaps a dolmen, crowned Mount Corneille. Legend tells us that during the third (some accounts say the fourth) century a sick widow had a vision of the Virgin Mary who told her to climb Mount Corneille and sit on the stone, and there she would be cured. So she was. She had a second vision of the Virgin who instructed her that the local bishop should build a church there in Mary's honour. This was completed by AD 430. Although it might have been expected that the pagan stone would be destroyed by the Christians, it was in fact left standing in the church and became known as Mary's Throne. In the eighth century it was broken up, but its fragments were preserved in the floor of what was known as The Angel's Chamber.

The combination of pagan and Christian history, and the mysticism of the area felt by so many, makes Le Puy a continuing place of interest for Catholics and New Age devotees alike.

Nuraghe Su Nuraxi, Barumini, Sardinia

Little is known of the origins of the Nuraghe people of Sardinia. Some scholars believe that they were a sea-going people that arrived on the island around 1500 BC, though from where has never been identified. They spread through the island, leaving evidence of advanced building capabilities and pottery design and manufacture, as well as evidence of a developed religion.

The Nuraghe people are named after the towers and tower-complexes that they left to history during their thousand year reign on Sardinia. The word 'nurra' means 'heap' or 'mound', and also 'cavity'. The towers are mounds with cavities within. Approximately seven thousand such buildings exist all over the island, though it is speculated that over thirty thousand once existed. Nothing comparable has ever been found anywhere else in the world. The layout would appear to have been designed to allow every nuraghe tower to be visible from at least one other; a simple form of protection.

While some earlier structures were just one isolated tower, others were much more complex; development included nuraghe with side projections, castle-like structures of nuraghe towers joined together, and whole villages of nuraghe developed around a central one.

According to tradition a fly, 'sa musca maccedda', lived in the entrance of the nuraghe. This fly was so huge that it could devour naughty or inquisitive children. Probably the legend can be related to the flies that helped carry the Black Death in Europe during the Middle Ages. The legend went on to say that 'sa musca maccedda' was guardian of a treasure hidden within the nuraghe.

The most significant complex is Nuraghe Su Nuraxi, in Barumini, which is centred around a three-storey tower built approximately 3,500 years ago. It has a clear fortress-like design; obviously the Nuraghe people were concerned with protecting themselves against invaders. Many visitors to the complex, though, have noted the magical, mystical qualities of the location.

Nor are the towers the only constructs of this mysterious civilisation. Archaeology has discovered giant's tombs, large structures to house the dead of eminent families. They are shaped like a T with the top-bar curved to form a semi-open space in which the ceremony of burial took place. The archaeologists also discovered sacred wells, sacred fountains and temples: evidence of religious beliefs amongst these people.

The Parthenon, Athens, Greece

The Parthenon is regarded as the product of the culmination of the development of Greek Classical art; it was created between 449 and 432 BC. The name Parthenon means 'apartment of the virgin'. Athena, in mythology, was a very tough and resourceful woman, patron of the polis of Athens and protector of all Greek poleis. (The polis was the name for the city-state, the political and social structure of the Greeks. It was the most structured form of democracy in the ancient world.) She was the daughter of Zeus and Metis, and the product of a curious birth. Discovering that Metis was pregnant, and fearing that their child might prove more powerful than himself, Zeus swallowed Metis whole. Later, suffering a terrible headache, Zeus had his own skull split open and Athena came forth from the wound, already clutching a spear.

The Parthenon in Athens stands atop the Acropolis: one of the most distinctive and well-known images of Greece, a natural outcrop of rock around which the city was built. The Parthenon was constructed to house a huge gold and ivory statue of the goddess Athena. It is a Doric temple, consisting of a rectangular floor with a series of low steps on every side, and a colonnade of Doric columns extending around the periphery. The larger of its two interior rooms, the naos, housed the statue, while the smaller room (the opisthodomos) housed the treasury. It was built to replace two earlier temples of Athena. To the Greeks, a temple was less a place of worship as such, and more regarded as the house of a god or goddess.

The Acropolis had been the site of temples dedicated to Athena and other patron deities for centuries. As such, it is likely that the erection of a statue of Athena there was probably both a political act, and one designed to ask Athena to act on the city's behalf, and to protect all its citizens. Its politicisation would have been to establish Athens as the leading polis of the area. One political leader, Pericles, can be regarded as the most instrumental person in creating the Parthenon. Indeed, the whole Acropolis was laid out in a design based on his inspiration. The Parthenon was constructed first, on the south side, then a gateway was built leading to the temple complex, known as the Propylaea, on the west side. In the south-west is a temple to Athena Nike. The Erechtheion (one of the most elaborate buildings) was erected to the north of the ruins of the old temple to Athena to hold the images of the gods and goddesses of the polis. The whole redesign took over fifty years.

In its history the Parthenon has been used as a Byzantine church, a Roman Catholic church, a Turkish harem, and a Turkish gunpowder store. On 16 September 1687, an attack on the Parthenon resulted in the powder store exploding, causing some damage to all parts of the Acropolis.

Pollution, and the large number of tourists, has caused considerable damage to the buildings on the Acropolis and the Greek government is taking steps to arrest this, and to preserve this sacred site.

St Peter's Basilica, Vatican City, Rome, Italy

The Grand Basilica di San Pietro in the Vatican, generally known as St Peter's, is the world-wide recognised symbol of Roman Catholicism. It is probably the best-known church of all, and it daily receives pilgrims and visitors from all over the world.

The original St Peter's Cathedral was the first basilica built under the Emperor Constantine, and was completed in AD 349. It was always believed that it was erected on the site of the tomb of the apostle, St Peter. In 1506, Pope Julius II laid the foundation stone of a new church which was to take a century to complete and eventually included the work of artists such as Bramante, Michelangelo, Antonio de Sangallo, Mandero and Bernini.

The Grand Dome of the Basilica, 136 metres high, was designed by Michelangelo, though it was not completed until after his death. The nave is 212 metres long. At the centre is the

Baldacchino, a canopy of gilded bronze designed by Bernini in the seventeenth century. The Basilica is 187 metres long and contains eleven chapels and forty-five altars. St Peter's is the largest church in Christianity, and the dome is the largest in Europe.

St Peter departed for Rome in around AD 60, and was almost certainly killed there during Emperor Nero's purge of AD 64. The early Christian Church in Rome commemorated this martyrdom of Peter (and the apostle Paul, who was also probably crucified in Rome) on 29 June each year, presumably because one or both of them was executed on that date during the Festival of Romulus. They may have met their deaths near the spot now occupied by the Vatican, and the belief has been prevalent in the centuries since that St Peter's body was laid to rest in the pagan cemetery on Vatican Hill where Constantine built his first Basilica, and where the Vatican stands today. However, it was always a matter of hot debate whether it was an historical truth, or only a reflection of Jesus's words to Simon (Matthew 16:18): 'You are Peter [from the Greek 'petros' meaning 'rock'] and upon this rock I will build my church.' Some scholars think that the belief that the Vatican was built over Peter's body was only symbolic of Jesus's statement.

An answer was to be found, however. In 1939 Pope Pius XI died and was to be buried beside Pius X. The authorities decided to use the opportunity to lower the floor of the crypt beneath St Peter's, known as the Sacred Grottoes, where many Popes are interred. During the work, the floor of Constantine's original basilica was found, and beneath that was a street of ancient Roman tombs dating from the second century AD. This street had been filled with tightly packed earth to provide a sound foundation for the basilica. They also found an inscription, dated to AD 300, on the wall of one mausoleum, reading: 'Peter, pray Christ Jesus for the holy Christian men buried near your body.' Further excavation located an open area seven metres by four metres, bounded on one side by a wall. In the wall was an altar-like structure which seemed to date from around AD 160, and it was positioned directly under the High Altar of St Peter's. (Gaius, in AD 200, had commented that

Peter's tomb was marked by a monument of sorts.)

During the excavations some team members found the bones of a mature man, and these were taken from their resting place and put into a wooden box. At the time, the fact that these bones had been removed was not communicated to all the team, and when the area in which they had been found was investigated it was concluded that there were no human remains. Quite why the bones were secreted away on the orders of the Monsignor in charge of the operation has never been resolved. It was not until 1952 that this error was discovered and the disinterred remains were located in the storeroom in which they had been placed. Examination showed that these bones had once been buried in the soil beneath the altar-like structure (called an aedicula). The body had once been wrapped in fine woollen, imperial purple cloth, embroidered in gold. This person had obviously been of high regard. Further examination showed that in the area where the bones had been found there were remnants of plaster from the supporting wall. On one fragment was an inscription which two years later epigraphist Margherita Guarducci was able to translate from the Greek as: 'Peter is within'. It is fairly certain that the actual bones of St Peter had indeed been located, giving proof to the claim of the Vatican being built over his tomb.

On 27 June 1968 Pope Paul VI undertook a simple ceremony in the excavated area beneath the High Altar where he carefully placed plexiglass boxes containing Peter's bones back into the repository where they had originally been found.

San Galgano Abbey and Hermitage, Italy

The Abbey of San Galgano has been described as the greatest Gothic building in Italy; even in decay it is still an imposing sight, haunting and moody. It was built in the twelfth and thirteenth centuries, one of the two largest Cistercian foundations. However, the Papacy assigned its income to a cardinal in the fifteenth century, the monks then abandoned the place, and it fell into ruin. The bell tower is rumoured to have collapsed during a Mass. Although the church is mostly a ruin, its roof gone, its cloisters and smaller buildings are being restored under the guidance of Benedictine nuns.

Saint Galgano Guidotti was the son of a petty nobleman. Following a vision of St Michael, he gave up his life as a knight and became a hermit. His friends and family visited his small hermitage to try to persuade him to return to his normal life, but he had no interest in doing so. He thrust his sword into a rock, turning it from a symbol of conflict to a symbol of peace, and it can still be seen there today. He died in 1181, at the age of thirty-three, and was canonised four years later. During those years his hermitage became what is now known as the Cappella di Monte Siepi – the chapel on the hill – the sword in the rock being its most famous display. The Cappella is situated above the abbey, offering a striking view of the ruins.

The whereabouts of St Galgano's body is unknown, though his head is preserved in Siena's Museo dell'Opera del Duomo.

His spirit may be more in evidence however. While in the chapel on the hill, during the making of a 1994 documentary for the BBC programme *Arena*, entitled 'Relics', the sound man for the TV production team tried to pull the sword out of the stone. His sound equipment broke down, and the interviews had to be taped on borrowed domestic recorders.

Sant' Agnese Fuori Le Mura (St Agnes Outside the Walls), Rome, Italy

This church is dedicated to St Agnes, the virgin martyr. Of the many virgin martyrs, St Agnes, whose feast day is 21 January, has been held in the highest honour by Rome since the fourth century AD. Although she had been revered since then, it is apparent from the diversity of accounts of her life and death that there was, at the end of the fourth century, no accurate and reliable record of the details of her martyrdom. Only her youth is undisputed; she was around twelve or thirteen years old at the time of her death.

The generally accepted story is that in AD 305 Agnes, a young Roman girl who had converted to Christianity, was murdered, probably as St Ambrose recounts, by the sword. She was put to death for refusing the amorous advances of a Roman suitor. As punishment she was stripped naked in public and, according to Prudentius, sent to a brothel before being put to death. According to the legend, while in the brothel, a young man sought to violate her but fell to the ground stricken with blindness. In other accounts he was restored to sight by Agnes's prayers. In both stories it is said that her hair grew long, miraculously quickly, to clothe her nakedness, and that an attempt was made to burn her to death but the flames would not touch her.

Her body was placed in a sepulchre on the Via Nomentana, and around her tomb grew up a larger catacomb that was given her name. The original slab which covered her body, bearing the inscription 'Agne sanctissima', is probably the one now preserved in the Museum at Naples. During the reign of Constantine, at the behest of his daughter, Constantina, a basilica was erected over Agnes's grave. Pope Honorius I in the seventh century built a church nearby, later restored by Pope Hadrian I. The last major work done on the church was under Pope Blessed Pius IX in the mid-1800s. This church is said to stand on the site of the brothel into which she was forced, and in the church garden are remains of Constantine's original basilica, which may have been more of a covered cemetery than a basilica in the true sense of the word.

In the apse of the church is a mosaic showing the martyr amid flames, with a sword at her feet. The Baroque canopy at the high altar dates from 1614, and the statue of St Agnes in the church is also from the seventeenth century. Her tomb is positioned below the high altar where she rests with her 'milk-sister' Emerentiana, the daughter of her nurse.

Since the Middle Ages, St Agnes has been represented with a lamb as a symbol of her virginity. On her feast day two lambs are solemnly blessed, and from their wool are made the palliums (bands) sent by the Pope to archbishops to mark their jurisdiction.

Santiago de Compostela, Spain

In the Middle Ages, Santiago de Compostela was one of the three holiest cities of Christian pilgrimage, the others being Jerusalem and Rome. Many regard it as having been the primary such destination; Rome was associated with the Papacy with which there was political tension in those times, and Jerusalem was a long trek not without its dangers.

Santiago de Compostela houses the grave of the apostle St James, in the House of Galicia. St James in Spanish is Sant Iago; hence Santiago. Alighieri Dante, in *Vita Nuova*, regarded those who visited Santiago de Compostela as the only true pilgrims. At the height of its fame as a pilgrimage site, Santiago de Compostela was receiving half a million pilgrims a year. St James's Way in Spanish is El Camino de Santiago, which also means Milky Way – perhaps symbolic of the belief that there were as many pilgrims as stars in the sky. Pilgrims expected complete absolution if they reached the grave; hospitals, bridges and hostels were erected along the route to make it more accessible. The pilgrimage, and the cult of St James, was seen by the clergy as a tool in the Christian resistance of Arab domination of Spain.

St James was one of the twelve disciples of Jesus. The Acts of the Apostles indicate that he was the first Apostle to suffer a martyr's death; he was executed by King Herodes Agrippa I around AD 44. He was particularly important to the Spanish on the basis of a tradition that states he once preached in Spain, in Galicia. The *Legenda Aurea of Jacobus de Voragine* points out that his preaching was not overly successful; he converted only nine people to his teachings. However, after his death his body was brought back to Galicia in a sail-less boat said to have been steered by God himself. The boat docked at Iria Flavia (now Padron), and sought a place for burial from the ruler, Queen Lupa. She was a pagan, but became converted to Christianity and had her palace turned into a church where St James was laid to rest.

The location of the grave was unknown for eight hundred years, but during the reign of Alfonso II (AD 789–842) a hermit called Pelagius had a vision which revealed to him the site of the grave which was bathed in a holy light. Bishop Theodomir of Iria Flavia declared it to be the grave of St James, Alfonso had a church built on the site, and St James was venerated as the divine protector of Spain.

Whether or not the site actually holds the grave of St James has been the subject of much debate and doubt; Alfonso may have had ulterior motives for wanting the site 'located', and the pilgrimages to Santiago de Compostela were certainly lucrative for the local area. It is known that the Cathedral of Santiago hired travelling storytellers to spread fabricated news of St James's miracles, something not uncommon during the medieval period.

The likeliest ulterior motive was that Spain needed a champion in its wars with the Arab Moors who had invaded the country in 711. St James is said to have appeared as a 'heavenly warrior' during the Battle of Clavijo in AD 84 and to the Spanish he became a fighter and 'moor-slayer'. 'Santiago!' was for many centuries the battle-cry of the Spanish conquistadors conquering new lands.

Of the pilgrimage to Santiago de Compostela, particularly via the most important French route known as the Camino Frances, the medieval *Liber Sancti Jacobi* (an eleventh century document included in the manuscript called the *Codex Calixtinus*) describes it as representing: 'the absence of evils, immortality of the flesh, an increase in virtues, forgiveness of sins, repentance to those doing penance, the right-minded way, the love of the saints, belief in the Resurrection, a prize to the blessed, drawing away from Hell, and receiving the protection of Heaven. A pilgrimage also distances us from tempting delicacies, keeps in check the fleshly desires that attack the bastion of the soul, cleanses the spirit, invites the person to a life of contemplation, humbles the proud, ennobles the low-born, and cherishes poverty.'

The Camino Frances roughly follows the ancient Roman road known as the Via Traiana. There is evidence that the route has been one of pilgrimage since Roman times, and possibly even a spiritual route from prehistoric times. Earlier pilgrims may not have stopped at Santiago de Compostela but continued to Finisterre, also known as the End of the Earth, a mysterious place replete with myth and legend.

Notable pilgrims to Santiago de Compostela included the French bishop of Le Puy, Gottskalk, St Francis of Assisi and St Bridget of Sweden.

A number of factors conspired to reduce the attraction of the pilgrimage: the Protestant Reformation in northern Europe, the reputation of the Spanish Inquisition, and the French civil war in particular. When, in 1492, the Moors had been ousted from their last stronghold of Granada, the cult of St James lost much of its purpose, reducing the motive for pilgrimage. Indeed, pilgrimage for a while became associated with criminals and the poor, and pilgrims became a suspect group.

The cult was still alive in Catholic hearts, however, perhaps best demonstrated by the effect of Oliver Cromwell's attacks on Ireland which resulted in a resurgence of Irish Catholics travelling to Compostela.

Further revivals occurred. The saint's remains had been hidden to protect them in 1518, but they were rediscovered in 1879. A papal bull in 1884 decreed the authenticity of the relics and 1885 was made a holy year of St James. Once again pilgrims from all over Europe travelled to Santiago. In 1937 James was officially restored as the patron saint of Spain, and in 1992 the Pope visited the site. Although numbers of visitors had waned, there are still many pilgrims annually, and the numbers are again rising.

MYSTICAL AND SACRED SITES IN THE MIDDLE-EAST

Bamiyan, Afghanistan

Bamiyan was a central tourist area in Afghanistan, situated around 225 miles from Kabul. The northern part of the valley is famous for steep cliffs into which were carved massive images of Buddha; one, at fifty-five metres high, was the world's tallest standing Buddha.

Buddhism was introduced into the area in the third century BC by the Mauryan emperor Ashoka. Afghanistan was already an important trade route, at the heart of the Silk Route, and those travelling overland from east to west had to journey through it. Accompanying the traders' caravans were Buddhist monks who taught their religion as they travelled, and it was from that area that Buddhism may have spread to China, Korea, Japan, Tibet, Nepal, Bhutan, and Mongolia. In the first centuries AD Afghanistan had many Buddhist monasteries and stupas cared for by many monks, and the area remained a significant Buddhist centre until the country embraced Islam in the ninth century. With such a rich Buddhist tradition, it was here that two great works of art were produced: the Buddhas of Bamiyan, carved out of the rockface. They were covered with a mud and straw mixture to create the face, hands and the folds of the robes, then plastered and painted: the smaller Buddha blue, the larger one red, with their hands and faces gold.

The area had developed into a religious centre under Kanishka the Great and the smaller of the statues of Buddha, thirty-eight metres high, was built during his reign. It stood in the Folladi and Kakrak valley which has thousands of ornamental caves which were then inhabited by yellow-robed monks. Two hundred years later the colossal 55-metre Buddha was carved. The two statues, and the area itself, were sacred for Buddhists from all over the world.

The facial features and the hands of the statues disappeared long ago, possibly deliberately defaced to reduce the impact of these idols. Similar damage was inflicted on the images in the ornamental caves nearby.

The wars in Afghanistan since 1980 have severely damaged the sites. Since October 1994 many archaeological artefacts, sculptures and works of art have been destroyed, and similarly art and religious artefacts stored in the Kabul Museum have come under attack by Taleban Muslim fundamentalists, on the basis that: 'Islam prohibits carving and worship of statues,' according to Sahar, a Peshawar-based news agency and the Taleban-sponsored weekly, Zarb-I-Momin.

In the mid-1990s, the area around the base of the larger Buddha was being used as an ammunition dump. This was possibly because of the dual advantage that opposition forces might be reluctant to harm the idol while the Islamic groups would not have regarded it as important, it being a 'false idol'. In 1997 a Taleban commander trying to take over the valley stated he would blow up the Buddhas the moment the valley fell into his hands. This was officially denied by the Taleban High Command in Kandahar after many international protests; indeed they promised they would protect the images on the basis that they represented part of the country's cultural heritage. Under pressure from SPACH (Society for the Preservation of Afghanistan's Cultural Heritage) the ammunition dump was removed and a General Office for the Preservation of Historical Sites established. After that time there was a controversy between the officials and the soldiers in the valley itself as some damage had been found inflicted on the statues.

Bamiyan changed hands twice during the month of February 2001 alone. UNESCO's Afghan expert Michael Barry commented at that time that: 'The entire archaeological legacy of a country is being destroyed.' On 27 February The Times reported (through its correspondent Zahid Hussain in Islamabad) that: 'Taleban authorities have ordered the destruction of all statues in Afghanistan, including the ancient statues of Buddha, citing Islamic prohibitions on icons.' They were to be demolished by officials from the Ministry of Vice and Virtue.

In the early part of 2001 it was reported that the destruction of the statues had been completed. One witness had claimed on 5 March 2001: 'I could see the Taleban soldiers firing anti-aircraft weapons at the two statues.' The leader of the Taleban forces, Mullah Omar, commented: 'Muslims should be proud of smashing idols. It has given praise to God that we have destroyed them.' On 9 March Muhammad Ashraf Nadeem, a spokesman, said 'The Taleban dynamited both of the statues and they are completely gone.' Although this caused an international outcry, Taleban leaders insisted that the policy of demolishing all statues would not be reversed.

Castle of the Jews/Wadi Kharrar, River Jordan

South-east of Jericho, less than half a mile from the River Jordan, is a Greek Orthodox monastery, referred to as Qasr el-Yahud (The Castle of the Jews), said by the Israelis to be the site where John the Baptist baptised Jesus in the Jordan. It was built in the fourth century AD and has been destroyed and rebuilt several times. The site contains the ruins of a Byzantine monastery, as well as a fortress and a church from the time of the Crusades.

However, it is not the only site claimed for the baptism. On the opposite bank of the river, about a mile to the east, Jordan has declared that Wadi Kharrar is the actual site, and at least part of the debate seems to have stemmed from attempts to corner the tourism market, and money, for the new millennium. 'This is the baptism site. Other sites have not been proven as far as any archaeologist is concerned,' Jordanian Tourism Minister Akel Beltaji claimed. A Byzantine monastery and three churches have been unearthed, along with a series of shallow pools they believe were used for baptism when the site rapidly grew into a pilgrimage centre in early Christianity.

The Vatican seemingly gave Wadi Kharrar a seal of approval. The Holy See's representative in Amman, Dominique Rezeau, said that Vatican theologians believe Jesus was 'most probably' baptised on the Jordanian side of the river. However, that was later downplayed during a visit to Wadi Kharrar by Pope John Paul II in the year 2000; his aides claimed that it was the baptismal waters of the Jordan that were sacred rather than any individual piece of land. At the Jordanian-sponsored site the Pope said in prayer: 'On the banks of the River Jordan, you [God] raised up John the Baptist, a voice crying in the wilderness . . . to prepare the way of the Lord, to herald the coming of Jesus.'

Then, to ensure his neutrality, the Pope made clear he would later visit the 'competing' site also.

Chapel of the Nativity, Bethlehem, Israel

Although the actual place of Jesus's birth is the subject of debate, it has long been accepted by Christians to have been at Bethlehem, to the south of Jerusalem. A cave-site held to be the birthplace was first mentioned by St Justin in the second century. Archaeological examination has suggested that the site was originally a sacred place dedicated to Adonis (an ancient Greek spirit representing the cycle of nature). It was Helena, the mother of Roman emperor Constantine, who built the first basilica on the site sometime around AD 326. The original basilica was destroyed during the Samaritan Revolt of 529 and was later rebuilt, somewhat extended and modified, by Emperor Justinian. This makes the Church of the Nativity one of the oldest churches in Christendom.

It was the only major church to escape destruction during the Persian invasion of 614, seemingly because, when they entered the place, they found a representation of the Magi from Persia, and decided to honour their ancestors by leaving the place untouched.

It was frequently visited by pilgrims during the Crusades.

The grotto (cave-site) of the nativity can be seen beneath the church, and a silver star marks the alleged spot where Jesus was born.

The Church of the Holy Sepulchre, Jerusalem, Israel

The Christian Bible tells us that Jesus was crucified by the Romans and buried in a rock tomb in a garden nearby, probably just outside the city walls, as was the tradition of the time. The enlargement of the city in AD 41 to 44 brought the site of execution and burial within the expanded city.

Jerusalem was destroyed in AD 70 and rebuilt by the Emperor Hadrian in 135, and named Aelia Capitolina. The tomb was covered in earth and paved over, and a temple dedicated to Venus was built atop it.

Sometime after AD 313 the Emperor Constantine's mother, Helena, converted to Christianity, following a vision her son had in battle prior to his becoming emperor, and she set out on a quest to find the True Cross. Torturing a Jew named Judas for the information, she apparently found the True Cross and the crucifixion nails in a rock cavity in the city which became known as the Grotto of the True Cross. This Grotto, one of the sacred sites of Christianity, is located beneath the Church of the Holy Sepulchre.

Constantine funded the building of Christian churches through-out the Holy Land and the Church of the Holy Sepulchre in Jerusalem was built over the rock tomb that had housed Jesus' body. The entrance to Christ's tomb had been sealed with a huge stone; it is said that this is the stone that is now preserved in the Chapel of the Angel under the dome in the Church.

In the seventh century Constantine's church was destroyed by the Persians; its replacement, funded by the Byzantine emperor, was destroyed in 1009 by Caliph al-Hakim who ordered its total obliteration. The Church and shrine were demolished and the tomb and evidence of its very being were virtually hammered out of existence. However, the Caliph's Christian mother sought to restore the tomb, the Caliph agreed, and the foundation of the tomb was found to be still visible beneath the rubble. By 1012 the shrine had been rebuilt. Further work was undertaken in 1037 by the Byzantine emperor Michael IV.

In 1099 Jerusalem was conquered by the Crusaders from the west who rebuilt the Church yet again, greatly embellishing the Edicule (meaning 'little house') containing the rock-cut tomb. Remnants of the restored structure, and the Edicule, are present within the modern-day structure.

In 1244 Jerusalem was sacked by Khwarismian horsemen who stripped the Edicule of its valuable ornamentation but left the basic structure unharmed.

In 1555 Boniface of Ragusa 'restored' the Edicule still further, and in doing so demolished masonry revealing the original rock-cut tomb. He constructed a more elaborate church over the tomb-site.

The modern church fell into some disrepair mainly because of lack of agreement between the Greek, Latin, Armenian and Coptic communities charged with its care. However, these groups began to work together more efficiently during the 1990s and this culminated in 1997 with a common dedication service for the newly restored dome.

In the late 1990s, a team of scientists led by Professor Martin Biddle of Oxford University were able to make close examinations within the church and the Edicule itself, using the most modern equipment. What exists today is, to quote Professor Martin Biddle: 'like an onion, with earlier Edicules being preserved within its walls like a succession of skins'. Biddle also added: 'There is strong evidence to suggest that the north and south walls of the original rock-cut tomb built at the time of Christ still survive inside the present structure.'

It is only fair to point out that Biddle's work, and much that is believed about the Church of the Holy Sepulchre depends on belief in the history of Jesus Christ, which is not accepted by all scholars. Biddle has been able to confirm that there is probably a rock-cut tomb dating from the time of Christ, not that it is Christ's tomb.

However, housing as it does what is widely accepted to be the Grotto of the True Cross of Christ, the place of crucifixion, the place of burial, and the stone used to seal the tomb of Christ, the Church of the Holy Sepulchre is therefore the most sacred site on Earth to Christians. It has been the object of pilgrimages since the time of Helena's patronage and apparently has lost none of its fascination for both pilgrims and scholars alike.

Dome of the Rock, Jerusalem, Israel

There has been human habitation in the area of Jerusalem for five thousand years. Excavations revealed that a town – named Ursalim, meaning Foundation of God – once existed on Mount Moriah, which is also known as Temple Mount.

David, founder of the Jewish kingdom made Ursalim his capital in around 1000 BC, renaming it Jerusalem, meaning City of Peace. The most precious object for the Israelites – the Ark of the Covenant – was allegedly brought to the city less than fifty years later. The Ark is the container in which the two tablets inscribed with the Ten Commandments are stored.

The Jews built their First Temple there in 957 BC, during the reign of David's son, Solomon. This Temple of Solomon is also central to the beliefs of the Knights Templar who would take part in the later Crusades.

Nebuchadnezzar II of Babylon ravished the Jewish treasures and destroyed the Temple in 586 BC. When the Jews returned to the area in 539 BC, they began construction of the Second Temple, completed by 515 BC. By now the whereabouts of the Ark of the Covenant was in question.

During the years of Roman rule, Herod the Great enlarged the Second Temple (and built the Wailing Wall). During later resistance to the Roman army of occupation Jerusalem was sacked, and the Second Temple destroyed in AD 70.

In AD 135, the Roman Emperor Hadrian constructed his new capital, Aelia Capitolina, on the ruins of the destroyed Jerusalem. He built a temple to the god Jupiter on the site of the Temple, but this was itself destroyed by the Byzantines when Christianity took hold. Jerusalem remained a Christian stronghold until 614 when the Persians sacked the city and destroyed the churches. They remained in power there for only a short time until 638 when, six years after the death of Muhammad, the Muslim Caliph Umar I occupied the city and built a mosque there, probably of wood and plaster and hence none of it remains to the present.

According to Islamic tradition Muhammad and the Archangel Gabriel flew to Temple Mount where they met with many prophets including Abraham, Moses, and Jesus. The Archangel led Muhammad to the pinnacle of the rock from where Muhammad ascended into the presence of Allah. Muhammad was then returned to Mecca; hence the importance of the two sites to Muslims.

It was on this site, that had once held the two Jewish Temples and the Temple to Jupiter, that the tenth Caliph, Abd al-Malik ibn Marwan, built the Dome of the Rock between 687 and 691. The Dome, known in Arabic as Qubbat As-Sakhrah, is regarded by many as one of the greatest, and most beautiful, Islamic monuments. The dome itself is twenty metres high and ten metres in diameter, and was once covered in pure gold (now removed in favour of aluminium). K.A.C. Creswell, an authority on Muslim architecture, commented that 'the building instead of being a collection of odd notes becomes a harmonious chord in stones, a sort of living crystal . . . some of the ratios involved . . . go right down to the very basis of our nature, and of the physical universe in which we live and move'.

In 1071 the Turks dominated the Holy Land and closed the pilgrimage routes, leading to the Crusades which again returned Jerusalem to Christianity. During this time the Dome of the Rock became a Christian monument, re-named the Temple of the Lord. Muslims recaptured the city in 1187 and it went through a succession of further changes until, by the middle of the nineteenth century, half of the population was Jewish. The city was proclaimed the capital of Israel in 1980.

Within the Dome, the rock itself – from where Muhammad ascended – can be seen protruding through the floor. Underneath the sacred stone is a cave-like hollow known as the Well of Souls. Here, it is said, the voices of the dead may sometimes be heard.

That one site should be so important to so many major religions, that each should build its sacred places on one exact spot, strongly suggests that the site has very special, mystical and sacred energy.

It was mentioned at the beginning of this passage that the original Temple on the site probably housed the Ark of the Covenant. The Ark has itself been the subject of great mystery. The researcher and writer Graham Hancock in *The Sign and the Seal* claims that it was removed from the Temple between 687 and 642 BC. It is said that it was then taken to Egypt and later to Ethiopia, where many believe it remains today.

However, author and researcher Richard Andrews, in his book *Blood on the Mountain*, is drawn to the claims of Lieutenant Charles

Warren who sought the Ark in 1870, and who concluded that it was hidden virtually under the Dome of the Rock itself. Excavation has never been permitted, but Andrews, using infra-red photography from a helicopter, showed that there is indeed an underground tunnel and chambers where Warren predicted they would be. Possibly the Ark – one of the most treasured artefacts of history – has never moved from its original resting place of three thousand years ago.

The House of the Virgin Mary, Ephesus, Turkey

The story told by an invalid German visionary, Katherina Emmerich, who lived between 1774 and 1824 was to have profound repercussions for Christians.

There was already an established story that after the crucifixion, St John the Apostle and Mary, the mother of Jesus, travelled to Ephesus in present day Turkey. According to those stories, Mary is said to have lived out her final years there. The minutes of the AD 431 Ecumenical Council of the Christian Church indicate that the Virgin spent at least some time living there, though whether it was the rest of her life is not specified.

Emmerich described in detail the Virgin's house in Ephesus in her *Life of the Blessed Virgin*, even though it is clear that she never left Germany. On 29 December 1812 while she was praying in bed with her hands stretched forth she was 'suddenly shaken by a divine force' and overcome by fever. A bright light covered her hands which suddenly took on the stigmata – the wounds of the crucifixion of Christ. The people at her bedside were, understandably, astonished, and her doctors were unable to offer explanation. In this state she had visions of the Virgin, including her death at the age of sixty-four, and received a detailed description of her house in Ephesus.

At the end of the nineteenth century catholic priests in Smyrna, and particularly one French clergyman named Gouyet, read Emmerich's account. Gouyet went to Ephesus to investigate it. He was astonished to discover that there was indeed a small chapel-like house on a hill, just a few miles to the south of the ruins of the city. It matched Emmerich's description of location and structure almost perfectly. He also discovered that it was a popular shrine, visited every year by Orthodox Christians on 15 August, and was locally known as Panaya Kapula – the Doorway to the Virgin.

In 1892 the archbishop of Smyrna proclaimed that the building was a place of pilgrimage. It was given a huge boost in this regard when, on 26 July 1967, Pope Paul VI visited the building, and later, on 30 November 1979, when Pope John Paul II attended.

In the book *Virgin Mary*, translated by Derbent Sumer, the setting is described: 'The view from the hill on which the house stands and the greatness of the sense of peace and serenity it awakens in one is beyond expression.'

Ephesus was also the site of a prominent and significant debate around the nature of the Virgin. In AD 431 the Council of Ephesus, the third general or ecumenical council of the Christian church, was held there. The assembly was organised by Emperors Theodosius II and Valentinian III, to resolve a controversy known as Nestorianism. This arose when Nestorius, patriarch of Constantinople, refused to grant to Mary the title 'Mother of God'. His view, and that of his followers, was that Christ was actually two separate entities: a physical human and a divine God, and that Mary was 'only' the mother of the physical person, not the divine one. This was in contrast to the accepted belief that Christ was one unified person: God and man.

Under St Cyril, patriarch of Alexandria, the council found against Nestorius and deposed him, condemning his doctrine. The council emphasised that Christ was unified as God and man, that he had two aspects but that they were inseparable. Mary was therefore confirmed as the legitimate mother of Jesus, God and man, and the council approved the title 'Mother of God' for her.

Ephesus had once also been the home of the Temple of Artemis, one of the Seven Wonders of the Ancient World, and had been famous through history for its sacred shrines. It was also the home of the fourth-century church of St John the Evangelist, lavishly rebuilt in the sixth century by Justinian I.

By the early fourteenth century, the harbour had silted up, the city declined and it was eventually abandoned. Excavations of the city began in 1963 and it is now a major tourist attraction, not just for pilgrims but for holiday-makers who go to see the recovered temples, many churches, a huge magnificent theatre, and the restored, marble Arcadian Way that runs from the theatre to the harbour.

The house itself is under the care of the Panaya Kapulu, the Society for the House of the Virgin Mary.

Jabal Hira (or Jabal Al-Nur, or Mount Hira), Saudi Arabia

This mountain near Mecca is effectively where the religions of Islam started. The north-east face contains a cave in which Muhammad rested and sought tranquillity and where he had visions that led him to becoming a prophet.

Islam is the most recent of the major religions to appear, and has roots that take it back to Judaism and Christianity. Within around three hundred years of Muhammad's death, Islam had spread throughout the world. It is estimated that today one-fifth of the world's population is Muslim.

Before Muhammad's revelations, the Arabs inhabiting the desert regions were mostly animists who believed in gods and spirits that inhabited the stones, rocks, trees and water-holes; they also believed in demons called jinns. In the towns of Arabia, where Muhammad was brought up, Jewish and Christian ideology was well known and followed by many of the people. The idea of a monotheistic religion – following one God – was therefore not novel when Muhammad brought his revelations to the people. Over a period of around twenty years Muhammad took that belief into the desert areas.

There is a common stem to the religions of Judaism, Islam and Christianity in that Abraham is regarded by all three as father of the Semites. The Arabian peoples regard themselves as the direct descendants of Ishmael, Abraham's first born son. Ishmael was the son of Abraham and the Egyptian woman, Hagar. Abraham also fathered a son, Isaac, late in his life, with his wife Sarah. The Jews and Christians are the sons and daughters of Isaac. Muslims believe in Jesus, but as a prophet and not as a god, and they believe that Christians are wrong to worship him. Muslims regard Jesus as having been a messenger from the true God, Allah. They also believe that Jews have turned their back on their own heritage by not following Islam.

According to tradition, when Adam and Eve were cast out of Paradise, Adam fell on a mountain in Sri Lanka (Adam's Peak) and Eve fell in Arabia. They wandered apart for two hundred years. Finally, they were allowed to come together again on Mount Arafat, near Mecca. Adam prayed that a shrine might be given to him which was similar to that at which he had worshipped in Paradise. The shrine was built, and when it was gradually eroded over time, Abraham and Ishmael rebuilt it, including a stone brought to them by the Angel Gabriel. (The stone is thought by some to have been a meteorite.) This shrine was known as the Ka'abah. The Ka'abah is considered to be the first House of God.

Muhammad was born in Mecca in AD 571, and there have been many unusual events associated with his birth and childhood. His mother said: 'When he was born, there was a light that issued out of my pudendum and lit the places of Syria.' It was also believed that: 'fourteen galleries of Kisra's palace cracked and rolled down . . . and some churches on Lake Sawa sank down and collapsed.' His young life had several tragedies; his father died before he was born and his mother died when he was just six years old. He was raised by his grandfather for two years and then by an uncle. He became a shepherd. He married a woman, Khadija, who bore him two sons who died in infancy and several daughters. One of his daughters, Fatima, is revered by Muslims.

Ill at ease with the state of the world Muhammad sought peace and meditation in the cave on the mountain. There he was visited by an angel, Gabriel, who told him he was to be a messenger of God, and gave him the first verses of the Koran. Muhammad was troubled by his visions, but his wife encouraged him to believe them. He did, and commenced a lifetime of preaching in the service of Allah.

Kidron Valley, Jerusalem, Israel

The Kidron Valley is located to the east of Jerusalem, between the Temple Mount (the site of the **Dome Of The Rock**) and the Mount of Olives. Kidron means dusky, or gloomy. It is a sacred site for Christians, Jews and Muslims.

Jesus travelled through the Kidron Valley many times when journeying to and from Jerusalem: including his journey to visit Lazarus at Bethany; when he rode in triumphal entry on a donkey from the Mount of Olives; and when travelling from the location of the Last Supper to the Garden of Gethsemane where he was arrested.

At the practical level, the Kidron Valley, which contains the Gihon Spring, was the water supply for ancient Jerusalem. Hezekiah built a tunnel that allowed water to flow, undetected by enemies, from the spring to within the walls of the city.

The Church of the Assumption is in the lowest point of the Kidron Valley. The original church was built by the Byzantine Emperor Theodosius I in the fourth century, on the place where Mary is believed to have been buried. The church has been destroyed and rebuilt several times; the present structure dates from the time of the Crusades. The shrine allegedly houses the tomb of the Virgin Mary, her remains having been brought from Mount Zion. It is the place of her Assumption to Heaven.

The Jews believe that the Messiah will come from the east, passing over the Mount of Olives and through the Kidron Valley before arriving on the Temple Mount. For this reason, for centuries, Jews have buried their dead along this line so that when the Messiah comes he will pass directly over their graves. There are several ancient rock tombs visible today.

Muslims believe that the Kidron Valley will be the location of Judgment Day, where God will raise the worthy to Paradise, according to the quality of their beliefs and the good they have done in life, leaving evil people to journey to hell.

Mahram Bilqis, Yemen

Excavation of a temple site at Mahram Bilqis, thought to date from three thousand years ago, was started in 1951 by the late American archaeologist Dr Wendell Phillips. However, this work was halted in 1952, when the team had to abandon the site due to political unrest in the area.

Excavations began again only in 1998, when researchers from the University of Calgary, working in a project with the American Foundation for the Study of Man, were invited to resume work. The AFSM President who received the invitation was Wendell's brother, Merilyn Phillips Hodgson. He said: 'In the beginning, my goal was to see my brother Wendell's dream come true to return to the Mahram Bilqis. Now it is my passion to excavate it and see the greatest of Yemen's cultural heritage monuments come alive again.'

The Mahram Bilqis (Temple of the Moon God) lies buried under the sands of the southern Arabian desert in northern Yemen and is believed to have been used throughout the reign of the legendary Queen of Sheba. It was a sacred site for pilgrims throughout Arabia from around 1200 BC to AD 550. The project's field director, University of Calgary archaeology professor, Dr William Glanzman, said: 'The sanctuary is packed with artefacts, pottery, artwork and inscriptions, opening a new door to the ancient civilisations of southern Arabia. We've probably excavated less than one per cent of the site, with many of its treasures still buried far beneath the sands. This is the largest and one of the most important pre-Islamic sanctuary sites in Arabia.'

Mahram Bilqis is located near the ancient city of Marib, capital of the Queen of Sheba's kingdom, which is mentioned in both the Bible and the Koran. Hers was the most powerful of the five ancient states of Southern Arabia. It was on the Arabian Peninsula's main caravan trading route, and therefore became a wealthy and important centre.

The ruins consist of eight limestone pillars from the front of the temple, half-buried in the sands. Behind the site's peristyle hall is a wall of thick limestone blocks covered in inscriptions. The temple's foundations are still buried some ten metres below the sands. Excavation to date has uncovered large numbers of animal bones, suggesting the sanctuary was used for animal sacrifices. When archaeologists have completed their work there is an outline plan to restore the temple to its sixth-century state.

Glanzman commented: 'The ancient builders of this temple used extremely advanced engineering techniques. To reconstruct it, we first have to understand how the original stone masons carved the blocks and then teach the Yemeni masons these skills. We're hoping to rejuvenate crafts and masonry skills that have lain dormant for more than fourteen hundred years.' He went on: 'In many respects, the Queen of Sheba's kingdom was the cradle of the Arab civilisation and the Mahram Bilqis was at the very heart of this kingdom. This temple may well be considered the eighth wonder of the world.'

The Queen of Sheba appears in the Bible, in the Koran, where she is called Bilqis, and in Ethiopian legend where, called Makeda, she is credited with founding the first royal lineage. In southern Africa, the stone ruins of Great Zimbabwe (see entry) are said by the Mashona people to have been the palace of the Queen of Sheba, and they have their own legends about her.

In the Book of Kings in the Bible, the Queen of Sheba visited King Solomon in Jerusalem, taking with her gifts of spices, gold, and jewels, but she was herself overwhelmed by the wealth of King Solomon's state, and believed this was due to good fortune showered on his people by their God, Jehovah.

The excavations at Mahram Bilqis may offer insight into the reality of the Queen's life, whichever traditions have adopted her story.

Marduk Ziggurat, Babylon, Iraq

In the Mesopotamian plain between the Rivers Tigris and Euphrates, in modern Iraq, is a collection of dilapidated mud-brick buildings which is all that remains of the ancient city of Babylon.

Babylon was one of a number of communities built by the peoples of that plain around 5,500 years ago. A tradition of building which grew up in the area was the construction of temples in the shape of stepped pyramids, known as ziggurats. They were flat-topped, stepped towers, and were built to honour a chosen god. Babylon was one of the most influential cities on the

Mesopotamian plain and its ziggurat honoured the god Marduk; in Mesopotamian religion Marduk was the chief god of Babylon and the national god of Babylonia. He was probably once the god of thunderstorms, later becoming known as Bel, and eventually just Lord.

The importance of this ziggurat to Marduk was such that it was many times destroyed and rebuilt, until it became the tallest tower on the plain.

Modern archaeology has located what seem to be its foundations: a square of earthen embankments over ninety metres on each side. The tower was probably at its most glorious during the reign of King Nebuchadnezzar II who lived from 605 to 562 BC. During this time the tower was ninety metres high, and, according to an inscription made by the king, was constructed of: 'baked brick enamelled in brilliant blue'. Also it is reported that: 'gold, silver and precious stones from the mountain and from the sea were liberally set into the foundations'. Its rebuilding needed the 'various peoples of the Empire, from north and south, from mountains and the coasts'.

The tower, called Etemenanki by the Babylonians, was not the only marvel of the city. It also held the famous Hanging Gardens, one of the Seven Wonders of the Ancient World, and two fabulous palaces built by Nebuchadnezzar.

The tower probably came to an end around 478 BC when the city was overrun by the Persian King Xerxes; it would have been left to decay back into the mud from which it was built. Even in 460 BC, after the tower had been deteriorating for many years, the Greek historian Herodotus visited the site and was impressed. He described it thus: 'It has a solid central tower, one furlong square, with a second erected on top of it and then a third, and so on up to eight. All eight towers can be climbed by a spiral way running around the outside, and about halfway up there are seats for those who make the journey to rest on.'

Although this tower is now lost to history, ziggurats still exist from which we can learn a great deal about this style of worship. The largest surviving, if somewhat damaged, such temple is in Iran, in what was once the land called Elam. Built in 1250 BC by

King Untash-Napirisha it once had five levels and stood over fifty metres high.

So why is this particular tower to Marduk, now not even in existence, so important? Because it is likely that it is the legendary Tower of Babel, the subject of one of the better known stories of the Old Testament, told in Genesis, Chapter II: 'Now the whole earth had one language and few words. And as men migrated from the east, they found a plain in the land of Shinar and settled there. And they said to one another, "Come, let us make bricks, and burn them thoroughly." And they had brick for stone, and bitumen for mortar. Then they said, "Come, let us build ourselves a city, and a tower with its top in the heavens, and let us make a name for ourselves, lest we be scattered abroad upon the face of the whole earth." And the Lord came down to see the city and the tower, which the sons of men had built. And the Lord said, "Behold, they are one people, and they have all one language; and this is only the beginning of what they will do; and nothing that they propose to do will now be impossible for them. Come, let us go down, and there confuse their language, that they may not understand one another's speech." So the Lord scattered them abroad from there over the face of the earth, and they left off building the city. Therefore its name was called Babel, because there the Lord confused the language of all the earth; and from there the Lord scattered them abroad over the face of the earth.'

The modern word 'babble' comes from the story of the Tower of Babel, but it must be remembered that Babel was also the ancient name for Babylon. Some scholars believe that the story of the Tower of Babel was a myth; what is clear is that a fabulous structure existed here at some time in the past and seems to have played some part in the origin of the Biblical accounts.

Mecca, Saudi Arabia

Mecca is the birthplace of the prophet Muhammad, who was born there in AD 571. He was the founder, and prophet, of one of the world's great monotheistic religions, Islam; its followers, Muslims, believe in one god, Allah.

Mecca is the most sacred of Muslim holy sites. It is known to Muslims as Umm-al-Qura, the Mother of Cities, and each year, during the Islamic month of Dhu al-Hijja, approximately two million Muslims go on pilgrimage there. Although chiefly associated with Muhammad, Mecca was a religious centre before his time, and there are several holy sites with the sacred precincts of the Great Mosque, al-Haram, which had religious significance in pre-Islamic times. The mosque is designed to be a replica of Allah's (God's) house in heaven, and holds up to three hundred thousand worshippers at a time. It also contains the sacred well known as the Zamzam, which is believed to have been used by Hagar, the mother of Abraham's son Ishmael.

Most sacred location of all is the Ka'abah, a windowless cube-shaped building in the courtyard of the mosque, draped in black cloth, believed to have been built by the Hebrew leader Abraham. Non-Muslims are not permitted in this most sacred of sites. On arrival in Mecca pilgrims dress in two white, seamless sheets to symbolise purity, and then make a ritual procession – called the tawaf – seven times around the Ka'abah in an anti-clockwise direction. If possible they kiss the Black Stone housed there. This was supposedly given to Abraham by the angel Gabriel, and is presented in a silver frame in the wall of the north-east corner of the shrine. It is oval in shape, and composed of seven small stones of different sizes and shapes joined together with cement. There is speculation that the stone is a meteorite. (One legend has it that the stone was originally white but blackened because of the kisses of sinful people.)

Wherever they are in the world, Muslims face Mecca to pray five times daily, at which time they are deemed to be joined to the Ka'abah by an invisible line known as the qibla. They are expected to visit Mecca at least once during their lifetime. These are two of the five basic tenets of Islam; the other three being: profession of the faith, that there is only one god, called Allah, and that Muhammad is his messenger; the giving of percentages of possessions towards the good of the community; and fasting during Ramadan.

Each year there is an annual pilgrimage to Mecca, called the 'haj'. Part of that pilgrimage is to visit one of three great pillars representing the Devil on the Bridge of Jamara, in the Mina Valley, in a ritual known as the Stoning of Satan.

There have been tragedies during these pilgrimages. In 1990 1,426 people were crushed to death during a stampede; in 1997 343 were killed and fifteen hundred injured when fire broke out; in 1998 118 pilgrims died and 180 were injured in a stampede at the Stoning of Satan ritual. In 2001 thirty-five people were crushed to death there during the first day of the Islamic feast of Eid-al-Adha.

The city was first mentioned by the Egyptian geographer Ptolemy, who in the second century AD called it Makoraba. Apart from its religious significance, its location on several primary trade routes made the city commercially important in ancient times.

Mecca has had a colourful past. It was controlled by the Egyptians in the thirteenth century, but from 1517 it was controlled for Turkey by the sharifs (descendants of Muhammad through Hasan, son of Muhammad's son-in-law Ali). The Turks were driven from the city in 1916 by Grand Sharif Hussein ibn Ali, later first King of Hejaz. In 1924 the city was occupied by Abdul Aziz ibn Saud, then Sultan of Najd, who made Mecca the religious capital of the Kingdom of Saudi Arabia. King Fahd adopted the official title of the Custodian of the Two Holy Mosques as an acknowledgement of his responsibility towards Islam.

In recent years there have been incidents in and around the mosque produced from the passion of religious conviction: in 1979 it was occupied for ten days by two hundred or so Muslim extremists, and in 1987 over four hundred people were killed nearby when Iranian demonstrators clashed with Saudi police.

Medina, Saudi Arabia

Medina, in ancient times called Yathrib (also called Medinat-en-Nabi, meaning City of the Prophet or Medinat Rasul Allah, meaning City of the Apostle of God), is one of Islam's most sacred sites.

At the age of forty, Muhammad was visited in Mecca by the

angel Gabriel after which he set about the task of converting his countrymen from their pagan, polytheistic beliefs, against considerable opposition.

In AD 622, opposition to Muhammad and his followers in Mecca had become so strong that he was persuaded to move two hundred miles north to Yathrib; according to some traditions Muhammad had been invited there to act as a peacemaker between warring factions. The event, known as the Hijra (migration), was a turning point in the life of Muhammad. In Yathrib he established the first Muslim community, and the Hijra became the start of the Muslim calendar. Yathrib soon came to be known as Medina.

Upon his arrival in Medina, the Prophet established the first mosque in Islam at Quba, a village on the outskirts. Called Masjid Al-Taqwa (Mosque of Piety), the mosque still stands, albeit modernised and enlarged. According to history, the manner in which the Prophet decided on its location was to let his camel loose, and choose the site where it stopped to rest. The whole Muslim community took part in the construction of this first mosque, which was simply an open courtyard surrounded by a wall made from bricks and tree trunks.

Once settled in Medina, the Prophet built another mosque adjacent to his house. Called Masjid Al-Nabawi (the Prophet's Mosque), the first structure on the site was a simple one supported by the trunks of palm trees, and was built by the Prophet himself.

Over time the community converted to Islam, though most Jews did not and were expelled or executed on Muhammad's orders, as he believed them to have sided with his enemies. One reason for the growing acceptance of Muhammad's authority in Medina was his military success in battles against the forces in Mecca. By 628, he had concluded the treaty of al-Hudaybiyya with the Meccans, making the status of his community equal to that of Mecca, and within two years he was able to take control of Mecca virtually unopposed. Those Meccans who had opposed him now also converted to Islam, and the Ka'abah, central to Islam, became accessible to the Muslims.

Muhammad died in Medina, from fever. He was buried on the

very spot where he died, which was in the house of Lady Aisha near the Prophet's Mosque. This mosque was enlarged by various Muslim rulers over time, and continued to draw pilgrims from around the world as Islam's second holiest site. By the eighth century AD, the mosque had expanded to include the grave of Muhammad over which a dome was constructed. The last major development was completed in 1992, expanding the mosque's area to over 160,000 square metres, allowing more than seven hundred thousand visitors to pray simultaneously.

Medina was the capital of the Muslim world until 661, when the caliphate was transferred to Damascus. The city of Medina was incorporated into the kingdom of Saudi Arabia in 1932.

Nemrut Dag (Mount Nemrut) National Park, Turkey

Nemrut Dag (mount Nemrud) is 2,150 metres high, located near the village of Karadut in Kahta county in the province of Adiyaman. Kings of the Kommagene dynasty ruled the region from 80 BC to AD 72. This kingdom was founded by Mithridates I, father of Antiochos I, and ended when it was defeated by the Romans in the Kommagene wars. It then became part of the Roman province of Syria.

The awe-inspiring ruins on the summit of Mount Nemrud are the famous tumulus (burial mound) and hierotheseion (sacred burial precinct of the royal family) of King Antiochos I, who ruled from 69 to 36 BC. King Antiochos declared that he had had the site built for the generations that were to follow him 'as a debt of thanks to the gods and to his deified ancestors for their manifest assistance'.

The tumulus is fifty metres high, and one hundred and fifty metres in diameter. It is constructed from stones and rocks of less than fifty centimetres across, and bounded by terraced courts carved out of the mountain. The court to the east side was the centre of a most sacred precinct; it is dominated by huge statues, an altar in the shape of a stepped pyramid, and walls of upright stones. A processional way connects the terraces of the east and west; huge statues of eagles guard either side of the entrance.

Reliefs depicting the Persian ancestors of Antiochos are displayed: particularly Dareios I, the founder of the Achaemenid dynasty on his father's side, and ancestor of Alexander the Great on his mother's. The carved relief of a lion in the west court is one of the more impressive sights; it is carved into a slab 1.75 metres in height and almost 2.5 metres long. The lion is decorated with nineteen stars and a crescent moon on the breast; the three larger stars on the lion's back emit sixteen rays, the smaller stars radiate eight rays each. The larger stars are identified as Jupiter, Mercury, and Mars, and it is believed that this lion represents the world's oldest horoscope. There is some debate about its intended meaning. Professor Otto Neugebauer has identified the horoscope as relating to 7 July 62 or 61 BC: the date on which Antiochos I was installed on the throne by the Roman general Pompey. However, Professor Dorner believes that the event represented is the establishment of the Nemrut Dag monument.

Excavations indicate that it is likely that the king's remains were placed in a chamber cut into the rock, which was then covered over with the tumulus. To date the burial chamber itself has not yet been excavated.

The ruins were re-discovered by Karl Sester, a German road engineer, in 1881, and in the following two years an expedition was organised by Karl Humann and Otto Puchstein to study them. Subsequent studies were undertaken by several groups up to 1989, when the area was declared a national park.

Petra, Wadi Musa, Jordan

Petra (meaning Rock) was the capital city of the Nabataean tribe: pre-Roman Arabs who dominated the region during the sixth century BC. It was located on an important trade route through the Middle-East, one which linked the region with China, India and southern Arabia, and its financing came largely through toll monies. It is effectively a rock-carved city, concealed up in the mountains of south Jordan. It contains over eight hundred monuments, almost all directly carved from the indigenous sandstone of the region, an outstanding tribute to the artistic and technical talents of the Nabataeans.

The city is familiar to film enthusiasts as the centrepiece of *Indiana Jones and the Last Crusade*.

Away from the centre of Petra is a temple known as El-Deir, meaning the Monastery. The long hike there passes fascinating small caves and buildings, including the Lion Tomb which features two of the carved beasts. The Monastery is a spectacular sight: fifty metres wide, forty-five metres high, and carved directly into the rock face. The inside is, as with most buildings in Petra, a simple square largely unadorned. This temple has been an important pilgrimage site, even since before the fourth century when it was used as a monastery, the reason for its present name.

Despite decades of excavation in the area archaeologists have not reached firm conclusions about the origins or development of the site. The city became a World Heritage site in 1985.

Quarantal, the Monastery of the Temptation, Israel

Less than fifty miles from Jerusalem is The Mount of Temptation, regarded as the place where the devil tempted Christ's faith. The Gospels (other than John) record that Jesus, after his baptism by John, journeyed into the mountains to fast for forty days. The devil came to him and asked that he make bread from stones, provoking the much quoted response 'Man shall not live by bread alone.' The devil then asked Jesus to throw himself from the heights and be protected by angels, which Jesus refused. Finally the devil offered Jesus great riches if he would pay devotion to him, which Jesus also refused.

A small cave on the mountain is deemed to be the place of Jesus's meditations. The original monks who later came to live there also occupied the natural caves in the cliffs. The first chapel was built at the site in AD 340 by St Chariton; this, though, was destroyed by the Persians.

The site became a place of pilgrimage for the first time during the Crusades. The present monastery was built there between 1875 and 1905 by a Greek Orthodox sect which bought the mountain in 1874. It houses a stone said to be the one on which Jesus sat during the Temptation.

Of all the significant Biblical sites, it is one less visited than most, perhaps because of its isolated position. For those spiritually inclined it is therefore a tranquil place of meditation.

Qumran, Israel

Qumran is an ancient settlement on the north-west coast of the Dead Sea: a ruin dating back to the time of the fall of the Second Temple. Nearby, in the surrounding hills, is the location where the Dead Sea Scrolls were found in 1947. The ruins, excavated in the 1950s, consist of a courtyard with outbuildings and a cemetery with over one thousand graves. One of the rooms excavated contained inkwells and was labelled a 'scriptorium'; and is thought to be where the Dead Sea Scrolls were copied. The site was served by a system of water channels, probably used for ritual purification. As no bedrooms or dormitories have been located, it is thought that the tribe lived for the most part in tents or caves.

Qumran is believed to have been the centre of a large religious community, probably one of the Essene tribes. The Essenes were a first century BC break-away group from the Jewish faith, who, facing persecution, moved out into the desert areas. The community was basically an apocalyptic sect, believing that the end of the world was soon to happen. (Their communities have been described by such writers as Philo of Alexandria and Pliny the Elder.) The Scrolls, written before the destruction of the Second Temple, mostly in Hebrew and Aramaic, represented the library of the sect.

In 1947 two Bedouin shepherds found, in a cave, a clay jar that contained seven parchment scrolls. These scrolls came into the hands of dealers in antiquities who offered them to interested scholars. When their age was recognised by E.L. Sukenik, he managed to acquire three of them for the Hebrew University, and parts of these were published by him in 1948 and 1950. The other four scrolls were smuggled to the United States, where three of them were published in 1950-1. Later they were again offered for sale. Yigael Yadin, the son of Sukenik and a leading archaeologist, bought them and returned them to Israel, where the Israel Museum in Jerusalem constructed a special exhibition site for the Scrolls called The Shrine of the Book, which was opened in 1965.

In the early 1950s, meanwhile, a team of scholars led by Father Roland de Vaux searched the cave where the first scrolls were found, as well as other caves in the region. Many more scrolls and thousands of fragments were found in eleven caves. The manuscripts were mostly written on parchment, some on papyrus. In some caves the manuscripts were carefully placed in covered jars, others appear to have been discarded thoughtlessly. Some of the worst-preserved manuscripts crumbled, and great care was used to recover what was salvageable.

One of the limitations of study is that the discoveries by Roland de Vaux in 1952, five years after the first scrolls were found, have never been published. Indeed the publication of the original finds was slow, partly because of funding difficulties, and partly because of the detailed attention of an editorial board.

The documents contain over one hundred copies of the books of the Hebrew Bible, many of which have survived only as fragments. Twenty-three of the twenty-four books are present, excepting the Book of Esther. Fragments of Septuagint text have also been identified. There are also 'commentaries' on the various books which provide evidence for the text of the Hebrew Bible at the end of the period of the Second Temple.

However, the origin of the Dead Sea Scrolls is hotly debated. Of Qumran, there are many scholars who think that the settlement was simply an administrative set of offices not connected to the Scrolls, and that the Scrolls were brought to the area from Jerusalem. Further debate has argued that the inhabitants of the site were not the Essenes at all. The most persuasive arguments for this are based on the Scrolls themselves, which some scholars believe do not reflect Essene lifestyles.

In 2001 a coffin and mausoleum were discovered at Qumran, just a few hundred yards from where the Scrolls were found. However, the graves had already been looted and much of the treasure lost. The discovery has re-fuelled the debate as to whether the site relates to the Essenes at all; they were a simple people, but the coffin seems to have been that of a wealthy man. It has been suggested that the community houses were in fact just part of one rich individual's villa.

In September 2001 the Vatican announced that it was to reveal much of what the Dead Sea Scrolls contained, and that it would allow revisions of the Bible to be made in accordance with the newly published information. The Vatican had for decades been accused of keeping the information secret as it was at odds with traditional teachings.

Suleimaniye Mosque, Istanbul, Turkey

The Suleimaniye is one of the most important and significant mosques in Istanbul. It was built between 1550 and 1557 by Sinan for the Ottoman Sultan Suleiman I, known as Suleiman the Magnificent. Other buildings in the mosque complex were completed in the following year. The mosque, based on the design of the Hagia Sophia Mosque (St Sophia), also in Istanbul, stands on an impressive site overlooking the Golden Horn, on the third hill (of seven) of Old Istanbul. Sinan, acknowledged as the greatest Ottoman architect, is reputed to have claimed: 'I have built thee, O Padishah, a mosque which will remain on the face of the earth till the day of judgment.'

The mosque is fronted by a courtyard entered through a magnificent portal. The courtyard is surrounded by arcades with columns of porphyry, marble, and granite, topped by twenty-eight domes. It has four minarets positioned at the corners and ten balconies. It is said that the minarets indicate that Suleiman was the fourth sultan of Istanbul, and that the balconies reflect his position as the tenth monarch of the Ottoman empire. The western portal of the courtyard is flanked by two-storey chambers known as the muvakithane, the house and workshop of the mosque astronomer. Other connected buildings include schools of religious teachings, a hospital, food kitchens for the poor, and a guest house for VIP pilgrims and visitors. The complex has always been, therefore, not just a place of worship but one that cared for and nurtured the basic and spiritual needs of its people. While the Hagia Sophia Mosque, built a thousand years earlier, has now been turned into a museum, the Suleimaniye has remained a place of worship.

The Suleimaniye mosque itself is square, topped by a huge dome supported by columns and arches. The interior is solemn, allowing for meditation and serenity, though highlighted by stained-glass windows designed by Sarhos Ibrahim.

Suleiman, and his Russian wife Haseki Hürrem (aka Roxelana), are interred in a walled garden to the south side of the mosque. Suleiman's tomb, or 'turbe' contains his own cenotaph flanked by those of his daughter, Princess Mihrimah, and the sultans Suleiman II and Ahmet II.

Just outside the main complex is the tomb of Sinan, who died at the astonishing age for the time of ninety-nine years old, at rest in the shadow of his greatest achievement.

Wailing Wall, Jerusalem, Israel

More correctly known as the Western Wall, the Wailing Wall in Jerusalem is said by some to be the holiest and most sacred place in all of the Jewish world.

Purists however point out that it is not a sacred site at all, but what makes it important is that it is the closest point that can be reached to the holiest site – the Holy Temple that once stood on Temple Mount (see entry for **Dome of the Rock**).

The hill on which Herod wanted to build his massive Temple was not big enough for the project, and therefore it was artificially expanded by building a huge platform supported by massive walls. The Western Wall of this platform was therefore not actually part of the Temple itself. It supports today not only the site of the Temple but the Dome of the Rock, and the El Aqsa Mosque.

For the most conservative of Jews the Western Wall is so important because they want to be near to the Temple, but they do not want to walk on the platform itself for fear of accidentally walking over the Temple site – the Temple's exact position is no longer known – and thereby accidentally desecrating it.

Jews from all over the world gather to pray at the Wall, and leave written prayers on slips of paper pushed into its cracks.

The Wall is known as the Wailing Wall because after the destruction of the Second Temple in AD 70, Jews were forbidden entry to Jerusalem, until the Byzantine era when they were allowed one annual visit on the anniversary of the destruction of the Temple. When they arrived they would weep over the ruins of this holiest of sites. Then, from 1948 to 1967 Jews were again forbidden to approach it when it was in the Jordanian quarter of the city. After the Six Day War, the Western Wall became, and remains, accessible again to Jews.

MYSTICAL AND SACRED SITES IN THE FAR-EAST

Adam's Peak, Sri Lanka

Rising from the jungles of south-west Sri Lanka is the isolated 2,243-metre high mountain known as Adam's Peak.

The mountain could arguably be regarded as one of the most significant holy places in the world. It was worshipped as a sacred site by the original inhabitants of Sri Lanka, the Veddas, who called the peak 'Samanala Kanda' (the butterfly mountain). It was named after Saman, one of the four gods that protect the island, and the fact that it attracts thousands of butterflies which arrive each year to die at the peak.

Since the time of the Veddas, it has become a sacred site for adherents of four major religions: Hinduism, Buddhism, Christianity and Islam. All four are practised on the Island, Buddhism being the prevailing faith, though on Sri Lanka it exhibits elements of Hindu and Islamic traditions.

At the summit is a depression some 1.5-metres long and seventy-six centimetres wide, shaped like a human footprint, which can be observed from a platform at the Buddhist temple and shrine erected to Saman. Rainwater collected from it is believed to have miraculous healing powers.

Hindus believe that the footprint was made by the dance of the god Shiva as she created the world.

Buddhists believe that the footprint represents that of Buddha, but that his actual print is below the visible depression. This hidden footprint is believed to be impressed in a giant sapphire, and was made during Buddha's third and last visit to the island.

Christianity claimed the footprint for its own when Portuguese Christians arrived on the island in the sixteenth century. They believed it to be the footprint of St Thomas who first introduced Christianity to Sri Lanka.

The name Adam's Peak derives from the Muslim Arab tradition that the footprint is that of Adam, marking the spot where he stood on one foot for a thousand years as a penance. In Islam, Adam was God's vice regent, regarded as the first Prophet Messenger. According to one Islamic tradition, Adam was the original builder of the sacred shrine, the Ka'abah in Mecca. He was expelled from heaven, but a merciful God placed him on Sri Lanka to lessen the shock, Sri Lanka being the most heaven-like domain on Earth. Muslims believe that Adam and Eve lived on Adam's Peak together after they were expelled from the Garden of Eden.

The peak has been a magnet for explorers for centuries. The Arab Ibn Batuta (1304–68) and the Venetian Marco Polo (1254–1324) both visited it, and it has since become a place of important pilgrimage.

Certain parts of the path leading up to the mountain are extremely steep, though it is no longer dangerous. Two stairways lead to the summit, described by some as probably the longest stairways in the world. Local rumour is that the climbing chains affixed to parts of the walk were placed there by Alexander the Great, though there is no historical evidence to support that.

Amritsar and the Golden Temple (Har Mandir Sahib), northern India

The site of the Golden Temple was originally a small lake in a forest, a place known to have been a centre of meditation since antiquity. Buddha spent time there in contemplation. The name of the lake is Amrita Saras, meaning Pool of Immortality or Pool of Ambrosia (Ambrosia being the legendary food of the gods).

The lake was also a place of peaceful meditation for the guru (holy man) Nanak, the founder of the Sikh religion. After his death the site was frequented by his disciples. The lake was enlarged during the leadership of the fourth Sikh guru Ram Das, and during the leadership of his successor, Arjan Dev, the Har Mandir Sahib, or Golden Temple, was built on an island there.

Ram Das also founded the city of Amritsar in 1574, the land having been granted to him by the Mughal emperor, Akbar. The city takes its name from the lake which now surrounds the Har Mandir Sahib; the lake also acts as a defensive moat around the temple, crossed only by a guarded causeway which is itself further protected by a security gate.

This Temple is the most sacred shrine and place of pilgrimage for the Sikh religion. The current temple dates from the early nineteenth century when it was reconstructed by Marajah Ranjit

Singh, the Sikh leader who conquered the Punjab. The temple is covered in gold leaf, hence its 'western' name. Most of the present decorative gilding, precious stones and marblework comes from Ranjit Singh's reconstruction period. Its architecture draws from both Hindu and Muslim styles.

The Har Mandir Sahib houses the Guru Granth Sahib, the holy book left by the guru Govind Singh, which contains a collection of devotional poems, prayers, and hymns composed by the ten Sikh gurus and various Muslim and Hindu saints. The site also contains the building known as the Akal Takht, the seat of Sikh religious authority.

The city of Amritsar gained further importance in Indian history when a massacre took place there that in many ways was a foundation-event for the independence of India. During the First World War the British government ruling India had activated emergency powers to oppose subversion on the sub-continent. Mohandas Karamchand ('Mahatma') Gandhi called on Indians to oppose those powers. On 10 April 1919, local representatives of Indian National Congress were arrested, and on 13 April twenty thousand unarmed Muslim, Hindu and Sikh civilian supporters, including women and children, gathered to protest in an enclosed public square known as the Jallianwalla Bagh. British troops under the command of Brigadier-General Reginald Dyer sealed the square, preventing any civilians from leaving, and then opened fire on them, killing 379 people and injuring between twelve hundred and two thousand directly or in the ensuing panic. More than any other single event, this massacre focused Indian public opinion against British rule, and set the seal on the process of revolutionary non-cooperation sought by Gandhi, which was to lead to Indian independence.

The significance of the Golden Temple came to the fore again in June 1984 when the Indian government sought to check Sikh protestors. The Sikhs were demanding greater self-rule for the Punjab as a Sikh homeland; the Indian government sent troops to occupy the area around the Golden Temple. In the ensuing confrontation hundreds were killed, the Akal Takht was almost destroyed, and the Har Mandir Sahib – which the Indian army was doing its best to avoid – was struck by a number of shells. Such a desecration of the holiest of shrines could not go unpunished. Indira Gandhi, the prime minister, had ordered the attack and as a direct consequence she was assassinated by Sikh members of her own security guard.

Throughout the day the area is alive with the sounds of hymns chanted to the accompaniment of flutes, strings, and drums. The combination of atmosphere, sights and sounds creates an almost trance-like state in people visiting the site. Pilgrims come not just to see the Temple, but also to immerse themselves in the lake, not so much cleaning the body as representing a cleansing of the soul. Near the Temple are huge pilgrims' dormitories and dining halls. Any visitors – irrespective of race or religion – are lodged and fed without charge.

Angkor Wat, Kampuchea (Cambodia)

Kampuchea's central landscape is dominated by a huge, low-lying plain containing Tonle Sap (the Great Lake). To the north of this lake are the ruins of Angkor. From the late ninth century until 1431 – when it was attacked and abandoned – Angkor Thom was the centre of the Khmer empire which ruled over a huge domain that reached from present-day South Vietnam to Yunan, China and to the Bay of Bengal.

The huge temple complexes built there over a period of three hundred years show the early influence of Hinduism in the region, and later of Buddhism. The most magnificent of the temples was Angkor Wat which was built between 1112 and 1152. Angkor Wat is regarded as one of the world's greatest architectural achievements, and spiritual centres. 'Wat' means place of worship, or religious education.

There are over one hundred temples remaining at Angkor, the surviving religious buildings of a huge social and administrative metropolis. The other buildings of the time – palaces, public buildings and houses – were made of wood and are long gone.

The reign of Jayavarman (aka Suryavaram) II between 802 and 850 represented the beginning of the Angkor era. Jayavarman returned from exile in Java and built the empire on the basis of the cult of the god-king. The temples at Angkor were built by his successors to house the lingas, the phallic emblems of the Hindu god Shiva.

Because the first building phases of Angkor were based on the Hindu god-king, the temples were built as representations of Mount Meru, the Hindu cosmic mountain. Each king built his own temple. Angkor Wat was built under Jayavarman II to present him as the incarnation of Vishnu, and also to house his body after death.

Angkor Wat is around 850 metres by one thousand metres in area. It is a west-facing stone building consisting of three concentric walled enclosures surrounded by a defensive moat. There were originally five lotus-shaped towers, representing the five peaks of Mount Meru; only one such tower now remains.

Jayavarman VII, who reigned from 1181 to 1219, was a Mahayana Buddhist who designed Angkor Thom to the north of Angkor Wat in an attempt to eclipse the earlier structure. It had a square moated enclosure, each side approximately two miles long, with moats ninety metres wide. The centre was a stepped temple complex, the Bayon, with five towers. Huge face effigies on the Bayon represent Buddha and Jayavarman VII. Subsequent rulers updated some of the effigies to eradicate earlier images and replace them with their own.

The introduction of Theravada Buddhism, which proclaimed spiritual advancement for all people through meditation, is believed to have been a factor in weakening the empire and its rigid social order. In 1431 Angkor was defeated by Thailand (then known as Siam).

After the defeat, the Khmers abandoned the city and it was virtually lost to the jungle for several centuries until wandering Buddhist monks came upon the ruins and recognised their sacred nature and intent. Unaware of their history, the monks invented fables about the structures, such as how they had been built by the gods in ancient times. The stories spread, and pilgrims from distant parts of Asia travelled to this 'mystic city of the gods'. The stories also encouraged Portuguese and other European explorers to study the city.

The monuments unfortunately had fallen into significant disrepair partly from general neglect as a result of political instability in the region and partly because the design incorporated aligning vertical joints in stone for artistic effect, but which caused weakness in the structure. The French explorer Henri Mouhot, brought Angkor to the world's attention in 1860. In 1908 the French mounted a restoration project which has continued to the present day. Angkor Wat has survived as a focus of Buddhist pilgrimage.

Theravada Buddhism is today the dominant religion of Kampuchea, followed by about 90 per cent of the population. Other influential religions practised are Hinduism, Roman Catholicism, Islam, and Mahayana Buddhism. The mountain tribes remain animists.

Arunachaleswar Temple, India

In *Pilgrimage in the Hindu Tradition* by Alan Morinis, he relates the legend of the sacred place of Arunachala, associated with the fire linga (phallic emblem) of Shiva.

After losing his wife, Sati, Shiva was walking, nude, in the forest when a group of women saw him. Aroused, they desired sexual union with him. Their husbands cursed Shiva's linga that it should fall off, which it did. As the god's phallus struck the ground, the gods Brahma and Vishnu watched as it turned into a bright column reaching through the clouds at the top, and into the earth at its base. Vishnu turned into a boar and dived to the bottom of the ocean to locate the base; Brahma took the form of a swan to fly up to its summit. Vishnu admitted that he had been unable to find the base, but Brahma lied that he had located the top of the column. Shiva saw this, and called out, naming Brahma a liar, and thanking Vishnu for his honesty. Vishnu requested, in response, that part of the linga be left in the form of fire on the hill of Arunachala.

This is the mythology behind the Arunachaleswar Shiva Temple which sits at the foot of the Arunachala hill. It is one of the largest and oldest temples in southern India and is vast, covering twenty-five acres of land. The shrine is adorned with stately towers, prakaaras and magnificent mandapams. The structure owes its majestic appearance to four towers – the eastern tower is called Rajgopuram and is the tallest at sixty-six metres. The shrine has five prakaaras and the walls are broad and high, resembling the rampart walls of a fort. There are 360 thirthas and four hundred lingas in the eight-mile circuit of the sacred hill. Around the hill, which has a widely known reputation for being a place of miraculous healing, are situated many hermitages used by holy men.

Every year in November/December the ten-day long Deepam festival is held to celebrate Shiva's manifestation through dancing and singing and fabulous processions. The festival is the subject of pilgrimage for many thousands.

Bodhi Tree, Bodh Gaya, India

Buddha was probably born sometime between 644 and 540 BC in the hills around north-eastern India and the Nepalese border. (Some traditions have him born later, in the fourth century BC.) He was named Siddhartha Gautama, the son of Suddhodana, ruler of the Sakyas people. It is said that miraculous events occurred at the time of his birth: his mother dreamt that the Bodhisattva (Buddha-to-be) entered her womb in the guise of a white elephant and caused her to give up wanting sex. Although his mother was not a virgin, Siddhartha's birth is believed to have been miraculous as it is not thought to have been the product of sexual union.

Sages predicted that he would become an enlightened individual and a religious leader. His father tried to isolate him from religion, and immerse him in wealth and material possessions, hoping that he would follow a destiny as a great king. However, when he left the protection of his palace grounds, he saw suffering in the world that he had never before experienced, and it turned him from what he saw as a shallow existence to a search for deeper meaning. At the age of twenty-nine he set out to understand the world.

For seven years he sought the help of gurus, and learned much, but he did not achieve his goal of enlightenment. He then journeyed towards the sacred forests of Uruvela (now Gaya, in north India), following visionary dreams and the footsteps of three previous Buddhas: Krakucchanda, Kanakamuni, and Kasyapa. He came to rest beneath a sacred fig tree, the Bodhi Tree.

There he entered a state of meditation and achieved enlightenment, becoming the Buddha (Enlightened One) of his age. He meditated for seven weeks near the Bodhi Tree before setting out to preach to the world. He spent the rest of his life travelling in north-eastern India and Sri Lanka, teaching and aiding in the setting up of monastic groupings for both men and women. He died at the age of eighty, was cremated, and his ashes distributed to ten shrines constructed to house these most precious of relics. His death had been accompanied by portents: earthquakes and showers of flowers.

Buddha did not write down his teachings, so what we know of his beliefs and work come down through history solely from the writings of his disciples. Three months after his death, five hundred of his followers gathered together at Rajagraha to agree upon what were to be disseminated as the most important of his teachings. Consensus was not found, and eighteen different sects developed, each holding its own interpretation of his work. Consolidation, and a measure of consensus, came much later.

Places important in the Buddha's life became sites of pilgrimage for Buddhists, arguably the most important being the Bodhi Tree where he had found enlightenment. Tradition holds that it is the same location where the previous Buddhas also found enlightenment.

Emperor Asoka built the first shrine there in 250 BC, and this was replaced in the second century AD by the present temple. There have been many refurbishments and repairs since. The present temple is fifty-five metres tall and houses shrines for the use of pilgrims. Behind the temple are the Bodhi Tree and the Vajrasana, where Buddha sat in meditation. The tree is not the original, but is believed to be a descendant of the actual tree under which Buddha meditated. As Hindus believe that Buddha was the incarnation of Lord Vishnu, this temple is also a sacred shrine for Hindus.

In 2000 a building project was announced which was the most recent to claim the label 'eighth wonder of the world'. An enormous bronze statue is proposed for the site, to be completed by 2005. The Buddha Maitreya (meaning 'universal love') will, at 150 metres high, be the world's largest statue. The Statue of Liberty would fit into one of its legs. It will sit on a throne, the height of a seventeen-storey building, which will house one million works of art, a library, prayer and exhibition halls, theatre, school and gardens. Within the statue itself a shrine behind the Buddha's eyes will be available to only a chosen few, but a shrine near the Buddha's heart will be available to all pilgrims.

Chaturmukha, Ranakpur, India

The Chaturmukha Jain temple, situated in the secluded valley of Mount Madri, is the largest, and most elaborate, temple in Ranakpur; built in the fifteenth century. It has been described as a 'haven of peace', a feast of carvings and corridors of white marble. It is said to be a work of art equal to the Taj Mahal and is one of the most important Jain temples in India.

The building of the temple began in AD 1390, and took fifty years to complete. It is an extraordinary three-storey construct with historical scenes portrayed on ceilings and domes. The temple is supported by 1,444 carved pillars, and no two pillars are the same. As an active temple, it is a beautiful setting for the white-robed Jain devotees who are regularly seen there in devotional rituals. In the main chamber or Gabhara are four huge marble images of Bhagwan Adinath, installed facing four different directions. The temple also has seventy-six smaller domed-shrines, four Rangamandapas (assembly halls), four Mahadhar Prasads (principal shrines) and a number of Devaku-likas (subsidiary shrines). These eighty-four shrines represent the eighty-four lakhs (cycles) of birth and death before eternal salvation. It also contains eighty-four statues of past tirthankaras depicting eyes of striking appearance; Jains believe that their god's energy can flow through the eyes of idols. In the north of the temple, there is a Rayan tree, and the footprints of Bhagavan Rishabhadevand of Shatrunjaya on a slab of marble, reminders of his life and preaching; this is an important place of Jain pilgrimage.

The temple is the realisation of the vision of four devout seekers: Acharya Somasundarsuriji, Dharanashah, the Minister to Kumbha Rana, Rana Kumbha and the architect Depaka.

The temple is available to the public from all over the world, and indeed caters for their needs including overnight accommodation in monks' cells. Every year thousands of art-lovers and spiritual seekers visit from all over the world.

Cheju Island, Korea

Cheju Island is a place of mystery, myth and legend. The island is replete with stone statues of the dwarf-like Tolharubang, a powerful fertility god. It is also a place where the number three has been of significance.

The first settlement on Cheju was, in legend, founded by three god-men, Ko-ulla, Pu-ulla, and Yang-ulla, who came forth out of one of the many caves on the island. Ancient Koreans worshipped the shamanistic spirits and, even though since that time Confucianism and Buddhism have come to the country, this nature worship has never been completely dismissed. Cheju is described as an 'island of three plenties and three lacks'. The three plenties are stones, wind and women. The three lacks are beggars, thieves and locks. The sea provides for the islanders' needs, and crime and poverty are rare. Islanders find it unnecessary to lock their doors and secure their possessions, and the traditional 'door' is actually three bars placed across an entrance; when one bar is missing it means that the house is unoccupied.

The three gods that created the island supported themselves by hunting and gathering. One day, we are told, while they were on the slopes of Mount Halla, they saw a wooden box floating in the sea off the eastern shore. They found inside the three daughters of the King of Pyoknang who had sent them to the island to be brides for the gods. The women were carrying seeds of grain, cattle and horses.

Archaeological evidence indicates that the island has been inhabited since at least the Palaeolithic period, when the inhabitants lived in caves. Stone and bone tools have been found all over the island. It is also clear that the island thrived during the Bronze Age, evidenced by dolmens and earthen jar burials typical of that period.

Historical records from the Korean Silla dynasty (57 BC to AD 935) indicate that the fifteenth generation of descendants of Ko-ulla were received at the Silla court, at which time the island of Cheju was called Tamna.

By the beginning of the Christian era, Cheju was an organised state trading with the mainland states of Koguryo (37 BC to AD 668) and Paekche (18 BC to AD 660) as well as Silla. Records from the Chinese mainland show that Cheju was also trading with the Han dynasty in China (206 BC to AD 220).

In AD 1105, the island was ruled as part of the Koryo kingdom, when it was known as Tamna-gun. When the Koryo kingdom was overthrown by the Mongols, resistance fighters fled to Cheju before being wiped out there. The deaths of the resistance fighters on the island have made it a sacred place for their descendants.

At 1,950 metres, Mount Halla is the highest peak in Korea, visible all over the island. The volcanic mountain is the spiritual, as well as the physical, centre of the island. Atop the mountain is Paeknokdam Lake (White Deer Lake), one of over three hundred crater lakes on the mountain. It is said that in ancient times enlightened sages, riding white deer, visited the site to enjoy its serenity and beauty. The lake, a sacred area, is surrounded by many grotesquely shaped rocks and cliffs that protect it. To the south, about two miles from the summit, is Youngsilgiam, a mass of granite rocks which are held to be, in island legend, the five hundred disciples of Buddha. The area gets its name from its resemblance to Youngshwi Mountain where Buddha taught his disciples.

Another famous, and sacred, site on the island is situated on the seashore of Yongdam-dong in Cheju City: the dragon-head rock known as Yongduam. It is uncannily reminiscent of a dragon on the shore, perhaps waiting to take off into the sky. According to legend, a dragon emissary of the Dragon King was sent to Mount Halla to pick a herb which would give the king eternal youth, but a mountain god captured the dragon and imprisoned it in the sea with only its head protruding.

Dunhuang, The Cave of the Thousand Buddhas, China

Dunhuang is situated in north-west China, on the ancient Silk Route: an all-important trading route much travelled by monks journeying between India and Central Asia. Dunhuang was a crossroads where foreign Buddhist monks and Chinese disciples came together in the third and fourth centuries AD.

The 'cave' is actually 492 caves known as the Mogao Caves, though sometimes the collective is known as The Cave of the Thousand Buddhas (Ch'ien-fo Tung). Virtually every cave contains images of the Buddha, in sculpture, painting or other artworks which represent today the largest collection of ancient Buddhist art in China. The frescoes contain presentations of famous images from various Buddhist sutras and stories; the most commonly depicted are Buddhas, Heavenly Kings, and Protective Warriors. Some of them are huge, over forty-eight metres in height in one case.

The first of these caves – the original Cave of the Thousand Buddhas – was founded in AD 366 by Chinese monks.

By the fifth century AD, Dunhuang had become a pivotal Buddhist area and the caves were a central part of the religious devotions there.

At each end of the valley in which the caves are carved are temples to the Rulers of the Heavens, and the valley contains huge bells used during prayer, and many smaller temples and priests' quarters.

There had been many texts found in the caves. In one of the cave temples a vast collection of around sixty thousand paper manuscripts and printed documents, dating from the fifth to the eleventh century AD, was found in 1900. They had been walled up in 1015; these texts included many Buddhist works, but also Taoist, Zoroastrian, and Nestorian scriptures. Most of the manuscripts were sold before any thought was given to preserving them.

Today the Cave of the Thousand Buddhas is one of the most perfectly preserved ancient religious sites in the world. It uniquely expresses the blend of Indian Buddhism with Chinese influence, and shows, in the images there, the development of Chinese Buddhism. The caves were opened to the public in 1949, and became a World Heritage site in 1987. They are an important pilgrimage site for Buddhists from around the world.

The whole area is replete with sacred sites. For example, to the south is the place where the Bodhisattva Guan-yin once made herself visible; pilgrims traditionally travel on foot to visit this holy site. The Chin-an, or Golden Saddle, Mountain contains a shrine said to be so powerful people dare not approach it; there is an annual ceremony of sacrifices there by the local chieftain. The Yu-nu, or Beautiful Woman, Spring is a pool where, according to tradition, a young boy and girl would walk hand in hand to drown in the waters as part of a ritual to gain the gods' fortune for that year's harvest. According to writer Daniel C. Waugh, during the Shen-Lung period, around AD 705, the Governor of the region, Chang Hsiao-sung, became angry at this tradition and erected an altar at the pool, and challenged the spirit of the lake to come to him. It did so in the form of a dragon which the Governor slayed with a bow. The dragon's head he cut off and presented to the Emperor who bestowed on him the title of Lung-she Chang Shih (Mr Chang of the Dragon's tongue).

Ellora (or Elura) Caves, India

The caves are a series of thirty-four imposing temples cut into over a mile of basalt cliffs near the village of Ellora, around twenty miles north-west of Aurangabad in India. They are approximately fifty miles from a similar series known as the Ajanta Caves, and were designated a UNESCO World Heritage site in 1983.

The southern twelve caves are Buddhist, dating from around 200 BC to AD 600 and contain probably the simplest designs and art in the series. The central seventeen caves are Hindu, dating from AD 500 to 900; these contain the most striking designs. The northernmost five caves are Jain and date from around AD 800 to 1000. Some of the caves, such as numbers six and ten, house both Hindu and Buddhist images.

The cave system served as monasteries and temples, and some caves included sleeping cells that were used by travelling monks.

The whole complex is regarded as the finest example in the world of cave-temple architecture and represents the greatest concentration anywhere of such architecture and sculpture. Most spectacular of the caves is number sixteen, a Hindu cave named Kailasa, or Kailasanatha, named after the sacred mountain in the Kailas Range of the Himalayas (see entry for **Mount Kailas**). This cave was excavated downwards, whereas the other caves were excavated horizontally; the result is that this cave-temple is filled with sunlight, illuminating the complex structures within. Some two hundred thousand tons of solid rock had to be removed during construction which began in the eighth century under the reign of Krishna I. The temple is fifty metres long, thirty-three metres wide and thirty metres high, spreading over four levels. It covers twice the area of the Parthenon in Athens, and is one-and-a-half times higher. The internal design includes monoliths, halls, stairs, a footbridge, a flat-roofed mandapam supported by sixteen pillars, doorways, windows, and sculptures, all hewn out of the solid rock. Its decorations include: a depiction of Vishnu transformed into a man-lion, battling a demon; a monument to Siva's bull Nandi; and life-size sculptures of elephants and other animals. The halls contain depictions of the ten-headed demon king Ravana shaking Mount Kailasa to show his strength, and many erotic representations of Hindu gods.

The Buddhist cave number ten is a chaitya-hall and is popularly known as Visvakarma. It has an intricate, ornamental façade provided with a gallery, and in the chaitya-hall is a wonderful image of Buddha on a stupa. Cave number twelve has seen seven images of Buddha depicting his seven incarnations.

Cave thirty-two is a Jain cave which houses a beautiful shrine, decorated with delicate carvings of a lotus flower on the roof, a yakshi (female earth spirit), and a statue of Parasnath. Other Jain caves depict images of Tirthankaras, and one of them also has a seated figure of Mahavira.

Thousands of pilgrims and tourists visit the cave systems each year.

Great Shinto Shrine, Ise, Honshu, Japan

As is probably true throughout the world, natural objects have been the focus of devotion and worship in Japan since the earliest times. Trees, rocks, mountains and water were all regarded as sacred and they would be honoured with tributes and decorations at certain times. The Japanese call the mystical force of nature 'ke'. Ke was believed to permeate all matter, known in Japanese as 'mono'. The result was 'mononoke'. Mononoke particularly accumulated in trees and rocks. As a result certain trees – the cryptomeria and the sakaki in particular – were considered deeply sacred. Such trees are used in the creation of wooden shrines, as the ke remains after felling and is therefore present in the shrine when built.

At Ise the Great Shrine (the Ise Jingu) is built amid a forest of giant cryptomeria trees. It is also positioned next to the Isuzu River and at the foot of Mounts Kamiji and Shimaji. The combination of forest, water and mountains means that it is in a place deeply imbued with natural energies. The shrine buildings are made of wood and are completely rebuilt nearby every twenty years; the empty site (known as the kodenchi) is then covered in white pebbles. Only one small wooden building (known as the oi-ya) is left on the vacated site and this contains a wooden post some two metres high, known as the shin-no-mihashira, which literally translates as 'the column of the heart' or 'sacred central post'. This post surrounded by stones is kept hidden always; it is regarded as deeply sacred as it represents the original natural world imbued with ke that the ancient Japanese would have worshipped. The next replacement shrine is later built over this retrained wooden post.

The shrine is basically two sets of buildings: the Imperial Shrine (the Kotai Jingu), which is also known as the Naiku (or inner shrine), dedicated to the Sun Goddess Amaterasu Omikami, and, four miles away, the Toyouke Shrine which constitutes the Geku (or outer shrine), which is dedicated to the Goddess of Cereals, Toyouke Omikami.

Each shrine has a number of buildings which include ancillary shrines, workshops, storehouses, and other support buildings; each has an inner precinct with a main sanctuary and two attendant shrines. The rooms within the shrines are raised on timber posts that themselves represent the column of the heart. The roof is not supported by the walls, but, importantly, by two posts at either end which go directly from the roof into the ground, symbolic of the contact with nature and the earth.

The present buildings are said to be reproductions of the shrine first ceremoniously built by Emperor Temmu and rebuilt by his wife, the Empress Jito, in AD 692. Temmu was the first Mikado to rule over a united Japan; he established Ise as the main shrine of Imperial Japan, choosing an already deeply sacred site because of the forests of cryptomeria trees. It is said, however, that a shrine has been on the site continuously for two thousand years, though the twenty-year renewal and rededication appears to be a process created by Jito. The last rebuilding was in 1993.

Building the new shrine takes around eight years, each stage of the construction being blessed by a religious ceremony. Nails, which could adversely affect the natural energies of the wood, are not used in the structure.

Jagatmandir Temple, Dwarka, India

Located in the state of Gujarat, the elaborate Jagatmandir Temple is sandwiched between the ocean and the town of Dwarka. It is one of the oldest and most revered of pilgrimage sites because tradition says that it was founded by Krishna who lived there until his death. The site was further enhanced when, in the seventh century AD, the sage Shankaracharya created a monastery there.

The present temple, the product of much rebuilding over the years, dates mainly from the eighteenth century.

Most significantly the site is visited by pilgrims because of its association with the Bhakti saint, Mira Bai (aka Meera Bai). Mira Bai is probably the most famous, and popular, of India's saints; she lived between approximately AD 1500 and 1550. She was a princess of Rajasthan, in north-west India, the daughter of Ratan Singh of Merta. At the age of thirteen, according to legend, she was married to Bhojraj, king of Mewar. Devoted to Lord Krishna, she left her home after her husband died and wandered in Rajasthan, devising and performing lyrical poetry and compositions devoted to Krishna. She created a part of the Bhakti movement, which advocates total devotion as the path of the realisation of God. Bhakti Yoga is a common religious devotion amongst India's population and insists in essence of invoking the presence of God through focusing on a statue or other representation of a religious figure; in Mira Bai's case her devotion brought forth to her the living form of Krishna.

Mira Bai lived out her last years in Dwarka. Since then, devotees of Bhakti yoga have made pilgrimages there as a devotion to her.

Jokhang Monastery, Lhasa, Tibet

The Jokhang Monastery, three floors high and filled with chambers, was built in AD 647, and is the earliest wood-and-masonry structure existing in Tibet. It is believed that the monastery was designed by Princess Wencheng of the Tang Dynasty.

The Mongol invaders sacked the monastery several times, and it recently suffered during the Chinese occupation of Tibet in 1959.

The building has undergone many reconstructions and developments, particularly during the reign of the fifth incarnation of the Dalai Lama in the seventeenth century. Many of the decorations are from the eighteenth and nineteenth centuries, and most of the statues date from the late twentieth century.

One image, however, is more ancient, and is held by many to be the most revered image in Tibet: the sacred statue of Jowo Shakyamuni, sometimes known as Yishinorbu (the Wishfulfilling Gem). It is housed in the Jowo Lhakhang shrine and is a figure of the adult Buddha in metal, 1.5 metres tall, decorated with huge jewels. One of only a few images traditionally believed to have been cast during the Buddha's lifetime, it was created by the celestial artist Visvakaram, with the guidance of the god Indra. The statue once belonged to the king of Magadha (Bengal, India) who presented it to Princess Wencheng's father, king of the Tang empire in China.

Mainly because of the Jowo Shakyamuni, the Jokhang Monastery is the most visited shrine in Tibet. The temple has never been under the control of any one sect of Tibetan Buddhism, and therefore is a highly venerated site for followers of all sects, as well as devotees of Bon-Po, Tibet's indigenous shamanistic religion.

There are three circuits in Lhasa which take pilgrims to the Jowo Shakyamuni statue. The Great Lingkhor encircles the city's old sacred district; within this is the Barkhor which circles the Jokhang Temple; and lastly the Nangkhor is a ritual corridor around the inner chapels within the Jokhang. Every day many thousands of pilgrims walk these three circuits, chanting, praying and spinning their prayer-wheels; some choose to prostrate themselves many times during the walk.

Konarak, India

Konarak, on the shore of the Bay of Bengal, is world-renowned for its magnificent Sun Temple, which was constructed by King Narasinha Deva I of the Ganga dynasty of Orissa in the mid-thirteenth century. As such it is one of India's most famous Brahman sanctuaries, and enshrines an image of Arka, the Sun God, patron deity of the region when the temple was constructed. The Sun Temple contains the history of royal, social and religious life all depicted in intricate carvings in stone.

The complex was designed in the form of a huge chariot drawn by seven horses, the chariot itself being on twelve pairs of exquisitely carved wheels, symbolising the divisions of time. There are also beautiful sculptures lifted from the Kama Sutra.

The main tower of Konarak once stood seventy metres high, but is now a stump. The Jagmohana (Porch) structure and the tower are both situated atop the stone platform supporting the twenty-four wheels. The Konarak Sun Temple also houses a Natamandira or dancing hall.

There are just two subsidiary temples left today, out of twenty-two that originally existed inside the temple precincts.

La'Vang, Vietnam

During one of many, almost continuous, power-struggles in Vietnam, King Canh Thinh, on 17 August 1798, issued an anti-Catholic edict and an order to destroy all Catholic churches and seminaries. He perceived that his rival was receiving too much attention from the Catholic church and sought to dissipate this threat. A persecution of Catholics and missionaries began then which continued until 1886.

During this suffering visitations of the Virgin Mary – the Lady of La'Vang – came to the Catholics of the country. The name La'Vang is said to originate from a forest known as La'Vang (which is the name of a tree growing in abundance there) but may also refer to the Vietnamese word for 'crying out', arising from the cries of those persecuted.

It was in 1798, at the beginning of the persecution, that Catholics sought refuge in the La'Vang forest from the nearby town of Quang Tri, in Central Vietnam. They suffered great hardship from the cold, from starvation, and from animal attacks. One night, while gathered together in prayer, they were visited by the apparition of a beautiful lady wearing a long cape and carrying a child in her arms. There were two angels at her side. The devoted recognised the Virgin Mary at once. She told them to pick and boil the leaves from the trees to use as medicine and also told them that, from that day onwards, those who came to that place to pray would have their prayers heard and answered.

Over the next hundred years the Virgin appeared to many in

the same place, and it became a site of most important pilgrimage for Vietnamese Catholics. A small chapel was erected there in the Virgin Mary's honour. However, the persecutions continued: one group of thirty Catholics were seized as they came out of their hiding place in the forest of La'Vang where they had been at prayer; they were burned alive for their beliefs. At their request, their remains were taken back to the little chapel for burial.

Despite these difficulties, hundreds of pilgrims fought their way into the forest, trying to protect themselves against animal attacks and risking capture, to pray at the little chapel.

After the persecutions ended in 1886, Bishop Gaspar ordered a church to be built in honour of the Lady of La'Vang. It took fifteen years to complete the work because of its remote and difficult location, and limited funding. When it was inaugurated by the Bishop in a solemn ceremony lasting from 6 to 8 August 1901, over twelve thousand people made it to the site to share in the experience. Bishop Gaspar proclaimed the Lady of La'Vang as the Protectorate of the Catholics.

So many pilgrims sought to pray at the site that in 1928 a larger church was built to accommodate them.

The Catholic Church studied the claims of those who believed their prayers on this site where indeed answered as the Virgin had promised they would be. In April 1961, the Council of Vietnamese Bishops selected the Holy Church of La'Vang as the National Sacred Marian Centre. In August of the following year, Pope John XXIII elevated the church to that of Basilica, but during the Vietnam War of the 1970s this replacement church was destroyed.

On 19 June 1988, Pope John Paul II, in a ceremony canonising 117 Vietnamese martyrs, publicly recognised the importance of the Lady of La'Vang and expressed his desire for the rebuilding of the Basilica. He hoped that it would be built there by 1998, to commemorate the two hundredth anniversary of her first appearance, but this was not to be. Indeed, the Pope was refused permission to visit the site by the authorities in 1999. Nevertheless, he took the opportunity of the anniversary to make the Lady of La'Vang the official patroness of the Catholic Church of Vietnam, and proclaimed in his speech: 'In visiting the shrine of Our Lady of La'Vang, who is so loved by the Vietnamese faithful, pilgrims come to entrust to her their joys and sorrows, their hopes and sufferings. In this way, they call on God and become intercessors for their families and nation, asking the Lord to infuse in the heart of all people feelings of peace, fraternity and solidarity, so that all the Vietnamese will be more united every day in the construction of a world based on essential spiritual and moral values, where each one will be recognised because of his dignity as a son of God, and be able to go in freedom and as a son toward the Father of Heaven, "rich in mercy".'

Maha Muni Pagoda, near Mandalay, Myanmar

Situated to the south of Mandalay, the Great Maha Muni Pagoda is one of the most magnificent in Myanmar (formerly Burma). The pagoda is named after the statue that it houses: the sacred Maha Muni image of Buddha. This statue originally belonged to Myohaung, a town in Rakhine State of Myanmar. The capital of Rakhine state from the sixth century BC to AD 350 was Dhannavati, and it was there that the Maha Muni was said to have been cast during the second century AD.

According to legend, during Buddha's lifetime there lived a heretic king named Pyar Zoombu who was arrogant and vain and refused to pay obeisance to the Lord Buddha. Buddha, however, recognised that, by looking deeper into the man, he could see there was wisdom that could be developed. One day, therefore, Buddha appeared to the king, himself dressed in kingly robes, an elaborate crown and an intricately ornamented gold sash, and seated on a majestic throne. The king was then able to see through his own egocentricity, repented his ways, and became a devoted disciple of the Buddha. To commemorate this incident, the King of the Rakhines and the local people immediately cast a replica image in bronze; this was the Maha Muni.

In 1784, King Bodawpaya had the statute brought to the then

royal capital at Amarapura. He had subdued the independent Rakhine people and annexed their lands to his own. Today the Rakhine people regard themselves as a separate people, and they equate the loss of their independence with the removal of this most sacred of images. King Bodawpaya knew the impact such a loss would have, and allowed it to be believed that he had managed to acquire the image's fabled magical powers to his own ends.

The royal capital was moved from Amarapura to Mandalay in around 1861. The building in Amarapura that the Buddha statue had been stored in burned down in 1884, and the statue was then brought to the new capital.

To Myanmar Buddhists the heavily gilded Maha Muni image is not regarded as just a representation of Lord Buddha but is an icon regarded as sacred in its own right. The reason for this lies in the belief that the image was actually created during the Buddha's lifetime. Because he was pleased with the image, it is said that he endowed it with his own spirit which would last for five thousand years. Tradition maintains that only five images of the Buddha were created during his lifetime: two in India, two in Paradise, and the Maha Muni (though in fact there are more claims throughout the world for images cast in the Buddha's lifetime than this). Archaeologists, however, believe the image was made during the reign of King Chandra Surya, who ascended to the throne in AD 146, around six hundred years after Buddha's death.

Thousands of pilgrims visit the Maha Muni daily, and many thousands also attend a festival in February. The image is now heavily gilded and is estimated to weigh over one ton. The gold crown is studded with precious stones such as rubies, sapphires, emeralds, jade, diamonds, and so on, all donated by pious devotees.

The Maha Muni Pagoda also houses statutes of lions, warriors and a three-headed elephant that were originally sited at the Angkor Wat in Cambodia (see entry). These are reputed to have healing powers and there are many thousands of claims of miraculous healing resulting from prayers made at the statues.

Mount Fuji, Japan

Also known affectionately as Fujisan, Fuji-no-yama and Fujiyama ('yama' means mountain in Japanese) this is one of the world's most famous volcanoes. It is situated in southern Honshu, near Tokyo, and is Japan's highest mountain, part of the Fuji-Hakone-Izu National Park. It rises to a height of 3,776 metres, the top being broken by a crater 610 metres in diameter. Its last eruption was from November 1707 to January 1708; and as it is so close to Tokyo a careful watch is maintained on its potential activity. Geologically, the mountain is actually composed not of one volcano, but three. Shin Fuji (or new Fuji), having extruded volcanic rock, has spread out and covered up most of the remains of the earlier peaks.

The legend of Mount Fuji's origin is that it arose from a plain in a single night in 286 BC. It is regarded as the most majestic, beautiful and mysterious mountain in all Japan. Fuji features in many Japanese legends, for example the story of Taketori Monogatari. There are several versions of which probably the best known is as follows:

In a time long past an old couple lived in Fuji city. They had been unable to have a child and both wanted one desperately, so they prayed. The man was a basket maker who wove baskets from bamboo and one day, while he was cutting canes for his work, he found amongst them a thumb-sized baby girl and took her home. The couple raised the child as their own, naming her Kaguyahime, which means the Shining Princess.

The child grew up to be an elegant, gentle, noble woman, recognised as the most beautiful in the area. She was courted by several important men including the emperor himself and, later, a local magistrate. She married the magistrate after he had wooed her with many gifts. Then one day she told her husband that she wished to go back to the place from whence she had come; she called it the Palace of the Moon, which she said was at the summit of Mount Fuji. Her husband could not bear to be parted from her and forbade her to leave, but she did anyway, on the night of a full moon. Grieving for his loss, her husband followed her as she climbed the slopes of Fuji. Arriving at the summit he found a large lake there, surrounding a huge and beautiful palace. Kaguyahime was there, but she was no longer human; she had reverted to her real form, that of a celestial nymph, and messengers of the moon had come to take her away. She put on a cloak of feathers which removed all memories of her life as a human, and the messengers carried her off. The magistrate knew that he had lost her, and in his deep sorrow threw himself into the water, drowning in its depths.

Being the primary natural wonder of Japan, Mount Fuji was, and is, an important religious centre. A joint Shinto – Buddhist sect (Fujiko) would make popular pilgrimages to the volcano. The most devout pilgrims were encouraged not only to climb to the top, but also to make a circuit of the eight 'peaks' at the summit. The climb was divided into ten sections with stops where shelter, food and rest were provided. At the fifth stop, the pilgrims could also walk around the mountain in what amounted to a separate pilgrimage.

Today, the ascent is equally popular with tourists, but there are still thousands of pilgrims who choose to make the journey. It is customary to take a 'Fuji walking stick', which is emblazoned with wood-burns marking each stop, and several protective amulets. Several religious sects regard Fuji as a sacred mountain; some believe that every Japanese should visit the mountain at least once in their life: akin to the requirement for all Muslims to visit Mecca in their lifetime. There are many shrines and temples to be found on the slopes.

Mount Kailas, Tibet

Also known as Gangdise, the Jewel of Snow, Tisa, and by other names, Mount Kailas is a mountain in south-western Tibet, which, at 6,716 metres, is the highest peak in the Kailas range, a 400-mile chain of mountains running parallel to the Himalayan chain.

One story of the creation of Mount Kailas is derived from the Ramayana (the Sanskrit 'Story of Rama'). To revive the wounded and dead soldiers of Prince Rama, Hanuman (the monkey ally of Rama) was sent to Mount Kailas to retrieve the sanjiwini, a herb which restores life. The mountain was near the mythical paradise of Shambala (see entry). However, Hanuman could not identify the plant, so he brought the whole mountain back with him. After the herbs had been collected, he threw the mountain back to its original location, but missed, and so Mount Kailas ended up where it is today.

The leading Tibetan Yogi, Milarepa, born in AD 1040, meditated in a cave at Mount Kailas before achieving perfect enlightenment. A story attached to this event is that there was a contest between Milarepa and a Bonpo priest, Nara-Bonchung, over who owned Mount Kailas. Whoever reached the summit would be regarded as the true Lord of Kailas. The priest set out early, banging on his drum as he climbed the mountain, but Milarepa waited until sunrise and rode there on the rays of the sun, beating his opponent. The priest dropped his drum, the marks of which can still be seen on the mountain. The two were reconciled when Nara-Bonchung was allowed to dwell on a neighbouring peak.

The peak is of significance to both Hindus and Tibetan Buddhists. Hindus regard the peak as the abode of the god Siva; indeed some hold it to be Siva himself in eternal meditation. Tibetan Buddhists regard it as Mount Sumeru, the cosmic centre of the universe. For this reason Buddhists will not fully climb to the peak out of respect. Tibetan Buddhists believe that the mountain is the home of Demchog, a god with four faces who wears a tiger skin and a crown made of human skulls. The mountain is also sacred to Jains and Bonpos. Jains believe Kailas to be Astapada, the place where Rishabha, their first saint, gained enlightenment.

Kailas has therefore been a very important place for pilgrimage for 2,500 years, until the middle of the twentieth century when the Chinese government restricted access. That restriction has been relaxed in more recent times, with two hundred Indian pilgrims a year allowed to make a visit and, since 1984, a number of European and other nationalities allowed on the mountain.

The pilgrim road that girdles the mountain reaches 5,486 metres, as high as is expected for pilgrims to climb out of respect. The 32-mile-long road winds round Kailas, which is an isolated peak, and contains many small cairns and dome-shaped chortens (monuments), and is festooned with prayer-flags. There are several monasteries along the route. The road is mostly used by the

Tibetan Buddhists who believe that one 'parikrama' atones for the sins of a lifetime and that the making of 108 such circumambulations offers enlightenment, or nirvana.

Most of the few Indian visitors find that a visit to nearby Lake Manasarovor is sufficient for their devotions. Indian pilgrims are thought to be mostly renunciates, rather than ordinary people in search of a place of devotion and worship; it is thought that for the ordinary pilgrim the difficulties of travel to the region, and the possibility of bandit-attack, discourage them.

The restrictions that were in place were eased slightly when His Holiness Sri Jayaendra Saraswathi Swami, the sixty-ninth Sankaracharya of Kanchi Kamakoti Peetam, along with twelve disciples, was given permission to perform the celebration of Vyasa Pooja on Guru Poornima Day (9 July 1998) at the banks of the sacred lake of Manasarovor, just below Mount Kailas. Vyasa Pooja represents the beginning of a four-month period known as Chaturmasa when Sanyasis (monks) vow to remain at a certain place throughout. This enables the insects to come out during the monsoon and not be inadvertently harmed by the Sanyasis moving about or treading on them. The ceremony was agreed between the governments of India, Nepal and China. The Chinese Government arranged a special delegation to meet with the Sankaracharya, according him full honours and accompanying him throughout the visit. The Chinese further gave permission for the erection of a statue of Adi Shankara – regarded by some Indians as the greatest philosopher, mystic, and poet – at the foot of Mount Kailas.

Lake Manasarovor is held to have been formed by the mind of Lord Brahma, and contains the thirthas (bathing places and crossing points to the divine realm) of the sacred Rivers Ganges, Yamuna, Saraswathi, and Bhagirati. Within fifty miles of the lake are the sources of four of southern Asia's greatest rivers flowing into India: the Tsangpo/Brahmaputra, the Indus, the Sutlej, and the Karnali. It is said that rain from heaven falls first on the god Siva (Kailas) in order to soften its blow, before draining into the sacred Ganges River. After his death in 1948 some of the ashes of Mahatma Gandhi were scattered into Lake Manasarovor.

Lake Manasarovor is round and said to represent the sun.

Nearby is another sacred lake, Rakastal, which is in the shape of a crescent moon. The two lakes are therefore held to represent the solar (man's inner consciousness) and the lunar (darker, demonic) powers. Perhaps the mystical aspect of the region is enhanced by two large hollows on Mount Kailas which give it, from certain angles, the appearance of a skull looking down on the plains below.

Mount Qomolangma (Mount Everest), Tibet

Mount Everest, the highest peak in the world, is sacred to many of the people in its extensive shadow. There are many myths about the mountain and the Himalayan range of which it is a part. Everest is known as the 'third Pole of the earth'. Its height made it, for centuries, beyond the reach of human endeavour and as such it was thought to be reserved for the gods. To some Indian pilgrims it was regarded as an embodiment of God, indeed a god in its own right. Tibetans regard the mountain as the Goddess Snow, or sometimes as the Third Goddess.

One Tibetan myth described the Himalayan region as once an expanse of ocean with an endless stretch of forest on its shore, a paradise replete with all kinds of animals and birds. Then, from the sea, came a gigantic five-headed demon which frightened the animals, but was subdued by five fairies who were created from five clouds. The fairies were asked to stay by the grateful denizens of the animal kingdom and became the five Himalayan peaks; one of them is Mount Qomolangma.

On 18 March 1989, the Qomolangma National Nature Preserve was established by the government of the Tibet Autonomous Region, to preserve this sacred national treasure. In 1994 the Chinese Government elevated the Preserve from regional to national status, affording it the same level of legal protection as treasures such as the Great Wall of China and the Ming Tombs. The Preserve protects the thirteen thousand square miles of land containing four of the six highest peaks on earth.

In this mystical area, special consideration is given to the extremely sacred Lapchi pilgrimage to the highest monastery on earth, and to the four hermitage sites of Buddhism's poet-saint Milarepa.

Nara, southern Honshu near Osaka, Japan

Nara is an ancient capital of Japan, the first permanent capital city of the country. Prior to that, the capital had moved to the palace of whichever emperor was ruling at the time.

From AD 710, Nara was a huge conglomeration of palaces, temples and shrines, and to this day has a number of impressive sacred sites. It preserves the world's oldest wooden structure, the Horyu-ji Temple, and also the world's largest wooden structure, the Daibutsu-den in the Todai-ji Temple.

Nara Park is famous for its deer roaming free around the shrines; they are regarded as divine messengers from the gods and treated with appropriate respect. In the park is one of the largest bronze statues in the world – a gilded statue of the Buddha over sixteen metres high, known as the Daibutsu – and the temples of Todai-ji and Horyu-ji, the latter containing the grave of Jimmu, the first emperor of Japan.

The Buddhist temple of Horyu-ji was founded in 607 by the Emperor's son, the Prince Regent Shotoku, shortly after Buddhism came to Japan. This original temple is believed to have been destroyed by fire in 670, and the present buildings, Sai-in (the West Temple), date from 711 when they were rebuilt. These are the world's oldest wooden structures still standing. The East temple (To-in), was built by 739 at the site of Shotoku's Ikaruga Palace, and dedicated to the Prince. Being made of wood these structures have required extensive maintenance over the centuries. For example, between 1933 and 1953, the buildings were carefully dismantled and rebuilt, with careful restoration and care. Many of the temple buildings are now designated as National Treasures or Important Cultural Assets. In 1993, UNESCO added the Horyu-ji and other Buddhist buildings in the area to its World Heritage List.

The Todai-ji temple complex was built in 743. By that time Buddhism was at its height, and serving as the state religion. It is at this temple that the Daibutsu resides. It is housed in the wooden

Daibutsu-den, forty-eight metres in height, which has the distinction of being the largest wooden building in the world. Impressive as it is, the present structure, which was built in 1709 to replace one lost to fire, is smaller than the original structure, being about 30 per cent narrower. Since its construction in 749, the Daitbutsu statue has been maintained and repaired many times; earthquake damage has taken its toll. The upper portion, for example, was recast in the second half of the twelfth century.

As one of the major sacred temples in Japan, Todai-ji also houses many other valuable artefacts, many of them designated National Treasures. Their repository, the Shosoin, is known as the Treasure House of the World.

Pagan, Myanmar

Tradition has it that Pagan (or Bagan) was founded by King Pyinbia in AD 849; his people had migrated to Burma (since 1989 known as Myanmar) from Tibet. The country's history as a united state began in 1044 with the reign of King Anawrahta; Pagan, in the Mandalay region, was his capital. The unification was consolidated by his son, Kyanzittha.

The state was a Hindu kingdom, with taxes from local villages supporting the central court. Over time much land was given to Buddhist monasteries, the Buddhist faith having been brought to the region by the Mons peoples who lived largely in the south of the country. The king was therefore supported by the Hindu faith, and was defender of the Buddhist faith. The unified state remained at peace for nearly 250 years until it was conquered by the Mongol warlord Kublai Khan in 1287.

During those 250 years the enormous number of pagodas for which Pagan is internationally known were constructed. It is recognised as one of the richest archaeological sites in the world. Many of the pagodas have deteriorated over time, but the remains of over five thousand are still to be seen. While in Britain we speak of huge numbers as 'like the grains of sand on a beach', in Myanmar they speak of 'as countless as the pagodas of Pagan'. It is said that it is impossible to move in Pagan without touching something sacred. The writer James Harpur comments in his book *The Atlas of Sacred Places*: 'In the history of the world, it is doubtful whether any city has expended so much creativity on raising shrines as Pagan did.' It is said there are over four million images of Buddha there, which include small carvings on stone slabs around the city.

The Shwezigon Pagoda is the main focus of pilgrimage in Pagan. It is the greatest temple of Anawrahta's reign, though it was completed by his son. A sacred relic of the Buddha is believed to have been put on the back of a white elephant by the king and the pagoda was built at the spot where the elephant knelt down. The Shwezigon is believed to contain the Buddha's collar bone, and one of his teeth. (Other accounts claim that it houses a copy of the Buddha's tooth, the original of which is said to be in Sri Lanka.) It is also the first major monument built in Burmese rather than the earlier Mon style, becoming a model for other, later, pagodas. The stupa of the Shwezigon pagoda is the only one covered with gold in Pagan. Interestingly there is a throwback to beyond Buddhism in the Shwezigon; Anawrahta placed wooden images on the terraces of the thirty-seven traditional 'nats'. These were the spirits that Pagan people believed in before the introduction of Buddhism. He decided that rather than try to eradicate the old faiths he would use them to encourage his people to discover the new ones.

The present day small village of Pagan and its environs – consisting of more than two thousand temples – were partially destroyed by an earthquake in 1975. The buildings are now being restored under a UNESCO conservation programme.

Potala Palace, Lhasa, Tibet

The Potala Palace, on the Red Mountain (Mar-po-ri), was built in the seventh century, and is world-famous as a combination of Chinese and classical Tibetan architectures. It is named after a mountain in southern India which is regarded as the seat of the Bodhisattva Avalokitesvara, the patron god of Tibet. Tibetan Buddhists recognise the Dalai Lama as the incarnation of

Avalokitesvara. The Palace covers an area of 410,000 square metres and stands thirteen storeys high.

It was traditionally the winter palace of the Dalai Lama, and since the time of the fifth Dalai Lama it had been a venue for major religious and political ceremonies. This Dalai Lama, known as the Great Fifth, reigned from 1645 to 1693, and his death was kept secret for fourteen years in order to allow for the completion of his palace with its golden roofs over the tombs of the Dalai Lama. (It should be remembered that the Dalai Lama is only one individual; his 'deaths' represent only his passing from one incarnation to another, and therefore the bodies within the tombs represent his several incarnations rather than his predecessors.) The Potala is a major pilgrimage site for Tibetan Buddhists.

It is said that the Red Mountain included a sacred cave, thought to be the dwelling place of the Bodhisattva Chenresi Avilokiteshvara, and it was used as a meditation retreat by Emperor Songtsen Gampo in the seventh century AD. In 637, he built a palace on the hill which, in the seventeenth century, was incorporated into the foundations of the existing buildings. Of more than one thousand rooms in the Potala, the ones considered most sacred are the Chogyal Drubphuk and the Phakpa Lhakhang, both remnants from the original palace. The latter room houses the sacred Arya Lokesvara statue.

The Red Palace (the Potrang Marpo), the highest part of the structure, contains the living quarters and tombs of eight of the Dalai Lamas, as well as temples containing thousands of statues of Buddha, demons and gods. The White Palace (Potrang Karpo) below houses temples and once contained the administrative offices of the Tibetan government.

It is said that more than two hundred thousand statues and ten thousand altars are located within the whole complex.

The Potala Palace has not been the home of the Dalai Lama since 1959 when he – the fourteenth incarnation – went into exile following the occupation of Tibet by Chinese communists in 1950. However, its value was understood by China's Cultural Relics Commission, and it was preserved during the Chinese revolution. The Potala was designated a UNESCO World Heritage site in 1994, and is now open to the public as a state museum, though some parts remain off-limits to visitors.

In August 2001 it was announced that the Palace had suffered much damage because of poor restoration work by the Chinese; a ten by twenty metre section of one of the main walls had collapsed. Attempts had been underway to make it the centrepiece of a 'theme park' being built on adjacent land to cater for an ever-increasing flow of tourists. Criticism of the project has been strong from Tibet as it is said that it will emphasise the Chinese influence and submerge the original cultural heritage of the site.

Prayag, near Allahabad, India

Allahabad, in the state of Uttar Pradesh in northern India, is one of the four sacred sites where the Kumbha Mela pilgrimage and festival take place. The festival is held at the confluence of three rivers, the Ganges, the Yamuna and the mythical river of spiritualism, the Saraswati. The other three sites are: Haridwar, also in Uttar Pradesh, where the River Ganges enters the plains from the Himalayas; Ujjain (in Madhya Pradesh), on the banks of Ksipra River; and Nasik (in Maharashtra), on the banks of Godavari River.

Observance of Kumbha Mela is based on the story that thousands of years ago gods and demons agreed to work together to obtain Amrita (the nectar of immortality) and to share it equally. But when the Kumbha (pot) containing the amrita was presented, the demons ran away with it, chased by the gods. For twelve days and twelve nights (equivalent to twelve human years) the gods and demons fought in the sky for the possession of the amrita. During the battle droplets of it fell to earth at the four locations where the festival is now held.

The pilgrimage includes a ritual bath at a predetermined time and place; religious discussion and debate; devotional singing; and the mass feeding of holy men/women and the poor. It is held four times every twelve years, once at each of the four sites. Each twelve-year cycle includes the Maha (great) Kumbha Mela at Prayag, near Allahabad, which is attended by millions of people.

What made this festival special in 2001 was that it coincided with the start of a new moon, something that would not occur again for 144 years. Because of this the usual ten to twelve million pilgrims who attend the Maha Kumbha Mela were swollen to an extraordinary seventy million people, with an estimated thirty-two million converging on the location on the day of the new moon, 24 January 2001, making it the largest gathering of humanity ever known.

The Maha Kumbha Mela is the most sacred of all Hindu pilgrimages. Amongst the pilgrims are thousands of holy men and women, all seeking to wash their sins away by bathing in the holy waters. On 24 January 2001, the millions were led by thousands of naked Hindu warrior monks who ran into the freezing waters, holding hands, dancing, and punching the air in ecstasy.

Rameswaram, India

The island of Rameswaram, sometimes called the Benares of the south, is the closest point in India to Sri Lanka. It is one of the most visited pilgrimage sites in India, with over ten thousand visitors a day.

Legend, as related in the Ramayana, has it that from here Hanuman leapt across the ocean to Sri Lanka in search of the captured Sita. Hanuman later returned with Rama, Lakshmana, and Sugriva's army of monkeys to build a bridge across the ocean and launch their attack on Ravana. After Rama's victory over Ravana he returned to Rameswaram to crown Ravana's brother, Vibhisana, as the new King of Lanka.

The island is famous for the Ramanathaswamy Temple which is itself world famous for its long and magnificent corridors, including the world's longest, and its elaborately carved pillars. The temple is dedicated to Shiva and is the most southerly of the twelve jyortilinga shrines. Pilgrims to Rameswaram bathe in the sacred waters of the Agnitheertam, a stretch of sea near the temple. Devout Hindus from southern India take sand from the banks of the sacred River Ganges, and then travel south to immerse it in the waters of Rameswaram. In performing this ritual with the sand, pilgrims ensure for themselves a place in heaven.

An important reason for Hindus to travel to Rameswaram is its significance as a place to perform the ritual known as shraddh. Shraddh are ceremonies carried out after the death of a parent or other relative, and are for the benefit of the person who has died, making it possible for the soul to be freed from the endless cycle of birth and death.

It is said that the original shrine was housed in a thatched hut until the twelfth century, and that then the first masonry structure was built by Parakrama Bahu of Sri Lanka. Much of the additions were carried out between the twelfth and sixteenth centuries. The present huge temple dominates the island. It has two towers, in fact gopurams (stylised gateways), thirty metres high, dating from the seventeenth century. The sides of the towers, and the interior of the temple, are highly decorated with sculptures depicting myths from the Ramayana.

There are also many sacred bathing pools within the temple area, known for their healing qualities. Pilgrims immerse themselves, clothed, in each of these pools before prayer.

The Sacred Mountains of China

Many cultures around the world have made mountains a sacred part of their beliefs. For some they are links to the centre of the world, such as Mount Meru for Hindus. In ancient Greece the gods were believed to dwell on Mount Olympus. In Japan Mount Fuji is a powerful national symbol of their beliefs. Mount Kailas in Tibet is a sacred mountain for Hindus, Jains and Buddhists. All of these mountains, and others such as Everest (Qomolangma), are described in this compilation.

In addition, it seems very clear that many of the most sacred and significant manmade structures around the world were designed to emulate mountains: the pyramids in South America and Egypt for example. Also, shrines and temples are often built either on hills or mountains or on the highest points of artificial structures, such as the Mounds of the North American Indians, or the Parthenon in Athens.

Mountains represent the pillars that hold up the heavens above the earth, or the corners of the known world. They were the dwelling places of sacred peoples, or immortals.

China has nine sacred mountains which are the object of regular pilgrimages, five important to Taoist belief and four sacred to Buddhists. The five most famous Taoist mountains are: Tai Shan in Shandong province; Heng Shan Bei and Hua Shan, in Shanxi province; Heng Shan Nan, in Hunan province; and Song Shan in Henan province. The four Buddhist sacred mountains are: Pu Tuo Shan, in Zhejiang province; Wu Tai Shan in Shanxi province; Emei Shan in Sichuan province; and Jiu Hua Shan in Anhui province.

Each of the Buddhist sacred mountains is regarded as a dwelling place of a Bodhisatva: a mythological spiritual being dedicated to helping all sentient beings to attain enlightenment.

Taoist belief has it that mountains are a medium of communication between mortals and immortals. They are places of retreat, of pilgrimage, and of contemplation. They offer a chance to co-exist with nature. Many of these peaks were ancient shamanic sites of great local importance and their religious significance dates back over five thousand years.

Tai Shan is the most important of these Chinese sacred mountains, not just because it is a dwelling place of the gods, but because it is an actual god itself. The ancient emperors regarded the mountain as the son of the Emperor of Heaven and it cared for and nurtured the people over whom it dominated. It is said that seventy-two emperors made a pilgrimage to Tai Shan to speak with the gods, including the first emperor, Shi Huangdi. There are many temples and shrines on the slopes, and two important temples on the peak: The Temple of the Jade Emperor and the Temple of the Princess of the Azure Clouds, daughter of the Jade Emperor. The latter is reputed to be a place of spiritual healing.

The Chinese are concerned that these places of pilgrimage are being lost to the pressures of tourism, and their meaning diminished, a comment that has echoes around the world at many sacred sites. Zhang Hua Ne, of the China Taoist Association, commented in an interview with reporter Martin Palmer of the International Consultancy on Religion, Education and Culture: 'These places are meant to be hard to climb, arduous to explore, for in that struggle lies humanity. To build cable cars is not just to disturb the natural balance. It is to deprive us of a sense of awe.'

Sanchi, nr Bhopal, Madhya Pradesh, India

The hilltop at Sanchi is crowned by over fifty Buddhist monuments, most of them stupas. The most magnificent, and worldrenowned, is the Great Stupa, sometimes known as Stupa Number 1. The structures were built between the third century BC and the twelfth century AD.

Sanchi therefore displays in this one region fifteen hundred years of the decline and fall of Buddhist art and architecture. Perhaps this is unexpected; Sanchi was not a specific place in the life of the Buddha. In fact it was selected by the Emperor Ashoka Maurya as an ideal place to demonstrate his conversion to Buddhism. He had converted some twelve years into his reign and became zealous in his devotions. Monks need to be near, but not in, major cities as they have a dual and conflicting need to beg to live, but also to have peace and quiet for their meditations. Sanchi met this requirement, being an isolated place, yet near the city of Vidisha. Ashoka's empire was great, covering all of India and Afghanistan and he took close personal control of affairs for all his reign. It is largely due to him that Buddhism was for a long time the dominant religion of India.

The Emperor built eight stupas on the hilltop, including the Great Stupa. He also erected a monolithic pillar. The Great Stupa as originally built was made of burnt bricks and mud, was about half the size of the present structure, and is contained within it. It underwent reconstruction in the second century BC and four elaborately carved gateways were added in the first century BC. These gateways have been regarded as some of the finest Buddhist art in India; the carvings depict scenes from the life of the Buddha. In around AD 450 effigies of the Buddha were erected facing the gates. The other constructions there were created over succeeding centuries, but as Buddhism declined as the major religion of India so the site became decayed and forgotten.

The relics of Sariputra and Maha-moggalana, the two most

prominent disciples of Buddha, were found at Sanchi by Colonel Alexander Cunningham in 1851. However, the stupas have suffered at the hands of other excavators over the years and amateur attempts at opening them have resulted in their decay or complete collapse. In 1822, a Captain Johnson opened up Stupa Number 1 from top to bottom on one side, creating a breach so big that there was a significant collapse. Stupa Number 2 was similarly partly destroyed. Ashoka's monolithic pillar was broken up by local vandals and used as a sugarcane press.

Between 1881 and 1884 a Major Cole put right much of his predecessors' damage. He filled in the breach of Stupa Number 1, set up the fallen gateways, and undertook other remedial work. Between 1912 and 1919 Sir John Marshall, Director General of Archaeology in India, brought the stupas to their present condition with a thorough renovation that included the dismantling and rebuilding of the south-west portion of Stupa Number 1, re-erection of its balustrades, reconstruction of the dome and balustrade of Stupa Number 3, and much other work amongst the other fifty or so constructions. A museum was built to house the artefacts found in the course of the work.

Shambala

To Tibetan Buddhists Shambala, the Hidden Kingdom, is believed to be a community of perfect and near-perfect beings whose role is to assist in the development of humanity. It is thought to be the repository of Kalacakra, the highest form of Tibetan mysticism. Although its location is unknown, and regarded by most scholars as a myth, its position is generally said to be either in the Gobi Desert, or in the Himalayas near Mount Kailasa. In any case it is not thought to exist in our material world, but in a spiritual dimension. It is said that Shambala can only be perceived by those of pure mind and spirit.

According to legend, Buddha preached Kalacakra to the holy men of India, and the teachings remained hidden for one thousand years. After that time, a scholar went in search of Shambala and met with a holy man who initiated him into the secrets of

Kalacakra. These teachings were taken to Tibet in AD 1026. Since then it has been a source of study for Tibetans: teachings that include science, astrology, and meditation.

The religious writings of Tibet describe Shambala in detail. The community is shaped like a lotus with eight petals, divided into eight regions surrounded by mountains of gleaming ice. The capital of Shambala, Kalapa, is in the centre and contains the ruler's palace, made of precious metals and jewels, and coral. In much the same way as Atlantis is held to have been a highly advanced civilisation, so Shambala is thought of as highly advanced – not just spiritually, but technologically. The roofs of the palace are said to contain special magnifying lenses that allow the inhabitants to study other worlds; aircraft and cars allow for travel through underground networks of tunnels. At the more spiritual level, the inhabitants learn telepathy, materialisation and de-materialisation, and telekinesis.

It is a land guarded by the supernatural, and by beings with supernatural abilities. These guardians are generally not seen, but some claims of sighting have been reported. The Yeti, the much-sought after Abominable Snowman of the Himalayas, has been held to be such a guardian in some beliefs.

Writer and explorer Alexandra David-Neel described these guardians of Shambala. She was born in Paris, France in 1868, and lived to be over one hundred years old, dying in 1969. She was an extraordinary woman. Both a Buddhist and an authority on Buddhism, she was the first European woman to explore Lhasa, the forbidden Tibetan city. To do this she had to cross the Himalayas in winter, virtually alone – no easy task. While in the Himalayas she saw a figure, which she took to be a guardian, moving through the snows and described him thus: 'I could clearly see his perfectly calm impassive face and wide-open eyes with their gaze fixed on some invisible distant object situated somewhere high up in space. The man did not run. He seemed to lift himself from the ground, proceeding by leaps. It looked as if he had been endowed with the elasticity of a ball, and rebounded each time his feet touched the ground. His steps had the regularity of a pendulum.'

The reality of Shambala is implied by Tibetan texts that seem to describe historical accounts of the Hidden Kingdom. They give the names and dates of the Kings of Shambala intertwined with known events in the material world. It is said that the first king was Sucandra who came from the north of Kashmir, bringing the teachings of Kalacakra. He had requested the teachings of Buddha Sakyamuni which were given to him on the full-moon day of the third month, at the stupa of Dhanakataka in the south of India.

The writings say that there will be thirty-two kings, each of whom will reign for one hundred years, and during their rule, the material world will deteriorate. When spiritually unenlightened people have gained dominance over the earth, then the veil which hides and protects Shambala will lift to reveal the kingdom to them. Afraid of the power of Shambala, the barbarians will unite under an evil ruler and attack it. The thirty-second king of Shambala, Rudra Cakrin, will destroy the evil ruler and all his followers.

Some claim the predictions for the material world have already come to pass, and many Tibetans believe this further proves the existence of the Kingdom. For instance, predictions have included: the disintegration of Buddhism in Tibet – while not actually true, it has certainly suffered during the years following the Chinese revolution; the expansion of materialist thinking throughout the world – which seems to be correct; and the upsurge of warfare in the twentieth century – which is undeniable.

Shambala is regarded by Tibetan Buddhists as the spiritual centre of the world, and has been equated to the Hindu Paradesha, and the Jewish and Christian Garden of Eden. It is sometimes described as Shangri-la and Agartha.

It is said that those who seek Shambala never return. Perhaps they find it and choose not to leave; perhaps they die in the attempt.

Shwedagon, Myanmar

The Golden Stupa of the Shwedagon Pagoda has long been the spiritual symbol of the Burmese peoples. It is a solid brick stupa, completely covered in gold.

According to belief, the original stupa was built during the Buddha's lifetime, in the sixth century BC. This makes the site a magical and mystical one for Buddhists, increasing its sense of being a holy place for contemplation. It is said to have been built originally to house the eight sacred hairs of the Buddha and relics belonging to three previous Buddhas, and is therefore the only structure in the world that preserves the items relating to four Buddhas. Again, this serves to make the site an extraordinarily sacred one.

Legend has it that two brothers, Tapussa and Bhallika, travelled from India, carrying with them the original sacred hairs of Buddha. On their journey across the ocean, they had two of the hairs taken from them by the King of Ajetta, and two more were stolen by the King of Nagas, who had transformed himself into the likeness of a human being and boarded the ship during the night. When they came to Myanmar, the arrival of the sacred hairs was celebrated for several days. Sakka, Lord of the Heaven, came down to earth to help choose a site for their storage and invoked the aid of four spirits: Sule, Amyitha, Yawhani, and Dakkhina.

Relics of three preceding Buddhas were found with the help of these spirits and were secured along with the sacred hairs brought by the brothers. Before placing them in the vault dug on the hill, King Okkalapa opened the container holding the hairs and eight flew up to the height of seven palm trees, emitting coloured rays of such intensity that the dumb could speak, the deaf could hear, and the lame could walk. A rain of jewels fell knee-deep.

A golden stone slab was placed on top of the vault by Sakka and on it was erected a golden pagoda. Over time the pagoda has been extended to its present size and splendour.

The Shwedagon Pagoda complex is majestic, impressive and beautiful. The main stupa, rising ninety-eight metres, is surrounded by a plethora of sixty or so smaller stupas and a similar number of shrines, pavilions and temples, all set on a huge marbled platform of fourteen acres. In the precincts of the pagoda are figurines of mythical animals, each set atop a red signboard at the eight points of the compass. These are a celestial representation of the days of the week. Myanmar Buddhists celebrate their birthday every week – celebrating the day of the week on which they were born – and they pray at the appropriate compass point representing their day. This day is very important to a Myanmar Buddhist; it dictates everything in their life from their prayers to when to have their hair cut.

In addition, many Myanmar Buddhists will also pray at the Saturday image of Saturn and the dragon. Saturn is a powerful planet, and can have evil effects on a person when their horoscope is under its influence. To appease Saturn a person must make an offering at that compass point.

Visiting a pagoda is a very important aspect of Buddhists' lives. They are guided by Karma, a law of balance, and seek to undertake good deeds. To meditate on the infinite compassion of Buddha while walking towards the pagoda is a good deed. To make offerings of flowers, candles, flags, streamers, and donations for the upkeep of the pagoda, are good deeds. Acts of giving, or dhana, are an important aspect of Buddhist teaching. Visitors can pour cooling water on a statue of Buddha to refresh it from the sun's glaring heat. These acts compensate for bad actions, and the more good karma that people accumulate the better their chances of being born into a better condition in their next life.

A visit to a pagoda is not just undertaken to contemplate Buddha, but also to spread goodwill and kindness to fellow beings who are on different planes of existence. The spirit world is populated by nats, many of whom are represented in the precincts of the pagoda in paintings and sculptures. These nats have specific functions, rather like Catholic saints are assigned patronages.

Another area on the site is the star-shape known as the Wish Fulfilling Place, where people contemplate in the hope of getting their wishes granted. Keep your wish a secret, and ring the large bell to attract the attention of the spirits, and who knows . . .

Missing from the Shwedagon, however, is the 300-ton, jewel-encrusted Dhammazedi bell, which has been submerged in ten metres of mud in the Irrawaddy River since 1608, when it sank while being looted by the Portuguese military commander Filipe de Brito y Nicote. The bell was named for King Dhammazedi who commissioned it for the pagoda. It is made of gold, silver and bronze and studded with emeralds and sapphires. The Burmese were so incensed by the theft that they attacked the Portuguese garrison, killed everyone there, and bamboo-staked the commander in the sun, where he took several days to die. It is believed to be the largest bell ever created and it is also said that when it is restored to the Shwedagon good fortune, peace and prosperity will return to Myanmar. In January 2001 a £6 million operation to recover the bell was announced, to be headed by English marine archaeologist Mike Hatcher, though the scheme had to overcome political concerns of the British Foreign Office regarding the present ruling regime in Myanmar.

Sravanabelagola, Karnataka, India

The hill of Sravanabelagola (also known as Vindhyagiri or Perkalbappu) is situated 1,222 metres above sea level, and 614 steps lead to the summit, where a huge statue of Sri Gomatheswar stands. It is twenty-one metres high, the tallest free-standing statue in the world, and was built in AD 981. Sri Gomatheswar was the son of the first Tirthankara, an enlightened sage of Jainism.

Sravanabelagola means 'the monk on the top of the hill'. This refers not only to the statue, but to the fact that hermits, mystics and ascetics have taken up residence and followed their devotions there since at least the third century BC. During the tenth century AD temples began to be built. The site became, and is today, one of the most important pilgrimage sites of the Jain religion.

The chief festival of Sravanabelagola is the Maha Masthaka Abhisheka. During this a scaffolding is built around the statue and over a million devotees come to chant mantras and pour thousands of gallons of milk, honey and herbs over the head of the figure. As these substances flow down over the body of the image, they are believed to acquire a powerful charge of spiritual energy. The charged substances are collected at the feet of the statue and then distributed to the pilgrims in the belief that they will assist in the quest for enlightenment. The festival is performed once every twelve to fourteen years. The next one will be held in 2005.

The Temple of the Emerald Buddha, Wat Phra Kaeo, Bangkok, Thailand

Wat Phra Kaeo was built by King Rama I in 1782, on the east bank of the Chao Phraya River, specifically to house The Emerald Buddha, which is the most celebrated image in Thailand and sits atop an eleven-metre tall gilded altar, protected by a nine-tiered umbrella. The Buddha is carved from a single, solid block of jadeite. Thais regard the Emerald Buddha as the most sacred of all images of the Buddha, and believe that its well-being guarantees the prosperity and continuance of their nation.

An act which shows the importance of the Emerald Buddha to Thais occurred at the beginning of World War Two. Field Marshal Phibun Songkran believed that Japan would win the conflict and on 14 December 1942 signed an agreement with the Japanese. Judith Stowe, in *Siam becomes Thailand*, commented: 'To emphasise its solemn and binding nature, the treaty was signed by Phibun and Tsubokami in front of the Emerald Buddha, considered the most sacred object in the whole of Thailand.'

As with many ancient accounts, the stories of the Emerald Buddha are submerged in legend an myth. There has been little done to unravel that myth, though there are many good academic texts which examine the stories. The history of the Buddha is generally accepted as follows.

In AD 1434, during a storm, lightning struck a stupa in the town of Chiengrai in northern Thailand, revealing within a Buddha statue covered with stucco. This statue was taken to the abbot who, one day, noticed that the stucco on the nose had flaked off and that the image within was green. He took off the stucco covering to reveal the glory of the Emerald Buddha. It became an object of worship and pilgrimage. The town of Chiengrai was, at that time, under the rule of King Samfangkaen of Chiengmai. He three times sent an elephant to bring the Emerald Buddha to Chiengmai, but on each occasion the elephant diverted itself to Lampang. This the king took to be an omen that the spirits guarding the Emerald Buddha wanted it to reside in Lampang, and it was allowed to remain there for thirty-two years, until 1468, when King Tiloka had it brought to Chiengmai and, according to one record, installed it in a large stupa called Chedi Luang. The image stayed with the kings of Chiengmai until 1778.

Then, King Taksin conquered the region. One of his officers, General Chakri, later Rama I, brought the Emerald Buddha to the then Thai capital at Thonburi. The temple took two years to build, and the Buddha was placed in it in 1784. Rama I had two robes made for the Buddha, one a golden diamond-studded coat for the hot season and the other a gilded robe for the rainy season. Rama III later added a robe of enamel-coated solid gold for the colder season. The ruling monarch personally changes these robes as each season begins, ensuring good fortune during that period of his rule.

The lap of the seated Emerald Buddha is just over forty-eight centimetres wide and the figure is sixty-six centimetres high. The face has a gold third eye inset above the eyebrows. The eyes look downward, creating an overall tranquil appearance. The nose and mouth are diminutive and the mouth is closed; the ears are elongated, to show the figure's divine status. The Emerald Buddha was carved sitting upon a platform, while this base itself stands on a gold lotus blossom. The right leg rests on the left one, suggesting it was carved in northern Thailand not long before its first discovery. However, scholars have pointed out that the Buddha sits in an attitude of yogic meditation, and therefore looks like the Buddhas of Southern India and Sri Lanka; the attitude of meditation has never been popular in Thai images of the Buddha. Its origins remain somewhat uncertain therefore.

In 1788, Rama I had the Holy Buddhist manuscripts (the Tripitaka) revised, and a copy of the new version was then installed in the library inside the Temple of the Emerald Buddha. During the celebration of this event, sparks from fireworks fell on the roof of the library and burnt it down, but fortunately the Tripitaka was saved in time. A new library was later built nearby.

In front of the Temple of the Emerald Buddha, on the east, eight towers were constructed. They were dedicated to the important elements of Buddhism: the Buddha, the Dhamma (Law), the Sangha (Buddhist monks), the Bhikshuni (Buddhist nuns), Pacchekabodhi Buddhas (Buddhas who attained Enlightenment but never preached), the Chokravati (great emperors), the Bodhisava (the Buddha in his previous lives) and the Maitreya (the future Buddha).

The mystical powers attributed to the Buddha image – including that of purging evil spirits and disease – its association with the ruling leaders of the past, and the powers associated with other Buddha images, have all contributed to the Emerald Buddha becoming a potent religio-political symbol of Thai society. The king is regarded as the personal caretaker of the Emerald Buddha, and the possession of the image symbolises the legitimacy of the monarch.

The Temple of the Emerald Buddha underwent extensive renovations in 1882, 1932 and 1982 to coincide with the one hundredth, one hundred and fiftieth and two hundredth anniversaries of Bangkok.

Varanasi (formerly Benares or Banaras), northern India

Situated in Uttar Pradesh State, on the north bank of the River Ganges, Varanasi is the holiest of cities for Hindus. It is the most visited pilgrimage destination in all of India: one of the seven Holy Cities, one of the twelve jyortilinga sites, and one of the Shakti Pitha sites (Shakti in Hindu represents the power of the supreme goddess). Originally known as Avimukta, and also Kashi which means 'where the supreme light shines', this centre of worship has been inhabited for more than three thousand years. From the name Kashi, the city is also known as the City of Light. It is just a few miles from Sarnath, the site where Buddha preached his first sermon.

Despite its antiquity, the current city has few buildings dating from before the late sixteenth century AD. Muslim armies from the eleventh century onward destroyed many of the ancient Hindu temples and erected mosques on their foundations. Qutbuddin Aibak's armies were said to have destroyed more than a thousand temples in 1194 alone, and Shah Jahan, most famous as the builder of the Taj Mahal, had seventy-six temples demolished.

The city houses more than fifteen hundred temples, perhaps the best known being the jyortilinga Vishwanath (or Golden Temple), rebuilt in 1776, dedicated to Shiva and housing the image of Shiva in the form of a black stone linga set into a solid silver altar in the floor. Another prominent place of worship is the Jnana Vapi, or Well of Wisdom, which is said to have been dug by Shiva himself; its waters carry the liquid form of jhana: the light of wisdom.

Hindu pilgrims travel to Varanasi from all over the world and there are records of them having done so since the seventh century. Huge groups gather along the banks of the scared River Ganges, where terraced landings, known as ghats, lead down to the water. Hindus believe that immersion in the Ganges cleanses them of sin and that death on its banks is a wonderful thing and leads to salvation. The Ganges is said to have fallen from heaven; to drink even one drop of its water is said to be sufficient to cleanse the sins of a lifetime. Bottles of Ganges water are prized possessions, and often administered to the dying.

The level areas of the ghats are used for funeral pyres. Those who come to Varanasi with the intention of dying there are called jivan muktas, meaning those who 'are liberated while still alive'. Hindus believe that cremation at the holy city ensures moksha, the final liberation of the soul from the cycle of birth, and rebirth (known as samsara). The dead and dying are brought from far-flung places for cremation at Varanasi. In *Banaras – City of Light*, author Diana Eck states: 'Death in Kashi is not a feared death, for here the ordinary God of Death, frightful Yama, has no jurisdiction. Death in Kashi is death known and faced, transformed and transcended.'

Encircling Varanasi is the sacred path called Panchakroshi Parikrama. Pilgrims start at the Manikarnika ghat where they bathe in the Ganges, then take five days to walk the fifty-mile path clockwise round the city, visiting 108 shrines during that time. Even more popular is the Panchatirthi sacred path starting from the Asi ghat and proceeding along the banks of the Ganges, with five stops to bathe in the waters at designated tirthas (fords, or crossing places). At each stop the pilgrims recite the samkalpa, a vow of worship, which combines their stop at a crossing place in the river with a crossing place to the spiritual world.

Virupaksha Temple, Hampi, India

The first settlement in Hampi dates back to the first century AD. A number of Buddhist sites from that time have been found in the area.

Hampi, on the banks of the Tungabhadra River, was the centre of the Vijayanagar Empire, which dominated the region from 1336 to 1565. The greatest of its rulers was Krishnadevaraya who reigned from 1509 to 1529. The empire was founded by two princes, Hukka (or Harihar) and Bukka, and was celebrated for its power and wealth. Successive emperors were great patrons of art and architecture, as reflected in the many ruins at Hampi.

Hampi amounts to a mediaeval village surrounded by shrines and temples; it is still very much an active place of worship. The heart of the complex, and the place of sacred pilgrimage, is the fifty-metre high Virupaksha Temple complex, built to honour Shiva. (It is also known as the Pampapati Temple.) It was built in the fourth century, almost a thousand years before the emergence of the Vijayanagar empire. Pilgrims sleep outside all night, waiting to get into the temple at first light. They then walk past lines of saddhus in the 700-metre long avenue that leads to the entrance. The avenue passes abandoned colonnades that were the approaches to the king's palace. The temple's first gate is topped by a pyramidal tower covered with sculptures and carvings; a second gate further in leads to a large court in the centre of which is the Bhuvanesvari shrine. This is magnificent and atmospheric, lit by hundreds of oil lamps and candles housed in small holes in the wall. There are many images to be seen, the main one being a round stone linga which is the object of much veneration.

On the opposite bank of the river is Anegondi. There are many myths surrounding these twin towns. In one of them Pampa, the daughter of Brahma, became the wife of Lord Shiva and encouraged him to live in the area.

There is a large-scale project of restoration, excavation and protection of the ruins at Hampi, with much government involvement; it was listed as a World Heritage site in 1987. Other major buildings at Hampi include the Vitthala Temple with its stone chariot, the wheels of which once actually rotated; the monolithic statues of Lakshmi, Narasimha and Ganesa; the Krishna temple; and many Jain temples.

Hampi is famous for the annual Purandara festival, held in January/February in the Vitthala Temple, to celebrate the birth of the medieval poet-composer, Purandar.

Xi'an (Sian), China

Xi'an is famously known as the site of the Terracotta Army, and the excavations at the burial site of China's first emperor, Shi Huangdi (sometimes known as Ch'in Shih Huang Ti) who lived between 259 and 210 BC, may yet reveal some of the most fabulous artefacts relating to death rituals seen in the world.

Shi Huangdi was the founder of the Qin (or Ch'in) dynasty. It is probable that China gets its name from this dynasty. In 246 BC, at the age of just thirteen, he ascended the throne of the feudal state of Qin, one of seven main kingdoms. It was a violent time, known as the Warring States (Zhan Guo) period. Shi Huangdi continued a process, started by his predecessors, of uniting the feudal states into which China at the time was sub-divided, and created a unified country, declaring himself emperor in 221 BC.

He abolished the feudal system, and the ruling families of the old states were forced to live in Shi Huangdi's capital. The country was then divided into thirty-six provinces or commanderies (later enlarged to forty-two), further sub-divided into counties. These commanderies each had a civil governor, a military commander, and an imperial inspector, all appointed by the emperor.

As part of the unification process Shi Huangdi standardised laws throughout the country, created a common currency, and standardised weights and measures and the written language. He brought the defence and economy of China under centralised control. As part of the country's defences, he began construction of a major part of what was to become the Great Wall of China, built to keep out invading Huns. A huge project, it consisted both of new building and the linking of existing walls that had been constructed by the various kingdoms. The social and political structures he set up lasted virtually unchanged for two thousand years, until the revolution of 1911 that ended Imperial rule.

One of his least popular actions, in 213 BC, was the burning of all books that disagreed with his philosophies and beliefs about history, an act that was continued by his son who took power after him. The aim was mainly to eliminate the teachings of Confucius. There was an ironic footnote to this act; Shi Huangdi preserved in his palace only books he approved of, but people hid and buried the books they believed important. When Shi Huangdi's palace burned down, his approved books were destroyed; the hidden ones he disapproved of survived and were collected together by the leaders of the dynasty that followed.

Shi Huangdi was also known to bury alive those who disagreed with him; over four hundred and fifty dissenting scholars were known to be killed in this way. When his eldest son objected to his actions, he was banished to a border region. Perhaps understandably, Shi Huangdi was not a popular ruler, despite his achievements, and survived several assassination attempts.

If one word characterised Shi Huangdi's life it was: death. He was obsessed by it throughout his life. Immediately he became emperor, he set about building his tomb, a task which took the efforts of over seven hundred thousand forced labourers. In his last days he became paranoid, secretive and fearful. Not surprisingly, he was afraid of assassination and spent years searching for an elixir of immortality. He became obsessed with the mystical, surrounding himself with alchemists, magicians and three hundred astrologers, their task being to procure this remedy. Ironically, Shi Huangdi died after travelling to an island (probably Japan) in search of the elixir. Having prepared his tomb throughout his life, a huge complex on Mount Lishan, Shi Huangdi was buried in it.

The tomb was officially discovered in 1974 and is still to be studied in detail. In that year, peasants digging a well unearthed pieces of terracotta. When they reached over three metres down into the earth they discovered what was described as 'a pottery man': a full-size (even slightly larger-than-life) figure made of terracotta. In fact they had accidentally broken into an outer chamber of the tomb complex which, it would be discovered over the next few years, contained somewhere between six thousand and eight thousand full-sized figures: an army to protect the emperor in his afterlife. Many ranks of the army were represented, and every soldier's expression is unique; it is thought that each one represents a real, living soldier of Shi Huangdi's time. They were originally painted in bright colours, and in their hands they carried real weapons: crossbows, swords, scimitars, and so on. Along with the figures were terracotta horses and chariots.

The first archaeologist to work on the find was Yuan Zhongyi, who became leader of the excavations and director of the on-site museum. Examination of the first chamber took three years, and the second and third chambers were located shortly afterwards. The Chinese, once reticent towards foreign visitors, have been very accommodating to tourists wishing to see the terracotta army, and have organised tours to watch the work underway, enclosed the site in a huge building which protects it from the elements, and built a museum. Two million visitors a year now visit the site, bringing much-needed wealth to the country.

Despite the efforts to date, little of the tomb has yet been excavated. What is speculated – mostly based on the writings of Sima Qian, an historian writing around one hundred years after Shi Huangdi's death – is extraordinary. According to Sima Qian, and indeed to legend, the tomb is actually a vast underground city, possibly fifteen storeys high and covering twenty square miles. It includes a palace with a banqueting hall capable of seating one hundred people, a cemetery and protecting walls. The chambers contain a three-dimensional model of China. The Yangtze and other prominent Chinese rivers are reproduced in mercury, and a mechanical device keeps them constantly flowing. The rivers are populated by waterfowl made of gold and silver. The heavens are reproduced on the tomb's ceiling – an underground planetarium with the sun, moon and constellations made of pearls.

To prevent grave-robbers stealing the riches it is said that concealed crossbows were installed which would automatically be triggered, killing intruders. (That said, it is almost certain that tomb-robbers did break in and plunder the complex centuries ago.) Security was furthered by the designers and labourers being entombed within, to prevent them revealing the secrets of the emperor's last resting place. Hu Hai ordered that women of the palace who had not given birth to boys should also be entombed there. To hide the whole 'city' from prying eyes, trees and grasses were planted over the mausoleum to disguise it as an ordinary hill.

MYSTICAL AND SACRED SITES IN AFRICA

Aksum (or Axum), Ethiopia

Aksum is an ancient town in northern Ethiopia, once the seat of the kingdom of Aksum, and now a tourist town and religious centre.

In the central square, 126 granite obelisks stand, or lie fallen and broken. One fallen obelisk, measuring thirty-four metres, is believed to be the tallest ever erected. They range from virtually plain blocks to intricately inscribed and carved works. Some, because of the nature of the artwork on them, give the appearance of being tall, slender buildings. One of the most recent carved obelisks heralds the adoption of Christianity into the region. At least twenty-seven carved stone thrones have been unearthed in the ruins of the ancient palace in Aksum.

Ethiopia's heritage can be traced back to cultural and trading exchanges as far back as the late first millennium BC. Arabian immigrants arrived in the Ethiopian highlands from beyond the Red Sea, bringing with them their religious beliefs and a tradition of monumental stone building that would be a major influence on the region's own architectural and religious traditions. Perhaps most famous is the eighteen by fifteen-metre stone structure at Yeha, composed of three-metre sandstone blocks fitted together without the use of mortar, which is thought to have been created in the fifth or fourth century BC. It was probably originally a temple to a south Arabian deity.

Christianity was at first followed only by Aksum's royal elite, but in the later part of the fifth century AD it spread to the general population through missionaries fleeing into Ethiopia from the Roman empire. These worshippers were drawn to the Ethiopian Orthodox Church because it maintained the monophysite doctrine (the argument over the duality of Jesus) after this was branded heretical in AD 451 by the Council of Chalcedon.

The Ethiopian Orthodox Church has survived to the present day. Some of the most famous examples of Ethiopian Christian art post-dating the Aksumite period are the rock-cut churches of Lalibela (see entry).

Aksum has long been regarded as a holy city for the Ethiopian Orthodox Church. According to tradition, the Church of St Mary of Zion contains the Ark of the Covenant, which was brought there by King Menelik I, son of the Queen of Sheba and King Solomon of Israel, as described in the thirteenth-century Kebra Negast, The Book of the Glory of Kings.

Over the centuries, the church there has been destroyed and rebuilt several times; the present structure dates from the seventeenth century. A second church of St Mary of Zion was built near the old structure in 1965 by Emperor Haile Selassie I.

Giza, Egypt

The Giza Plateau is now a tourist attraction, part of Greater Cairo. The three main pyramids on the plateau include The Great Pyramid of Khufu (Cheops).

The Great Pyramid is generally believed to have been built by Pharaoh Khufu, of the Fourth Dynasty, in about 2560 BC, to serve as his tomb. According to the Greek historian Herodotus, when he visited the pyramids he was told by priests that it took around twenty years to construct, though there is considerable dispute as to how it was achieved.

The Great Pyramid was 147 metres high when built, though it has lost almost ten metres over time. It was originally cased in limestone, most of which has been removed, but a similar crown of limestone still exists on the neighbouring Pyramid of Khafra (or Chefren), indicating what it would have looked like. For over four thousand years it was the tallest man-made structure on Earth. The sides are precisely aligned to the cardinal compass points, and the precision of those sides, each 751 feet (approximately 229 metres) in length, is astonishingly accurate.

The Great Pyramid alone could accommodate St Peter's in Rome, the cathedrals of Florence, Milan and Westminster, and St Paul's in London.

To the south lies the pyramid of Khufu's son and heir, Khafra; a third pyramid, much smaller than the other two, was built by King Menkaure (or Mycerinus), who was probably a brother of Khafra. Little is known of these three pharaohs and their bodies have not been found, probably having been looted many centuries ago.

Despite a plethora of theories concerning the pyramids – from being sources of power-generation to beacons for alien spacecraft – it is almost certain that their main function is as tombs from which the Kings could commence their voyages to the afterlife.

It is the nature of Egyptian belief about the afterlife that may have shaped the pyramids. It is probable that the Egyptians believed that they would gain the protection and blessing of their deceased Pharaoh who, in death, dwelt with the gods. The greater the pyramid's size, the greater the blessing on the living. It is possible that they were not built by slave labour, as often supposed, but by a workforce proud of their achievements and who were rewarded for their efforts with a good living. The pyramids were probably a source of pride for workers and other citizens alike.

Along with the Pharaoh's mortal remains the tombs would have contained food, jewellery and other implements of use in the afterlife. Many may have been plundered but intact tombs discovered, such as that of King Tutenkhamen, give an indication of the variety of materials buried with the King for his use.

Ancient Egyptian writings speak of the spirit 'ba' which left the body on death to travel to the next life, but which remained dependent on the physical body for its own well-being; hence the need to protect the physical body after death with embalming and protective entombment. The texts also refer to 'ka', a lifeforce that was born with the body but which lingered after its physical death; the food and liquids left in the tombs were thought to provide nourishment for ka.

In all three pyramids, passageways lead to the burial chambers. The Great Pyramid contains several corridors, galleries and shafts, and at the heart is the King's Chamber housing the King's sarcophagus. This is made of granite, which also lines the chamber.

The form of the pyramid is probably designed to represent a link to the stars, the home of the gods; British Egyptologist I E S Edwards suggested that it was designed to emulate shafts of sunlight streaming down to earth through the clouds, again a representation of the light of the gods. The pyramid is probably a development from the mastaba, a low rectangular structure covering a rock tomb, connected by a vertical shaft. This may have developed into a step pyramid, such as the fabulous example at Saqqara (see entry), the tomb of Djoser of the Third Dynasty. In turn, the Giza pyramids may be the ultimate development of this tomb style.

Robert Bauval and Adrian Gilbert, in their book *The Orion Mystery*, speculate that the three pyramids are designed to reproduce the stars of Orion's Belt in the Orion constellation, and that the shafts inside the Great Pyramid are aligned precisely to Orion, adjusting for the time the pyramid was built. The whole structure was therefore a home on Earth for the God Osiris, who normally dwelt in the stars. What were once thought to be air shafts leading outward from the King's Chamber and the Queen's Chamber turn out to have been accurately aligned with the stars Orion and Sirius: the stars sacred to the King and Queen respectively. The shafts may have been designed to 'target' those stars, to send the souls of the Pharaoh and his consort there. By working back to the time when the shafts in the pyramid aligned with the stars precisely, Bauval and Gilbert speculate that the pyramid was built in the year 10,500 BC, far earlier than generally supposed.

The other mystery of the Giza Plateau is the Great Sphinx. The Sphinx is almost twenty metres tall, carved from a limestone outcrop and is severely weathered. It has spent time buried up to the neck in sand, and there have been various other periods when it was more fully exposed, as at present. It is thought to represent the sun dog and there is debate whether the body is more canine or feline in nature. The face is thought to be that of Pharaoh Khafre, near whose pyramid it stands. It was originally thought to have been built around 2500 BC, but various theorists have since suggested that it could have been built much earlier: anywhere from 7000 BC to 10,500 BC, a date in line with Bauval and Gilbert's speculations above. Part of the controversy is based on whether the erosion of the sphinx was by wind or water, if by water then it is believed that it has to have existed at a time when rainfall was much more extensive. However, all of the assumptions relating to this are hotly challenged and debated.

There are fascinating paranormal connections to the Sphinx;

perhaps the most fascinating are the utterings of the 'Sleeping prophet', Edgar Cayce, who when in trances claimed that there were hidden areas below the Sphinx and that, near the end of the twentieth century, a Hall of Records would be discovered there. Some modern researchers have suggested that such a Hall does exist, but that it is being kept secret. Those opposed to conspiracy theory dispute this.

Another feature of the Giza Plateau is the museum now housing the world's oldest surviving boat, the Sun Boat, which was discovered in 1954. It may actually have brought the body of the pharaoh to the pyramid for burial, or it may have been intended as transport for his spirit into the afterlife. In all, five boat pits were located, and two boats recovered. Some scholars believe they were funerary boats, with indications that they were actually used on the Nile, but the absence of sails suggests they were not, and may have been intended as solar boats for Khufu, reincarnated as the God Re, to use on his voyages across the sky.

Zahl A Hawass, director-general of Egypt's most significant archaeological sites, has said: 'You have to know that the ancient Egyptians who made this civilisation were really normal people like us. They were not giants; they were not people who came from Atlantis or outer space. We have to learn that those people believed in God, and they did all this building because of their beliefs. If you believe in something you can do it. This is a very important lesson that you have to understand from the past to improve the future.'

Great Zimbabwe

Great Zimbabwe was once the capital of a large, indigenous state that existed between the Limpopo and Zambezi rivers. It is today a complex of stone walls and ruins, and is perhaps the finest, and certainly the largest, example of over fifty madzimbahwe: towns with stone walls thought to be regional centres.

Great Zimbabwe is believed to have been the major sacred and ritual centre of the ancestors of the Shona people. It was started in around AD 1130 and occupied for two to three hundred years.

Excavation of the site has located grey-green soapstone bird images, a number of fragments of decorated soapstone dishes, and many beads and ceramics, which were probably originally imported, suggesting strong trading links developed around the area. Indeed, it seems that Great Zimbabwe was the centre of a complex structure of trading routes which linked together many areas of southern Africa, as well as connecting with Arab traders who had established a foothold on the Indian Ocean coast.

The town was divided into two areas. Most of its ten thousand or so inhabitants would have lived close together in mud-and-thatch huts. The elite – a small, ruling and religious group – would have lived in the centre of the town, in houses protected from general view by high stone walls.

The focal point of the town of Great Zimbabwe is a high granite outcrop, on the summit of which is a set of stone-walled enclosures. One of these enclosures was undoubtedly a place of worship; research after the site was rediscovered in the nineteenth century revealed altars and also carved stone birds which would have represented the souls of the former rulers. The other large hill enclosure probably contained the residence of either the ruler or the leading shaman.

Much of the architecture – stone towers, monoliths and altars – suggests a religious purpose. The word 'zimbabwe', while mainly meaning 'stone houses' also means 'venerated houses'. The site appears to have been mostly associated with the god who would be asked to provide rain to make crops abundant and healthy. Chief god of the early religion practised here was Mwari – the creator. The practitioners were the Mbire, an early Shona people, who also worshipped mbondoro, the spirits of the ruling dynasties. Great Zimbabwe remained a ritual site for the Shona people into the nineteenth century.

Analysis of the original use of the site has been limited and the results unclear, but efforts have been made to apply knowledge drawn from the ethnography of the Shona people, in particular looking at aspects of their mythology. This work has mostly been undertaken by researcher Thomas Huffman, who believes that the circular Great Enclosure, situated in the valley, was probably an initiation centre for young women, and that the layout of the town in general is a symbolic arrangement of male and female space. Alternatively, if the hill enclosure was the residence of the shaman, then the Great Enclosure may have been the residence of the rulers.

Jenne, Mali

Jenne was once one of the greatest centres of trade, learning and religion in West Africa. As a result of caravan contact with Islam, the kings of Mali, in around AD 1300, became Muslim. It is best known for the so-called Friday Mosque, named because Muslims pray together on Fridays, which is the largest mud-brick building in the world. The present one was reconstructed in 1906–7, the third of a series of such mosques dating from the thirteenth century. Although it is a relatively modern structure, the site itself is regarded as having been sacred for a much longer period.

Nearby, the large mound called Jenne-jeno (ancient Jenne) is claimed by oral tradition as the original settlement. Much ancient broken pottery has been found at the site. Excavation in the 1970s and 1980s show that the mound is composed of over five metres of debris, accumulated during sixteen hundred years of occupation beginning around 200 BC. The original settlement arose on a patch of relatively high ground, which protected it from flooding, and consisted of a few circular huts of straw coated with mud daub. By around AD 450 it was around sixty acres in area.

These discoveries, and the fact that this represents the earliest known urban settlement south of the Sahara, contributed to the entry of Jenne-jeno, along with Jenne, on the list of UNESCO World Heritage sites.

Lalibela Rock Churches, Ethiopia

Roha was a religious and pilgrimage centre in north-central Ethiopia, and capital of the Zague dynasty for around three hundred years. Lalibela, who ruled from the late twelfth to the early thirteenth century, had the churches constructed in his capital in an attempt to replace Aksum as the most prominent Ethiopian city. The popularity of the churches, which still today attract thousands of pilgrims, eventually caused Roha to be renamed after this most distinguished monarch.

The churches were carved out of solid rock, entirely below ground level, and offer a variety of styles. Grecian pillars, Arabesque windows, ancient swastika and Star of David carvings, arches, and Egyptian-like buildings can all be seen.

The general approach was to excavate trenches in a rectangle, thus isolating a solid granite block within. The block was then carved externally and internally, working from the top downward, and the interiors were hollowed out and given vaulted ceilings. Some of the churches were quarried enlargements of caves. Archaeologists have calculated that it would have taken the work of forty thousand people to carve the elaborate church buildings from the rocks.

The work is attributed to divine intervention. Legend has it that Lalibela was drugged by his jealous brother, Harbay, and was carried to heaven by angels. There he spoke with God, who told him to return to earth to build the churches. Lalibela did as he was commanded, but, to assist him in his huge task, the angels worked through the night with him.

The churches are arranged in two main groups, connected by underground passageways. One group includes the House of Emmanuel, the House of Mercurios, Abba Libanos, and the House of Gabriel, all carved from a single rock hill.

The House of Medhane Alem (Saviour of the World) is the largest church, thirty-three metres long, twenty-three metres wide, and ten metres deep. The House of Golgotha is the repository of Lalibela's tomb. The skill of the craftsmen who created the churches has supported those who believe that there was a well-developed Ethiopian tradition of architecture in the past.

Luxor and El-Karnak Temples, Egypt

Luxor represents the southern part of ancient Thebes, El-Karnak occupying the northern part. The temples there are held by many

Angkor Wat, Cambodia: the temple complex was built between AD 1112 and AD 1152 and is regarded as one of the world's greatest architectural achievements (*PA Photos*)

Varanasi, India: the holiest of cities for Hindus who gather along the banks of the Ganges on these terraced landings known as 'ghats' (*Hulton Archive*)

Virupaksha Temple, India: this temple in the centre of Hampi was built to honour Shiva and is a place of sacred pilgrimage (*Paranormal Picture Library/Penny and Spencer James*)

Xi'an, China: the fabulous tomb of China's first emperor, Shi Huangdi, is guarded by thousands of life-sized figures known as the Terracotta Army (*Paranormal Picture Library/Jackie Watt*)

The entrance to the Temple of Luxor, Egypt which was built by Amenhotep III on the site of an older temple (*Paranormal Picture Library/Adrian and Maureen Pruss*)

The Forecourt of Amenhotep III adjoining the Hypostyle Hall at Karnak, Egypt (*Paranormal Picture Library/Adrian and Maureen Pruss*)

St Catherine's Monastery at Mount Sinai is the oldest active Christian monastery in the world and is situated on the presumed site of the Burning Bush seen by Moses (*Paranormal Picture Library/Adrian and Maureen Pruss*)

The Great Serpent Mound, Ohio, USA: serpents are often symbols of transformation as when they shed their skins they can be said to be 'reborn' (*Hulton Archive*)

The Devil's Tower, Wyoming, USA: this site has been a sacred location for native Americans since before written records began (*Paranormal Picture Library/Steve Gamble*)

The Inca settlement of Machu Picchu was once an important religious centre, perhaps a place of training for priestesses and brides for the Inca ruling families (*Hulton Archive*)

Monte Alban in Mexico flourished from around 500 BC to AD 500. At its peak it had a population of around 25,000 (*Paranormal Picture Library/Adrian and Maureen Pruss*)

The Temple of the Inscriptions at Palenque, Mexico is the burial place of the ruler Pacal (*Paranormal Picture Library/Adrian and Maureen Pruss*)

Shiprock, New Mexico, USA: the 'winged rock' of Navajo legend (*Hulton Archive*)

The Pyramid of the Sun at Teotihuacan in Mexico is one of the largest structures ever built in the western hemisphere (*Paranormal Picture Library/Adrian and Maureen Pruss*)

Uluru, Australia: the most sacred site for aboriginal people and a place of spiritual potency where many 'song lines' and 'dreaming tracks' come together (*PA Photos*)

to be the most complicated examples of architecture in Egypt. The Karnak site was known as Ipet-isut (meaning 'most select place') by the Egyptians of the time. Thebes was the capital of Egypt from around 2000 BC, reaching its peak during the New Kingdom. Although the mud-brick palaces of Thebes have long disappeared, the stone temples have largely survived.

The site of the Temple of Luxor was occupied by previous temples, and was already considered a sacred site before the erection of this huge structure. It remains a place of pilgrimage and worship today.

The Temple of Luxor was built by Amenhotep III on the site of an older temple dedicated to the local triad, Amun, Khonsu and Mut. Later, Horemheb built an avenue of sphinxes to connect the Temple of Luxor with the Temple of Karnak for the procession during the Opet Festival. Ramses II added the entrance hall, pylons and obelisks.

The Temple is situated close to the Nile, and has been in almost continuous use as a place of worship. During the Christian era its hypostyle hall was converted into a Christian church, and the remains of another Coptic church can be seen off to the west. A mosque was built over the hidden Temple ruins, and when the Temple was discovered the mosque was preserved as an integral part of the site.

The Temple was central to the Festival of Opet, which was designed to reconcile the human and divine aspects of the Pharaoh. A procession of images of the current royal family began at Karnak and ended at the Temple of Luxor; in later centuries this was achieved by barge down the Nile. Huge crowds of soldiers, dancers, musicians and officials walked alongside the barge procession. Once they reached the temple, the Pharaoh and his priests entered, and there the mortal form of the Pharaoh was united with his divine essence, known as 'ka', so that the Pharaoh was transformed into a divine being. This festival therefore secured the powers of the Pharaoh's rule.

Two miles away is the Temple of Karnak. This actually comprises three main temples, some smaller enclosed temples, and several outer temples. It took a succession of Pharaohs over thirteen hundred years to develop the site. Of the main temples, the Temple of Amun, is situated in the centre of the entire complex. The Temple of Monthu is to the north, and the Temple of Mut to the south.

Most striking of the features of the Temple complex is the Hypostyle Hall, considered by many to be one of the world's greatest architectural masterpieces. Construction of the Hall began during Ramses I's reign, continued under Seti I and was completed by Seti's son, Ramses II. The walls, ceilings and columns were painted with natural earth tones. The difference in height between the central and the aisle columns provided natural light through clerestory windows with vertical stone slats. The arrangement must have produced a sense of a forest carved in stone, with slatted beams of light producing almost rainforest-like areas of light and shadows. The Hall was originally roofed, the ceiling being twenty-five metres high and supported by twelve sandstone columns in two central rows of six, each capped with papyrus capitals. Each row is flanked by seven rows of smaller columns thirteen metres high; a total of 134 columns in all. The outer walls are covered with scenes of battle: either genuine victories or images of ritual symbolism.

The Hypostyle Hall leads through to the narrow court where there once stood several obelisks. One of these, twenty-one metres tall, was erected by Tuthmosis I, father of Hatshepsut. Beyond this is the only remaining obelisk of Hatshepsut, which is thirty metres tall; Hatshepsut was an exceptional woman who dared to challenge the tradition of male rule.

When he acquired power, Tuthmosis III, who was Hatshepsut's successor, built a high wall around her obelisk, probably to hide it rather than go to the trouble of tearing it down. Or perhaps he feared some kind of divine punishment if he desecrated it, and found hiding it an acceptable alternative.

Deeper into the complex is the original heart of the Temple, the sanctuary, or Holy of Holies. The sanctuary visible today was built by Philip Arrhidaeus, brother of Alexander the Great, but it was constructed on the site of the original built by Tuthmosis III, and contains blocks from that sanctuary and several original inscriptions.

The Temple of Karnak is the largest religious building ever created. The area of the Temple of Amun alone would house ten typical European cathedrals. The Hypostyle Hall, at over five thousand square metres, remains today the largest room of any religious building in the world.

As with all Egyptian temples, it is believed that the Temple of Amun symbolises the original island of creation from which everything formed, and the columns are stone representations of vegetation thought to have been growing there. According to myth, the earth was once covered only in water from which an island of mud emerged. From this island a reed plant grew on which Horus, the falcon-god, perched. The whole temple recreates this myth in stone.

Mount Sinai

According to the Bible (Exodus 3), Moses had encamped at the foot of Mount Horeb, called the Mountain of God, and tended sheep there. At that time an angel of the Lord appeared to him from the Burning Bush, and he heard the voice of God speak to him from within, telling him that he would send him to Egypt to bring his people, the people of Israel, out of Egyptian oppression and to 'a good and broad land, a land flowing with milk and honey' (Exodus 3:8). Moses was told by God that 'you shall serve God upon this mountain'.

When Moses led his people out of Egypt, they travelled for three months and then came to the wilderness of Sinai where they camped by the same mountain (Exodus 19). Moses climbed up and God told him that his people would be 'a kingdom of priests and a holy nation' (Exodus 19:6). God said that he would come down on to the Mount – the Bible here refers to it as Mount Sinai (Exodus 19:11) – on the third day, when he would appear to all the people.

On the third day thunder, lightning and a thick cloud, followed by a trumpet blast, announced to the people that they could go to the foot of the mountain. Mount Sinai was wrapped in smoke, because the Lord descended upon it in fire (Exodus 19:18), and God commanded Moses to climb the mountain where God recited the Decalogue, generally known as the Ten Commandments, and a series of ordinances which became the Law, or Torah, forming the basis of Jewish traditions.

Moses then built an altar at the foot of the mountain, and twelve pillars to represent the twelve tribes of Israel.

Later, during a stay of forty days and forty nights on the mountain, Moses received the Commandments from God set out on Tablets of Stone. On his way down, he found that his people had melted down the gold of their jewellery and ornaments and had created a statue of a golden calf, which they were worshipping. In anger, he smashed the Tablets, new ones being created to replace them after he had subdued an uprising amongst the people.

The location of Mount Sinai is unknown, but the most popular candidate for its location is in the mountains at the southern tip of the Sinai Peninsula where there is Jabal Katrinah which has two peaks: the northern one now named Horeb and the southern called Jabal Musa (the Mountain of Moses). Jabal Musa is traditionally considered to be Mount Sinai.

One pilgrim to the site in AD 330 was Helena, mother of the Roman emperor Constantine, who ordered a chapel to be built at the foot of the mountain, at the presumed location of the Burning Bush. Later, the building was extended and fortified on the orders of Emperor Justinian between 527 and 565 AD. It is now St Catherine's Monastery, held by many to be the oldest working Christian monastery in the world. It was designed to hold the bones of St Catherine of Alexandria, stored in a marble reliquary in the Basilica. The Monastery also houses a small tenth-or eleventh-century mosque, probably built to appease the Islamic authorities of that time. A small chapel, known as the Chapel of St Triphone (also known as the Skull House), houses the skulls of dead monks. Although established and patronised through most of its history by the Russian Orthodox Church, St Catherine's Monastery now falls under the auspices of the Greek Orthodox Church.

Although it is a site much visited by millions who believe that Jabal Musa is indeed Mount Sinai, there are other locations suggested, including one in Saudi Arabia.

The main references in respect of Mount Sinai being located in north-west Saudi Arabia are in the writings of Harvard professor Frank Cross, but Chuck Missler in *The Real Mount Sinai?* and Howard Blum in *The Gold of Exodus* suggest that the location might be the 2,500-metre high mountain in Saudi Arabia, called Jabal al Lawz. This is based on a visit to that location by 'two adventurers' – to use Howard Blum's phrase – Bob Cornuke and Larry Williams. The pair apparently found that the vegetation there was suitable for grazing, in keeping with Moses having kept sheep there. In a natural amphitheatre between the mountain's two peaks Missler suggests that 'the most momentous drama in history had been played out'. Just to the south is a huge area Cornuke and Williams believe could be the battlefield of Rephidim (Exodus 17). They also discovered what is described as an altar of stacked boulders and pictograms that might represent the Apis bulls of Egypt; the speculation is that this could be the altar for the Golden Calf.

The whole area is a military-protected site, part of a five-million-dollar-plus Saudi/American military installation called Operation Peace Shield, and the 'adventurers' had to sneak in to examine the site. Despite that, when they found a cave similar to the one where Moses slept, they felt unable to enter it; although having completed a daring and dangerous foray to see the Mountain, they felt the power of the cave too strong to break through. It is alleged that during the building of two nine-metre tall radar towers on the summit of the mountain, a worker vanished, later to emerge from the cave in a delusional state.

Of course, if the most sacred mountain in Jewish tradition were to turn out to be in Arab territory it would have considerable ramifications. Some speculate that the very suggestion is part of a plot to destabilise the Jewish faith. More tongue-in-cheek, one Israeli official commented to Howard Blum: 'This could only happen to the Jews. After all these years we find Mount Sinai and guess what, it's in Saudi Arabia.' It should be borne in mind, however, that Mount Sinai is not only sacred to Jews and

Christians, but also to Muslims, as Moses is also a Muslim prophet.

Other sites have also been suggested. One is Mount Karkom in a remote part of the Negev Desert, close to the border between Israel and Egypt. It was examined in 1955 when the Jewish-Italian archaeologist Professor Emmanuel Anati visited the area. He found considerable rock art from the Middle Bronze Age, depicting religious scenes and people at prayer. One piece of rock art was a grid divided into ten spaces which Anati believes could be the physical representation of the Ten Commandments. Another piece depicts a snake next to a staff which, some have speculated, could be a reference to the Biblical passage where Moses casts down his rod and it turns into a snake (Exodus 7: 8–12). Anati discovered, at the site, twelve standing stones that could be the twelve pillars erected by Moses to represent the twelve tribes of Israel. Nearby is a cave that could fit the description of the cave in which Moses slept. Certainly the site has been a place of human dwelling since the Stone Age. During the Bronze Age there was much activity at the mountain, evidenced by numerous circles of boulders that were used for religious rites and burials. Several ruined buildings in the area have the appearance of having been early temples. The site has been called a 'kind of prehistoric Mecca with large groups of people coming to worship there'.

Another possible location is also in the Negev. In 1995 Dr Gerald Aardsma suggested Mount Yeroham as Mount Sinai. He believed that it was within the right distance from Egypt for the people of Israel to have travelled during the Exodus. By his reckoning they could have travelled no more than 630 miles at the outside; Mount Yeroham is just 150 miles from Egypt. Aardsma calculates that there must be a wilderness in front of Mount Sinai sufficient to allow the encampment of six hundred thousand people; this he believes would require 1,377 acres of land. He believes that Jabal Musa does not fulfil this criteria whereas Mount Yeroham does. The considerable quantity of pottery remains found on the plain at the foot of Mount Yeroham also suggests to Aardsma that it could be the site of a huge encampment, the six hundred thousand having lived there for a year. The pottery also appears to date from the correct time period. Aardsma points out that such a large number of people camping at one site would need a water supply, and there is a reservoir at Mount Yeroham whereas there is no such supply at, say, Mount Karkom.

Why is the identification of this mountain so important? To those to whom the mountain is sacred the answer is obvious; they want to know where a significant event in their religion occurred, and they want to be able to stand where Moses stood and perhaps feel the energy of the land of which God stated: 'the place on which you are standing is holy ground'. For the non-devout it is still an important quest; there is a continuing debate as to whether Moses was a real or fictional person, whether the Exodus was an event or a story. Although there is no Egyptian record of the Exodus, as might have been expected, scholars have pointed out that it would be unusual for a race to invent a history in which it was once a slave-nation. Confirmation of the location of Mount Sinai would therefore strengthen the claims of the Old Testament of the Bible to be history rather than mythology.

Ngome, Central Zululand

Between 22 August 1955 and 2 May 1971 there were ten reported visions of the Virgin Mary seen by Sister Reinolda May (also known as Sister Mashiane) of the Missionary Benedictine Sisters. Sister Reinolda was born in 1901 and left Germany in 1925, working in various missions until May 1938 when she went to work in Nongoma and nearby Ngome, in Central Zululand.

Sister Reinolda was a well respected, much loved and greatly valued member of the community, and one of the best-known missionaries in the area.

The first message she received was on the feast day of the Immaculate Conception. Shortly after Holy Communion, she saw the Virgin Mary standing close in front of her. As the sister described: 'Everything was seen in spirit. I was drawn into another atmosphere. Mary showed herself in a wonderful light more beautiful than the sun. She was robed all in a white, flowing veil from top to toe. Upon her breast rested a big host surrounded by a brilliant corona radiating life. She was a living monstrance. Mary stood upon the globe, hands and feet visible. I felt like entering a cloud, drawn by Mary, away from the earth. I had my eyes closed but I saw so much light that, for several days, I was very much dazzled by the beauty and light that I had seen.' Mary spoke to Sister Reinolda saying: 'Call me "Tabernacle of The Most High". You too are such a tabernacle, believe it. I wish to be called upon by this title for the glory of my son. I wish that more such tabernacles be prepared. I mean human hearts. I wish that the altars be surrounded by praying people more frequently. Don't be afraid. Make it known.'

Sister Reinolda saw the Virgin again seven times in the following three years. Mary desired that a shrine be erected for her 'in the place where the seven springs come together'. The sister's eighth vision was just after she had located a place where she thought the shrine should be built, and Mary confirmed in the vision that that was indeed the place where the shrine should be.

The classroom of the Ngome school building was used as a chapel in those days. A picture of Mary as seen in Sister Reinolda's visions was painted by a German artist, under guidance from the sister, and it hung there until the shrine – a chapel – was constructed. On Pentecost Sunday in 1966 a ceremony was held to open and bless the chapel.

It was twelve years before Sister Reinolda again saw Mary. On 23 March 1970 she had her ninth sighting, in strange circumstances. As the sister described: 'It was the second night after a horrible appearance of the devil. I was woken from my sleep. All around me was light. Mary Tabernacle of the Most High stood beside me. She took me into her arms and consoled me. She said: "I know about your anxiety. I stand by you. I shall not abandon you." Before she disappeared she said: "Look to the other side." There stood St Michael in armour and a lance in his hands. On his right stood a cherubim robed in white, his arms folded. After about two minutes they disappeared and so did the brilliant light. This was a great consolation for me.'

The tenth and final sighting of Mary took place on 2 May 1971, when Sister Reinolda was again visiting Ngome. The sister was in the chapel, praying with a small group of women. Suddenly she noticed that the picture of Mary was alive. She moved a bit forward and her face was unbelievably beautiful. 'I was so excited that I shouted: "Look at Mary!" I was convinced that the women, too, had seen Mary. I was so overwhelmed that I left without saying anything.'

In 1985 a bigger chapel was built on a rock opposite the first shrine and the picture was moved to this new location.

There have been many reports of miraculous healing at Ngome. One, related by Sister Reinolda in a letter to Father Ignatz Jutz, described a woman who had left an unhealed Caesarean section wound untended for too long, and it had become septic. Her doctor had confirmed that there was nothing to be done for her. Sister Reinolda took the painting of the Tabernacle of the Most High to the patient, Monica, who spoke to the picture as if it were a living person. Then Monica told the sister: 'I am not going to die. This lady is going to heal me.' Indeed, the wound spontaneously healed and the woman survived.

Similarly, a cancerous growth was found on the right side of the face of one patient, Sister Deotilla, serious enough to merit referral to a specialist – whom the sister refused to see, deciding to pray instead. Her doctor, H.R. Neuman, later confirmed: 'Sister Deotilla was examined by me on 27 April 1993. She was suffering from skin cancer of the right cheek. She was seen by me again on 10 June 1993, and I found although she had no treatment, all traces of cancer had disappeared.'

Ngome today is a most important place for pilgrims, one of the most important Marian shrines in Africa.

St Mark's Coptic Church, Zeitoun, Egypt

When the Holy Family fled Judaea they travelled to Egypt to seek refuge. According to Matthew 2:12–23: 'When he arose, he took the young Child and His mother by night and departed for Egypt, and was there until the death of Herod, that it might be fulfilled which was spoken by the Lord through the prophet, saying, "Out of Egypt I called My Son".' Tradition claims that the Holy Family rested at the site of what is now St Mark's Coptic Church in Zeitoun. The church contains a shrine dedicated to this visit.

The Christian Coptic Orthodox Church of Egypt is based on the teachings of the apostle St Mark, who brought Christianity to Egypt during the reign of the Roman emperor Nero in the first century AD. The Virgin Mary is especially respected by the Copts.

During 1968 there was a series of Marian visitations at St Mark's Coptic Church in Zeitoun, witnessed by thousands of people, Christians and non-Christians alike, photographed and televised. The hundreds of sightings took place at night, and the visions were largely luminous in nature. The last feast day celebrating the Virgin falls on 2 April and commemorates her under the title Our Lady of Light. It was at 8:30 pm on this day in 1968 that she was said to have appeared on the roof of the Church in a kneeling position, and surrounded by light. The first person to see her was a Muslim, Farouk Mohammed Atwa, who was at the time having a series of operations to deal with gangrene. When he visited hospital on the following day, for his next operation, he was certified completely healed. Although this first sighting only lasted a short time, the apparition was witnessed by several other people.

Over the next three years there were repeated visions of 'Our Lady of Light' on the roof of the church, sometimes two or three times in a week. Often the visions were accompanied by white doves flying around. Many lights were seen in the sky, for which no source could be identified, described by witnesses as 'beautiful diamonds . . . dropping from the heavens'. Up to a quarter of a million devotees would crowd by the church, waiting for a sighting, including Christians, Jews, Muslims, and non-believers. There were many reports of miraculous healings taking place during that period.

The apparitions were approved firstly by the Patriarch of the Coptic Church in Egypt, and later by the Roman Catholic Church whose Cardinal Stephanos investigated the claims and submitted his findings to Pope Paul VI in May 1968; the Pope approved them as visitations of Mary.

No messages were given during these times which makes them

slightly different to many Marian visitations when a witness claims the Virgin imparts a statement.

But the visitations did not permanently cease at the church. On 17 August 2000 they started again, and by October of that year it was estimated that two million people had witnessed the appearances. Again the phenomenon was largely luminous, seen at night, and was accompanied by strange lights and flights of doves; the Virgin was seen in full figure.

One woman interviewed by BBC television said she had had two sightings, both between three o'clock and six o'clock in the morning, when she had seen the Virgin Mary with outstretched hands and a light emanating from them. The sightings were accompanied by a smell of incense and large numbers of pigeons. Another witness, Marcelle Maurice, described seeing the apparition of the Virgin every night: 'I saw the Virgin Mary, flashing lights and big white doves.' This description was matched by that of another witness, Sarwat Hani Marzouk who said: 'I saw Mary, she was beautiful, wearing a blue veil. Light was emanating from her hands, then doves start flying, they were as big as ducks.' Each night the streets would be filled with pilgrims chanting: 'Come Mary, Come,' or 'Your Light is on the Cross', praying for her appearance.

Father Labib, of the nearby Orthodox Copt Dronka Monastery, had special wonder for the lights: 'If you look for the source of the light, you can't find it. This is light from heaven,' he said. British and Egyptian journalists who visited the scene confirmed that there were flashing lights in the sky, but that they too could not find the source. The secretary of the Council of Churches in Assiut, the area in which the sightings took place, told BBC reporters that people had been sleeping in the streets around the Church and standing on rooftops to catch a glimpse of the Virgin.

Not everyone was convinced. 'I haven't seen any light,' Father Baki Sedka, head of a neighbouring Protestant church told The Associated Press. 'I stayed up all night and I didn't see anything except a few pigeons. The appearance of a few pigeons doesn't justify a miracle. This case needs a lot of consideration before we can authoritatively assert these sightings.'

However, during a visit to the United States and Canada in August 2000 the head of the Coptic Church, His Holiness Pope Shenouda III, the 117th successor of St Mark, confirmed the validity of the report of the apparitions. He said that they were a message of comfort from heaven and one of confirmation of the faith of the Copts. He believed they were a sign that heaven is aware of their struggle and is pleased by their perseverance.

The Step Pyramid, Saqqara, Egypt

The Step Pyramid was designed for King Djoser (or Zoser), of the Third Dynasty, by his vizier Imhotep. It is situated in Saqqara, the main necropolis (cemetery) near Cairo and Memphis; it was built around 2630 BC.

The pyramid consists of a series of six levels of stone, decreasing as they ascend to around sixty metres in height. It is the 'bridge' between the old form of tomb architecture known as a mastaba, a low rectangular structure built over a shaft which descended to the burial location, and the smooth-sided pyramids for which Egypt is famous. It is probable that the Step Pyramid was a mastaba that developed during erection. However, while most mastabas were rectangular, the one beneath the Step Pyramid is square. This burial tomb is twenty-eight metres below ground, with a vertical shaft leading to it. It was sealed with a three-ton block of granite. Most of the outer casing of the pyramid is gone, and some of the core masonry has also been lost to time and erosion.

Saqqara was used for burials for thousands of years, and much of it is probably still to be discovered; yet much may be lost for ever. Excavations have been going on there for two centuries, and continue to this day. A statue of Djoser was found, a copy of which is erected in the Tomb Chamber of the pyramid for tourists to see; the original is in the Cairo Museum. Viewing of the pyramid by the public can only be achieved through an observation slit; archaeologists believe the roof to be too unstable and dangerous for large numbers of people to enter it.

The Step Pyramid's creator, Imhotep, is himself a fascinating individual, a mixture of fact and legend. He has been variously referred to as a physician, sage, architect, astronomer and, more frequently, high priest. He was later deified.

Recently new finds have been made at Saqqara. A French team of archaeologists led by Professor Jean Leclant discovered the remains of a previously unknown pyramid belonging to Queen Ankhnspepi. She was the wife of the Pharaoh Pepi I and mother of Pepi II who reigned during Egypt's Sixth Dynasty. Then in February 2001 it was announced that the tomb of a priest of the sun god Ra, from the time of Pharaoh Akhenaten, had been discovered there. Gaballah Ali Gaballah, secretary-general of Egypt's Supreme Council of Antiquities, commented: 'the sands of Saqqara still hold lots of secrets waiting to be discovered by future archaeologists.'

MYSTICAL AND SACRED SITES IN THE AMERICAS

Cahokia, Illinois, USA

The Cahokia Mounds State Historic Site, on the Mississippi River, houses the remnants of the largest prehistoric Native American city north of Mexico. It is presently administered by the Illinois Historic Preservation Agency and is a United Nations World Heritage site.

The city thrived between AD 1050 and 1250 and was abandoned around 1500. It covers an area of over two square miles and probably housed up to forty thousand people. Almost one and a half million cubic metres of earth had to be moved to create the complex of ceremonial mounds. One of these, the Monk's Mound – so named because a group of French Trappist monks set up a monastery there for a few years during the early 1800s – is the largest single prehistoric earthwork in North America. It was the site of the main temple, and alone covers fourteen acres, rising through four terraces to a height of over thirty metres.

The whole complex is thought to have been the largest political, social and religious centre in the North American south-east. It maintained cultural ties with similar settlements throughout the area, and was the centre of trading networks across North America. William R Iseminger, Cahokia's principal archaeologist commented: 'The ancient city was well planned. It included ceremonial mounds, open plazas, market places, ranked residential districts, workshop areas, and cemeteries.' Satellite towns ringed the main complex; for example, over forty similar mounds are believed to have been located in present day St Louis.

It appears that the mounds had various uses; some appear to have been built for purely aesthetic appreciation, some as land markings, some as places of burial, some for ceremonial purposes. The Monk's Mound, while largely ceremonial, may also have doubled as a 'town square' for public meetings. The Cahokia site contains the largest collection of such mounds in the country; there are sixty-eight remaining from a possible 120 that once adorned the site.

It has been estimated that it could have taken two hundred or more years to build the Monk's Mound in its various stages of expansion; possibly all done by people carrying earth in baskets.

The complex was contained within a log stockade, at first a double-walled structure, but later replaced by a single wall. At its centre was a 200-acre Sacred Precinct where the rulers, religious and political, lived and were buried. On the Monk's Mound would have stood a pole-framed temple with a grass roof, probably adorned with carved wooden animal figures and decorated with beads, feathers and cloth.

The site appears to have been abandoned, possibly because the natural resources of the site were overworked and exhausted and the people had to move on. Alternatively, climate change may have affected crop production, or the tribe may have succumbed to an aggressor.

Examination of the site has been revealing. One mound, known as Mound 72, contained the remains of a tall man buried around 1050. He seems to have died in his early forties and was laid to rest on a bed of twenty thousand shell-made ornaments and eight hundred ornamental arrow heads. The grave also contained mica, copper, a staff, and stones used in games. It is assumed that he was an important leader, but the full story appears to have been somewhat chilling. With him were buried four men with their heads and hands cut off, and fifty-three women aged between fifteen and twenty-five who were probably strangled. The supposition is that these were the victims of human sacrifice, as they were all from a similar age range and unlikely to have died naturally all at the same time. If so, then it is a large number of people to have been sent with the leader on his way to the afterlife, and more than has been found anywhere else in North America.

Nearby more burial sites and a charnel house were located, and 280 skeletons have been unearthed, many apparently thrown into their graves without ceremony. Some had been killed by arrows – the arrowheads were still within the bodies – and some were beheaded. Either they were a defeated enemy, or a crushed internal rebellion.

As with so many of the ancient communities, there is clear evidence that the people who lived at the site were advanced astronomers. On the outside of the stockade were located posts that indicate the exact point of the sunrise during the spring and autumn equinoxes; other posts appear to indicate the winter and summer solstices. Monk's Mound is so constructed that the sun seems to rise directly out of it at these key times. The ring of posts seems to have been a calendar, and was nick-named Woodhenge in deference to England's Stonehenge.

Bruce Smith, director of the archaeobiology programme and a curator at the Smithsonian Institution suggests: 'Through Woodhenge, and dealing with the sun, they could solidify their position as middlemen or arbiters and show the general populace how the sun moved, and predict it.'

Recent excavations have thrown up a possible surprise, however. There appears to be a stone structure beneath Monk's Mound. It was located by accident, when drilling was underway to construct a water drainage system under the Mound. William Woods, an archaeologist with Southern Illinois University at Edwardsville, said: 'This is astounding. It's so unexpected that it would never have entered your mind before.' The stone structure appears to be around ten metres long, and is buried around twelve metres below the surface of the terrace on the western side, above the Mound's base and therefore well within the Mound itself. It seems to be made of several large stones placed together. Stone of this nature does not naturally occur in that area, so it would have had to be brought there from afar, by humans with few tools, much as the stones at Stonehenge were brought from a distance. There's no question this is a unique discovery,' said Melvin Fowler, an archaeologist at the University of Wisconsin at Milwaukee who specialises in the region's archaeology. 'It's totally unexpected.'

Today's Cahokia village was created when the area was settled by a white population in 1699. The village is the oldest permanent white settlement in Illinois. It means 'wild geese', and is named after a group of Indians who lived in the area long after the Mounds had already been abandoned.

Chaco Canyon, New Mexico, USA
The fifty-three square miles of the Chaco Culture National Historic Park is regarded as one of the most important archaeological sites

in North America. The early peoples of the area managed to created what were the largest manmade structures in North America until the late 1800s.

It is where the Anasazi culture flourished (Anasazi is a Navajo word meaning 'the ancient ones'). Despite being a desert area a thousand years ago, the valley was the centre of Anasazi life. They built single large pueblos with huge rooms, surrounded by small communities, a technique that became a trademark for the region. The building style was to erect masonry walls with rubble cores and outer surfaces of shaped stones. This allowed them to build to over four storeys in height; extraordinary for the period. Eventually there were more than seventy-five such communities, most of them linked to Chaco by a road system. By AD 1000 there may have been as many as five thousand people living in and around Chaco.

Pueblo Bonito (beautiful village), one of the largest of the Chaco Canyon pueblos, is a prime example of their architecture, and reveals much about how the Anasazi lived. Rooms surrounded a central square, or plaza, and throughout the settlement were a number of meeting places known as kivas, which certainly had a ceremonial function. The total population of Pueblo Bonito was probably around twelve hundred people.

Although it was originally a farming community, it is thought that Chaco developed into a trading and religious centre. The settlements seem to have been abandoned quite quickly, probably as a result of drought in the area lasting as much as fifty years. Possibly the religious importance of the site diminished, either as a result of social changes, or perhaps because the drought indicated to the people that the area was out of favour with the gods. Evidence for this is suggested by the evacuation of a pueblo at Sand Canyon. There the kivas were burned, which many archaeologists believe might have been a final act of 'closing'. For whatever reason, the buildings were abandoned and the people had left by the end of the twelfth century.

The area has a mesh of 'prehistoric roads'; but this road system may have had more significance than just as a means of transport. It seems that while many roads link villages and dwellings, others go nowhere in particular and some stop dead at no destination at all. The archaeological evidence of the site is that the roads were not just worn into the ground by use, but were engineered and planned. So their leading nowhere had to have a purpose. There is a growing belief amongst archaeologists that the roads may have related to ritual and ceremony.

In the early 1980s the Chaco Canyon Research Center used aerial photography and ground survey, and equipment from NASA such as a Thermal Infrared Multispectral Scanner, and detected roads not visible to the naked eye. They discovered that as well as the roads leading nowhere in particular, they were also built with exceptional linear straightness, sometimes six metres wide, and climbing directly over features of the landscape rather than taking easier ways round them.

Some aspects of these features are reminiscent of the leys found in England and Europe, of the songlines of the aborigines, and of the lines at Nazca in Peru (see entry). Their religious significance may have far outweighed their practical uses. One of the more controversial claims of modern researchers is that the lines mark out the routes for 'astral travelling' or 'out of body travelling' of shamans during their journeys. As in Nazca, some of the lines seem to lead to small shrines where shamanistic observances might have been undertaken.

The area was made a National Monument in 1907, and designated as an Historical Park in 1980.

Chavin de Huantar, Peru

Of all of the ancient cultures I admire, that of Chavin amazes me the most.
Actually, it has been the inspiration behind most of my art.

Pablo Picasso

Chavin de Huantar is situated at the bottom of Cordillera Blanca's eastern slopes, at an altitude of 3,185 metres above sea level in the Huari province, approximately halfway between tropical forests and coastal plains. Positioned at the intersection of many major routes, Chavin de Huantar would have been a centre of trading as well as a religious and social location.

It was not the most obvious place to build a large ceremonial centre for an indigenous coastal people, but reflected the cosmological principles of the builders. The important images placed in the heart of the site, such as the Lanzon Monolith, were Chavin's equivalent of the Greek omphalos. The Lanzon was the supreme deity of Chavin de Huantar. This central place designated its mystical function as 'axis mundi', linked it to the pole star, and set out communication with both the celestial and underworld realms. The site also combined mountains and water – it is at the confluence of two major rivers – and therefore was a symbol of the power of nature. It conferred great power on the shaman priests who could converse with the gods there.

The site was discovered around a hundred years ago when farmer Timoteo Espinoza was working on the land and accidentally lodged the point of his shovel in an enormous rock. It proved too difficult to move the stone, but with the help of other farmers he succeeded and discovered that the stone was flat and measured over two metres long. On it was carved the image of a creature with an enormous head and the teeth of a cat. Timoteo took the stone home and for years his wife used it as a table. Then, one day, an Italian traveller, Estela Raimondi, met with Timoteo and visited his house, where he found himself sitting at the table for a meal. He examined its carvings, recognised the importance, and today it resides in the National Museum of Anthropology and Archaeology, and is known as the Estela Raimondi stone. It represents one of the most important artefacts of the first High Culture of Chavin.

Chavin de Huantar, Peru's religious centre of the most advanced civilisation of the pre-Incan era, was constructed in 327 BC and involved the skills of architecture, ceramics, sculpture, textiles, hydraulics and acoustics. Its mysterious pyramid structures have led to various theories to explain the true purpose of the temple which is known to locals as The Castle. The belief that it was a temple was emphasised by Ernst Middendorf, a German historian who studied in the area more than a century ago. He based this theory on his observation that the truncated pyramid of the edifice was a common architectural form of pre-Colombian temples in Peru. In his book *Peru: Observations and Studies of the Country and Its Inhabitants Over 25 Years*, Middendorf also cites the presence of two idols, one of which he believed was used for general worship and the other probably 'for a secret cult'.

In one of the corridors of the Old Temple the image of a terrifying god of stone dominates the scene. The Lanzon Monolith is five metres high, with an imposing face and bulging eyes. It is locally known as 'the drinker of blood', and a vessel found nearby suggests it might have been connected with sacrifice. Hungarian investigator Tiberio Petro Leon says: 'The monolith of Chavin is a wanka which in quechua means "stone of power" and which has an eminently religious character. If we look closely, we note that it has the form of the eye tooth of either a jaguar, an orang-utan or a tiger . . . This monolith represents the anthropomorphic image of a child just born, or soon to be born.' Leon believes this represents the spiritual, non-physical, aspect of Man. The monolith also brings together the three elements of the cosmic trilogy of Chavin: eagle, serpent and feline. These are said to be the fearsome gods who punish men or who drive out evil by showing their fierce teeth. These three elements could also represent air, water and earth: the habitats of these three creatures. At the time, it was believed that shamans could become jaguars and interact with the supernatural. They achieved this by taking hallucinogenic drugs such as huacacachu or villca as part of their rituals. Sculptures that decorate the Old Temple show this transformation of the priests, and artefacts found there include mortars, pestles, conch-shell trumpets, and more, all thought to be associated with Chavin rituals.

The New Temple on the site seamlessly picks up from the Old Temple, and appears to have been involved with the same worship, practices and rituals as the Old Temple. It did not replace the Old, and may have been a new extension built and used while the Old Temple was still in operation. The Lanzon, in a different stance, is depicted there also; its right hand holds a Strombus shell representing male forces, and the left hand holds a Spondylus shell, which represents female forces.

In one part of the New Temple, the Gallery of the Offerings, many human bones were found amidst animal bones and cooking pots, suggesting the practice of ritual cannibalism.

The area flourished between 900 and 200 BC, after which the Chavin civilisation began to disappear.

Chichen-Itza, Mexico

The sacred city of the Itza peoples, known as Chichen-Itza, is situated some seventy-five miles to the east of Merida, capital of Yucatan, Mexico. Chichen-Itza means 'mouth of the well of Itza', and it is thought to be one of the most important archaeological sites deriving from the Mayan culture. It is approximately six square miles in area, and used to contain hundreds of buildings, represented now mainly by mounds. The thirty or so buildings that remain are therefore of great importance.

The remains can be divided into two groups. The first, from around the sixth to the seventh centuries AD, relates to the Mayan Period. The second group contains influence from the Toltec Period from the tenth to the early thirteenth century. Because of the many steep-walled sinks (called 'cenotes') in the area, it is clear that there was a good source of water.

During the Mayan period of flourishing arts and sciences Chichen-Itza became a significant religious and ceremonial centre. The buildings from this period indicate this clearly: the Red House, the House of the Deer, the Nunnery and its Annexe, the Church, the Akab Dzib, the Temple of the Three Lintels and the House of Phalli.

As their civilisation diminished, for reasons not yet known for certain, the Mayans left their religious centres, opting instead for smaller settlements, and cities such as Chichen-Itza were used only for burial of the dead and certain religious rites. It would be the tenth century AD before Chichen-Itza was resettled.

The Toltec religion of the Itza peoples was based on human sacrifice. It seems that men, women and children were killed, particularly at the Cenote of Sacrifice, in honour of the Rain God. There is, it must be said, some dispute about this: the cenotes are very steep sided, and it has been suggested that children at play could easily have fallen in accidentally. However, the existence of ritual artefacts in the sink-hole do point to some sacrificial use, which would in any case be in keeping with the Toltec rituals.

The most famous building on the site, and virtually the symbol of Chichen-Itza, is Kukulcan's Pyramid, also known as El Castillo: a square-based, stepped pyramid some twenty-three metres tall. It was created for astronomical purposes. During the vernal equinox (20 March) and the autumn equinox (21 September), at about 3pm, sunlight bathes the western balustrade of the pyramid's main stairway, causing seven isosceles triangles to form. These create the image of the body of a serpent some thirty-seven metres long that, as the sun progresses, creeps downwards until it joins the serpent's head carved in stone at the base of the stairway. The feathered serpent is a strong motif, and may be connected to agricultural rituals. This image is so popular that literally thousands of people visit at each equinox to see it.

The serpent may relate to ancient legends of the Mayans and Toltecs. Toltec history claims that in AD 987 the ruler, Quetzalcoatl, was defeated and then expelled on a raft of serpents. In the same year Mayan history claims that a king named Kukulkan – the Serpent God – arrived and made Chichen-Itza his capital city.

The pyramid further relates to sun-worship. Each of the four staircases has ninety-one steps, a total of 364, and combined with the top platform this creates 365 – the days of the year. The sides are also divided into eighteen sections, representing the months of the Mayan calendar.

Beneath the pyramid is an earlier construction over which El Castillo was built: an example of the custom of superimposing one monument on a previous one. In the antechamber of the earlier temple was the reclining figure of a Chac-mool (Red Claw), a messenger of the gods. Inside the shrine was the sculpture of a fierce-looking jaguar that probably served as a throne for the priests.

El Caracol (the conch shell) is another astronomy-related

structure. It is a giant observatory which would have been used for rituals. Its stone dome has windows aligned towards certain stars at certain times.

The Great Ball Court (Juego de Pelota) – an early playing field for a ball game – is the largest of its kind in the Mayan world. There are eight other, smaller, such ball courts at Chichen-Itza, but the Great Ball Court was built on a grander scale than the others. The length of the playing field here is 135 metres. There are indications that it was not a gentle ball game; carvings on the wall show, for example, a figure with blood spurting from his headless neck, while another player holds the decapitated head in the air. Either this is an early example of dark humour, or a reference to human sacrifice, or the game was used as a replacement for war with all its attendant gore.

After 1194 the city was finally abandoned. Quite what happened is unclear; unfortunately it was a policy of the Spanish who invaded Mexico to burn books and kill the Mayan priests, so much of the history was lost, probably forever.

Copan, Honduras

Copan contains the most southern ruins of the Maya culture dating from the classic period, between AD 400 and 800. It is located in the western part of Honduras, between the Motagua River and the Copan Valley.

The ruins are an astonishing complex of temples, plazas, a ball court, an acropolis and stairways. The acropolis is divided into two courts; the west court displays two temples constructed by Yax Pac, one as a doorway to the next world. Foremost amongst the stairways is the Stairway of Hieroglyphics, the longest known text left by the ancient Mayan civilisation. Sixty-three steps are each carved with at least 2,500 hieroglyphics, and were built in 756 by Smoke Shell, the fifteenth ruler. The steps exhibit an ornate array of sculptures: gods, animals, birds, and mythological beings. The texts are believed to be a lineage tree recording the lives and deaths of all Copan kings from Yax Kuk Mo to Smoke Shell. A clay figurine of Yax Kuk Mo, founder of Copan, was located at the site next to the Tomb of the Royal Scribe and is presently on display in the Copan museum.

The plazas contain thirty-eight stelae (stone pillars), altars and several pyramids, the highest being forty metres. Most of the stelae were erected between 711 and 736 by the thirteenth ruler.

Las Sepulturas (the graves) is a small site about a mile from the acropolis, and has revealed a great deal about how the Mayan elite lived before the collapse of Copan. It was the residential area, and takes its name from the Mayan practice of burying the dead in rock catacombs below family dwellings.

The city once housed twenty thousand people, including artists, astronomers and scribes. It was a major centre of religion and was also the social centre of the territory. The city appears to have begun to fall into decay in 738, after the capture and decapitation of the thirteenth ruler. However, collapse seems to have been brought about by ecological disaster, and human remains at the site show much disease and malnutrition. An unfinished altar commissioned in 822 by the last pretender to the throne, U Cit Tok, is representative of the monarchy's final days.

In 1952, responsibility for maintaining the area was transferred to the Honduras Archaeology and History Institute, and in 1980 UNESCO declared the Archaeological Park of Copan Ruins a World Heritage monument.

One tomb, that of Copan's 'Red Lady', was a central feature of the city, but fell prey to looters in February 1998. They broke into the tomb during the night and stole the treasures from the stone slab that had housed her body. Her skeleton and much of her famous jade had already been removed by archaeologists, but the thieves stole some two thousand of the beads that had decorated her body, and many jade figures.

Devil's Tower, Wyoming, USA

The Devil's Tower is the remnant of a volcanic extrusion about sixty million years ago and rises some 390 metres. It has been a sacred place of worship for some of the Native American tribes since before written records began. There are several legends to account for the origin of the mountain; the most generally known is a story common to several tribes including the Kiowa, Arapaho, Crow, Cheyenne and Sioux. According to that legend seven girls were playing in the forest when they were pursued by a giant bear. They fled, but the bear was catching up with them. In a desperate last bid, they stood on a small, low rock and prayed to the Great Spirit to save them. The rock gradually grew upwards towards the sky, lifting the girls up and away from the pursuing bear. Angry, the animal tried to climb the growing mountain to catch the girls, but it kept falling backwards to the ground. The claw marks of the bear's desperate attempts to scale the mountain can be seen all around the circumference, in the deep vertical striations that characterise the shape. The mountain continued growing until the girls were pushed into the heavens and they became the seven stars of the Pleiades.

The tribes know the mountain as Mateo Tepee (or Mato Tipila), which roughly translates as Grizzly Bear Lodge. The first white surveyors, who 'discovered' it in 1875, named it the Devil's Tower, after an old Indian name: the Bad God's Tower.

The Tower is a highly regarded, sacred vision quest site for many tribes. Sitting Bull is known to have visited it to gain the mystical insight needed to defeat the white invaders. New Age followers have continued to use the Tower in this way to the present day. Many Native Americans believe that there are benevolent spirits dwelling on the almost flat peak; the most famous is the Thunderbird, a giant eagle with a wingspan that can block out the sun. It sits atop the Tower looking over, and protecting, the tribes.

Strange light phenomena seen around the Tower have added to its mystery, and created a strong UFO folklore in the locality. In 1977 it achieved international fame as the centrepiece of the film *Close Encounters of the Third Kind*, where it was depicted as the chosen landing place of extraterrestrial visitors.

The site became the first US National Park, proclaimed so by President Theodore Roosevelt in 1906.

Easter Island, Pacific Ocean

Situated some 2,300 miles from the west coast of Chile, Easter Island is the world's most isolated inhabited island. It was formed as a triangle by three extinct volcanoes.

The original inhabitants were Polynesian settlers who probably travelled in canoes from the Marquesas Islands, led by Hotu Matua, and landed around AD 400. Easter Island's native name, Rapa Nui (meaning Great Rapa), was given to it by Tahitian sailors in the 1860s as it reminded them of Rapa, an island in French Polynesia. The majority of the island's modern population are descendants of these settlers. Today, slightly confusingly, the land, the people and the language are all known by the name Rapa Nui.

The first Europeans to discover the island were the occupants of a Dutch ship under the command of Admiral Jacob Roggeveen who encountered it on Easter Day in 1722, thus giving it its European name. Early settlers also dubbed the island 'Te Pito O Te Henua' ('the Navel of The World').

It is most famous for its huge stone statues, known as moai. Many weigh over fifty tons and stand ten metres high. They were carved at one of the most famous sites on the island, the volcano Rano Raraku. There are still several statues abandoned in various stages of production, including one, very close to completion, that would have been the largest on the island. These partially finished statues offer some clues to how the statues were formed, carved from the rock, then transported to the edge of the Island where they were erected facing inward. They were almost certainly created for the same reasons that other monuments around the world were erected: for sacred, ritual and religious purposes.

As to how they were erected, it is probable that, once the statues had been hewn from the rock, they were hauled on to felled trees and rolled across the island. Using leverage they were probably then tilted a few centimetres at a time by piling rocks and stones beneath them, until they came to a more erect angle, at which point pits could be dug beneath them into which they would eventually drop. With the use of ropes and levers, they could then be finally positioned. However, most are not 'buried' but stand on platforms; presumably they were erected on them using a similar technique but involving ramps to reach the appropriate height.

Easter Island has been the subject to some curious analysis. Psychologist Werner Wolff in his *Island of Death*, published in 1948, theorised that the statues were carved and left in the volcano so that, when it erupted, they would be thrown across the island directly on to their bases. Also, needless to say, space aliens have been credited with creating the statues, a theory largely promoted by writer Erich von Daniken.

These theories are based on the belief that ancient peoples did not have the skills to create of move such huge monuments. Increasingly, we find from research that indeed they did, and in fact the Polynesians had a long tradition of stone-working prior to their colonisation of the island, so extraordinary hypotheses are not needed.

The 'why' is more important than the 'how'. Why the people of this small island chose to exhaust their resources erecting huge numbers of these moai is the true mystery, and one that suggests their beliefs were very strong, and their carvings very sacred. Several researchers have pointed out that the sheer human effort used to create all the moai was probably – per head of population available, and as a percentage of natural resources diverted to the work – greater than the proportional effort used in creating the pyramids in Egypt.

The moai are believed to be carved images of dead chiefs or, possibly, gods. It is thought that after death, perhaps in battle, fallen heroes were laid to rest under the shadows of the moai and covered in rocks, to ensure their passage to the next world. There are variations in the moai: some have red rock topknots, some have coral eyes, some have elaborate carvings. Most of them are positioned around the coast. Perhaps most surprising to visitors, and not always apparent from photographs of the island, is that the statues faced inland, with their backs to the ocean. This suggests that they were not erected as guardians of the island, watching over it for marine invasion, as might have been expected, and must have had another function.

The moai are generally erected on an ahu, or platform base, under which a particular hero or leader was buried. Each ahu was constructed of neatly-fitting stone blocks, and usually supported four to six statues, although one ahu, known as Tongariki, held fifteen. Within many of the ahus are the burial vaults of clans or individuals.

The physical work needed to carve the moai and ahus indicates to archaeologists that at some time in the Island's past an excess of food resources was easily available, which allowed the population to indulge in its passionate beliefs to such an extent. If so, then what happened?

The population must have outstripped the island's food resources, and the almost total destruction of the palm forests to provide rollers to move the carved statues probably led to famine and tribal war. It is likely that a cult of cannibalism grew up on the island. Between the 1600s and the 1800s, Peruvians raided the island to capture natives as slaves; they introduced new diseases which, together with the famines, virtually decimated the population. Only after the Chilean annexation in 1888 did the population begin to grown again.

During this war between the tribes, or perhaps during the disintegration of old beliefs into new beliefs (see below), almost all of the moai were torn down by the islanders. Most were knocked face down, itself probably a symbol of the destruction of belief.

The moai probably represented 'mana': a mystical amalgam of power, prestige and wealth. The islanders believed in ancestor worship, and the moai represented a clan's most revered forefathers endowing mana on the living leaders of the day. The bigger the moai, the more mana was bestowed on the leader. Perhaps toppling the statues face down into the earth was regarded as a way of taking the mana from the rival clan, a symbolism of the expression biting the dust. However, at some point the whole cult of the moai lost its capacity for belief. In a short space of time, remarkably swiftly considering the abandonment of the statues in progress, the cult died and the statues were no longer of use in either belief or anti-belief. Arguably the fact that the largest statue on the island is one that was abandoned in the preparation suggests that a particularly significant leader may have died who was to have been greatly honoured, and perhaps the cult could not survive his death.

As the moai cult faded so the islanders turned to a new belief system: the 'birdman' cult (Tangata Manu). This consisted of each tribe selecting athletes from amongst its number to compete to bring back the first egg of the breeding season from the nests of the sooty terns on the nearby islet of Moto Nui. The winning tribe ruled the island for the ensuing year; this tradition served into the nineteenth century. One of the island's volcanoes has many petroglyphs depicting the birdman, who was seen as the representative on earth of the creator god Makemake. The winner of the competition was taken to the south-west exterior slope of Rano Raraku, where he remained in seclusion for a year. Presumably he was there to commune with the gods of the cult, perhaps a form of shamanic purpose. The birdman ritual was still in existence when Europeans arrived on Easter Island and is therefore historically documented.

There is some evidence, albeit ambiguous and tentative, that the islanders developed a written language; if so, then theirs was the only formal, written language in Polynesia. The evidence is in the form of twenty-four wooden tablets (ronga ronga) but they have never been translated.

Easter Island is arguably one of the most important sacred sites on Earth, not that its own particular beliefs were more or less important than any others, but because it is an isolated 'test bed' where the imposition of one culture on another, and the imposition of one belief on an earlier one, can be studied. Added to that, the self-inflicted destruction of its eco-system serves as a warning for global ecological care; a study of this island may offer many much-needed lessons.

In 1935 Easter Island was declared a national park and an historic monument by the Chilean government, and in 1953 the Chilean Navy took over the administration of the island. Its main industry today is tourism, despite its remoteness.

It has one further claim to fame that reflects the modern world in which it now exists; it houses a specially constructed runway that can be used for an emergency descent of the American Space Shuttle.

Great Serpent Mound, Ohio, USA

The Great Serpent is the largest and best known of America's 'effigy' mounds. It is an earth mound and was carved in around AD 1070, across a forested hilltop called Brush Creek near modern-day Peebles in Ohio. It is approximately six metres wide, 1.25 metres high, and around 411 metres long. Its jaws are five metres across, and stretched around an egg which it appears to be about to swallow. Its purpose is unknown, but its speculated use as a burial mound appears not to be correct; no traces of human remains have been found in studies of the Great Serpent Mound, though there were remains in two other mounds nearby.

Serpents are often a symbol of transformation, based on snakes shedding their skin and being 're-born'; perhaps the Serpent Mount represents such a symbol. No artefacts have been discovered in the Mound, but there were artefacts found at the nearby Fort Ancient village and these have been carbon-dated to approximately the same time as the mound was built. Therefore the builders and those who occupied the village were around at the same time, and may have been the same people.

Snakes played a significant role in Fort Ancient culture, and two other snake effigies in Warren County have been identified as originating from the Fort Ancient culture. Although these other mounds are built from stone, they are similar to the Serpent Mound in that certain features align with the summer solstice. Indeed, Great Serpent Mound has alignments to both the summer and winter solstices.

According to the Archaeological Institute of America, the date the Mound was carved, AD 1070, roughly coincides with two significant astronomical events recorded by Chinese astronomers: the explosion of the star that created the Crab Nebula, which was visible on earth for two weeks in 1054, and an appearance of Halley's Comet, which illuminated the sky in 1066 in its brightest recorded showing. The latter might have looked like a fiery serpent to the occupants of the ridge. Perhaps the image was intended to recreate something in the heavens that the Fort Ancient people were inspired by.

Gaudalupe, Our Lady of (Basilica de Nuestra Senora de Guadalupe), Mexico City

There were four apparitions of Our Lady of Guadalupe according to Luis Lasso de la Vega as he recorded them in 1649.

The first was in early December 1531, at daybreak, when a poor Indian, Juan Diego, was at the base of the hill known as Tepeyacac (just north of modern Mexico City) and heard, coming from the top of the hill, singing which he thought must be that of birds. He looked towards the sounds which then ceased, and the silence was broken by a voice calling to him by name. He walked towards the voice, and at the summit of the hill he could see a woman standing there. Her clothes shone brightly, the plants around her feet glistened like gold, and the earth around her sparkled. He bowed to her, and she said to him: 'Juanito, the most humble of my sons, . . . Know and understand well . . . that I am the ever Virgin Holy Mary, Mother of the True God for whom we live, of the Creator of all things, Lord of heaven and the earth.' Mary told Diego that she wanted a temple built to her at the site, and that he should travel to the Bishop of Mexico with this message. He confirmed: 'My Lady, I am going to comply with your mandate.'

Diego sought out the bishop, Franciscan Father Juan de Zumarraga, and delivered the message, describing what he had seen. He was disappointed that the bishop did not appear overly moved by his description, though Father Juan promised he would ask to see him again when he had had a chance to think about what he had been told. Later that day, Diego returned to the hill where he had seen the vision, and again the Virgin was waiting for him on the same spot. When he saw her he bowed down and told her that his reception had not been an enthusiastic one. The Virgin again implored him: 'I command that you again go tomorrow and see the bishop. You go in my name, and make known my wish in its entirety, that he has to start the erection of a temple which I ask of him. And again tell him that I, in person, the ever Virgin Holy Mary, Mother of God, sent you.'

On the following day, Sunday, before dawn, Diego left home to travel to Tlatilolco, where he would attend church and then see the prelate. He again relayed the message from the Virgin regarding the building of her temple, but the bishop was still doubtful and asked for a sign. He did not say what sign he required.

Diego later returned to the hill and there, for the third time, met with the Virgin. She told him: 'Well and good, my little dear, you will return here tomorrow, so you may take to the bishop the sign he has requested. With this he will believe you.'

On the Monday Diego had to attend to the needs of a sick uncle, Juan Bernardino, who wanted a priest because he believed he was dying. The following day, Tuesday, before dawn, Diego went to fetch the priest, but avoided passing near where the Virgin had appeared to him so that she would not detain him and delay him in his quest to help his uncle. However, her apparition appeared to him, descending down the hill, and looking towards their previous meeting point. She asked him: 'Where are you going?' He bowed to her and said: 'My uncle. He has contracted the plague, and is near death. I am hurrying to your house in Mexico to call one of your priests, beloved by our Lord, to hear his confession and absolve him, because, since we were born, we came to guard the work of our death. But if I go, I shall return here soon, so I may go to deliver your message.'

On hearing this the Virgin replied: 'Do not fear that sickness, nor any other sickness or anguish . . . Are you not under my protection? . . . Do not be afflicted by the illness of your uncle, who will not die now of it. Be assured that he is now cured.' Diego was consoled by this, and asked that he could take a sign to the bishop. He was then sent by the Virgin to the top of the hill and told to collect a sign from there.

Yet again he had trouble getting to see the bishop, and had to wait a long time. He showed the flowers he had collected to the bishop's servants and they were astonished, knowing them to be out of season. They went off to tell the bishop what Diego had with him. The bishop, hearing what he was carrying, realised this might be the sign he had asked for, and called Diego to him immediately.

Diego told him: 'She sent me to the top of the hill, where I was accustomed to see her, and cut a variety of rosas de Castilla. After I had cut them, I brought them, she took them with her hand and placed them in my cloth, so that I bring them to you and deliver them to you in person. Even though I knew that the hilltop was no place where flowers would grow, because there are many crags, thistles, thorns, nopales and mezquites, I still had my doubts. As I approached the top of the hill, I saw that I was in paradise, where there was a great variety of exquisite rosas de Castilla, in brilliant dew, which I immediately cut. She had told me that I should bring them to you, and so I do it, so that you may see in them the sign which you asked of me and comply with her wish; also, to make clear the veracity of my word and my message. Behold. Receive them.' He showed the flowers to the bishop, scattering them on the floor. As the bishop looked down, he could see the image of the Virgin on the cloth that had carried the flowers, and he and the others present fell on their knees. The bishop begged forgiveness for having doubted. The cloth with the image was taken to the chapel, and the following day the bishop asked Diego to show him where the temple should be built.

Diego took the bishop to the spot, then excused himself so that he could attend to his uncle's needs for a priest. The bishop asked his servants to accompany Diego, and they were able to see when they arrived that the uncle was fit and well, and cured. His uncle confirmed to Diego and the others that when he had found himself cured, he too had seen a vision of the Virgin, and that she had told him all about her appearances to Diego and of his trips to the bishop. The uncle was also taken to the bishop to tell his story.

In time the temple was built, erected on the spot where Diego had seen the Virgin. It was used to house the cloth with the image of the Virgin on it, and has been a place of sacred pilgrimage ever since. It is now the huge Basilica of Nuestra Senora de Guadalupe. It is said that the image on display there has significantly contributed to the Christian conversion of over eight million Indians. Despite the centuries, the cloth shows no sign of decay.

On 14 January 2001 it was announced that a study of the image of the Virgin had produced an astonishing find. Peruvian Engineer José Aste Tonsmann, of the Mexican Center of Guadalupan Studies, at a conference at the Pontifical Athenaeum Regina Apostolorum, claimed that digital examination of the eyes of the Virgin Mary on the imprinted cloth shows a reflection of thirteen people. The same images are present in both eyes, but in different proportions, exactly as might be expected when human eyes reflect what is before them. The report stated that: 'Tonsmann says he believes the reflection transmitted by the eyes of the Virgin of Guadalupe is the scene of Dec 9, 1531, during which Diego showed his tilma (nb the cloth), with the image, to Bishop Juan de Zumarraga and others present in the room.' Tonsmann believes the image was not painted by human hand, and points out that Richard Kuhn, a Nobel Prize winner in chemistry, had already found that the image did not use natural, animal or mineral colourings. As there were no synthetic colourings in 1531, this also makes the image harder to explain. (In 1979, Americans Philip Callahan and Jody B. Smith had also discovered that there was no trace of paint on the cloth.)

According to Tonsmann, his analysis shows that in the room, reflected in the eyes, are, amongst others, a seated Indian looking up; the profile of a balding, elderly man with a white beard which resembles a portrait of Bishop Zumarraga; a younger man, possibly the interpreter Juan Gonzalez; and an Indian who is possibly Juan Diego himself.

Interestingly, the site was a sacred one even before these visions. The hill of Tepeyacac had once had a temple on it dedicated to Tonantzin, an earth and fertility goddess, also a virgin. It had been a place of pilgrimage for those living in the Aztec city of Tenochtitlan. That earlier shrine was destroyed in 1521 on the orders of Cortez.

Head-Smashed-In Buffalo Jump, Alberta, Canada

The buffalo was sacred to the North American Indians because of their total dependence on it for food, materials and tools. As such, the movements of the buffalo – which dictated the nomadic movements of the tribes – and activities associated with them became sacred rituals. Locations where intense activity relating to the buffalo took place became sacred sites.

Situated some eleven miles north-west of Fort Macleod in Alberta, at the foothills of the Rocky Mountains, is the world's largest and oldest buffalo jump. Known as Head-Smashed-In (or estipah-skikikini-kots in the Blackfoot language), it was in continuous use by the native peoples for thousands of years. It was designated a UNESCO World Heritage site in 1981.

It is a significant location for one of the most important practices of the native North American Indians. Buffalo jumps were common on the northern plains and were used to kill herds which were stampeded over a precipice. The Indians would then use a camp below the jump to carve up the carcasses. Little was wasted – meat would be eaten, skins would provide clothing, dung was used for fire material, bones would be made into tools and even the ribs were used to make runners for sleds.

Head-Smashed-In is a ten-metre-high cliff, some three hundred metres wide. The butchering and cooking camp, half a mile across, is nearby.

At the top of the cliff is the original grazing range which has some five hundred stone cairns in evidence which were used to direct the herds towards their fate.

Over ten thousand buffalo are said to have died at Head-Smashed-In.

Izamal, Mexico

Izamal comes from the Maya language meaning 'deity of the creation, dew from the sky'. The city is famous for its yellow and white painted buildings, the mustard colour being known as 'Izamal yellow'.

In the centre of the city stands the Franciscan convent dedicated to San Antonio de Padua. It is an impressive church with a closed atrium, and half point arches regarded as the second largest in the world after those in the Vatican. This most sacred church was built between 1553 and 1561. It is constructed on the remains of a

Mayan base that was once part of one of only four great temple-pyramids sacred to Itzamna, Lord of the Sky, a principal deity of the Itza Mayans.

The church houses a carved, wooden image of the Virgin Mary, sumptuously clothed and bejewelled. The original was brought from Guatemala on the orders of Bishop Diego de Landa in 1558, but this was burned in 1829, after which it was substituted by a twin that is still on display today.

The figure is associated with many miracles. Because of these, the Virgin of Izamal was crowned in 1949 as Queen of Yucatan and, in 1970, declared as patroness of the archdiocese. In 1993 Pope John Paul II visited the monastery. This shrine to the Virgin had once been the most popular pilgrimage site in south-east Mexico, though interest waned until recently, but following the Pope's visit it has again become a most popular sacred sit.

The Virgin is particularly associated with alleviating the frequent plagues that befell the peninsula in colonial times, and many personal healing miracles are attributed to her by Catholics. Other devotees of the site have suggested that perhaps the credit should go, or jointly go, to the earlier building on the site – the Mayan pyramid. Martin Gray, photographer and writer on sacred sites, has pointed out that Izamal had been a pilgrimage site since 1000 BC. The city was regarded by the Mayans as the home of Kinichkakmo, a manifestation of the sun god, and of Itzam Na, a god of healing. Gray believes that the healing powers may be a combination of several factors: the Marian statue; the earlier dedication to the god of healing; the possible factor that the site was already regarded as having powerful earth energies, which caused the Mayans to dedicate the site in the first place; and a psychic field that could have built up over the centuries, caused by devotion and prayer at the site.

Machu Picchu, Peru

If there is one single symbol of the Incan Empire of Peru it is the ruined fortress city of Machu Picchu (meaning Old Peak).

The Incas as a cultural force existed from around AD 1200 to

1532. Originally, they were a tribe that moved into the upland valleys of the Southern Andes and founded the town of Cuzco as their capital and centre. From around 1438, under three principal leaders, they engaged in a programme of conquest, creating a substantial empire.

The first of these leaders was Inca Pachacuti, who later gave his name to the whole tribe. From around 1438 to 1463 he expanded the empire out from Cuzco to much of the nearby mountain lands. Between 1463 and 1471 Pachacuti and Topa Inca further conquered the coastal lands to the north; and from then until 1493 Topa Inca led a massive expansion of the Empire south as far as the River Maule, using force, threats and diplomacy. From 1493 the Empire was in the hands of Huayna Capac until it was swiftly devastated by the arrival of the Spaniards under Pizarro.

The sophistication of their Empire is best demonstrated by their road system which, given the mountain terrain they were dealing with, is comparable in achievement to the Roman road system. Twelve and a half thousand miles of roads, threading through the mountains, linked the whole Empire which was divided into four sections ruled by relatives of the reigning Inca.

Machu Picchu is a former fortress city of the Empire situated high in the Andes, some fifty miles north-west of Cuzco. It is located on a ridge between two peaks, around six hundred metres above the Urubamba River, at a height of around 2,200 metres above sea level, and covers about five square miles of terraces built around a central plaza and connected by several stairways. The terraces were used for growing crops.

Houses in Machu Picchu consist mostly of one-room stone dwellings; the walls are largely standing but the roofs have long since disappeared. The buildings are arranged around internal courts, and there are several tombs apparent. The structures give ample evidence of advanced engineering skill and superior craftsmanship; for example, many of the building blocks weigh over fifty tons yet they are so perfectly made, and fitted together with mortarless joints so precise, that even a thin knife blade cannot be inserted between them.

The city was discovered in 1911 by Hiram Bingham, an

American explorer from Yale University, engaged at the time in searching for Vilcabamba, the last refuge of the Kings of the Incan Empire. The city's origins and history are unknown, its date of occupancy is unknown, and it is not mentioned in the writings of the Spanish conquerors of Peru. Bingham thought that Machu Picchu could have been the fortress city that was the last stronghold of the Incas of Cuzco as they fled the Spanish invaders.

There is a strong suggestion that some of the larger buildings were not private dwellings, but were used for religious observances. It is generally considered that Machu Picchu was once an important religious centre, which survived largely intact because it managed to remain hidden from the Spaniard invaders. One theory has it that it was an important centre for training priestesses and brides for the Inca ruling families.

It is probable that one of Machu Picchu's functions was as an astronomical observatory. The Intihuatana stone (the Hitching Post of the Sun) is believed to be an indicator of the date of the winter solstice and other significant celestial times. Each midwinter, the Incas would have held a ceremony at the stone, to tie the sun and prevent its northward movement in the sky. Shamanic legends say that when people touch their foreheads to the stone it can enhance psychic sensitivity.

Intihuatana stones were the most sacred objects of the Incas, and for that reason were sought out and destroyed by the Spanish invaders. It was believed that when the Intihuatana stone was broken at an Incan shrine, the gods that protected that place would be forced to depart. As the Spaniards did not reach Machu Picchu, both the stone and the gods are believed to be still present.

The site of Machu Picchu is beautifully set off by the peak of Huayna Picchu, a mountain which rises up steeply behind the city and which has ruins clearly visible on its top. For those visiting Peru, particularly for those with an interest in the early cultures of South America, a trip to Machu Picchu is an essential highlight. Unfortunately, however, the ruins are in danger of being destroyed by erosion. In *The Times* of 8 March 2001, it was revealed that Japanese archaeologists from the Disaster Prevention Research Institute at Kyoto University had discovered that the ridges on which the ruins stand are crumbling away at a rate of twelve centimetres a year, and have weakened so much that a total collapse is a possibility at any time.

The Majorville Medicine Wheel and Cairn Site, Alberta, Canada

Medicine wheels are generally rings of concentric stone circles and straight lines radiating out from a central hub or cairn. Smaller stone circles, called tipi rings, are often found in close proximity to the medicine wheels. The use of the term medicine indicates the presumed religious significance of the structures to the native peoples.

There are forty-six of these structures in Alberta, representing around sixty-six per cent of all known medicine wheels. This suggests the phenomenon possibly originated with tribes from this part of the world.

The Majorville Medicine Wheel and Cairn is located to the south of Bassano, Alberta, on a high hill near the banks of the Bow River. It was first examined in the early 1970s and is thought to date from around 4,500 years ago. It consists of a large cairn, nine metres in diameter, constructed of stone and prairie soils and situated in the centre of a medicine wheel. The medicine wheel itself is twenty-seven metres in diameter and has about twenty-eight spokes radiating from the cairn. The core of the complex is built on three hills, over nine hundred metres above sea level. The Majorville Medicine Wheel itself is on the north-east summit with a smaller medicine wheel situated on the middle summit. On the south-west summit are cairns and a one-ton granite block. The hills are connected by observation lines for the Winter Solstice sunset and the Summer Solstice sunrise.

Although the purpose of medicine wheels is uncertain, many researchers believe that they – and particularly the Majorville Cairn – represent a sun effigy, the centrepiece of a huge temple dedicated to the sun, moon and the morning star. Many researchers believe that the accuracy of the solstice lines is so precise that the people who constructed the Majorville Medicine Wheel must have been as scientifically advanced as those who constructed Stonehenge.

Medicine wheels certainly had ceremonial purposes, possibly linked to the fertility of the buffalo on which the natives were totally dependent. The artefacts found at Majorville – which number almost three thousand – bear this out.

It is likely that the medicine wheels served several different purposes over the centuries. Some were related to tribal mortuary customs; some researchers believe they were used for ceremonial functions such as the Sun Dance, and others believe they served an astronomical purpose as a primitive calendar or solar observatory. This last theory has fallen from popularity in recent years and has been challenged by many astronomers.

Little is known of the culture of the wheel builders as the plains Indians left scant evidence of their occupation between the last Ice Age and the arrival of the white settlers. Theirs was a nomadic lifestyle and one almost certainly based on the migrations of the buffalo. The white settlers of the 1800s – fur traders and missionaries initially – brought the people out of the Stone Age and in doing so effectively destroyed their culture. The first published records of studies of medicine wheels in western Canada were made by surveyor George Dawson in 1885. Unfortunately, by the time any practical interest in the structures arose, the cultures that might have explained them were already decimated.

The circular shape and presumed uses of the medicine wheels are reminiscent of the stone circles of Europe. These similarities have implied to some researchers that there may have been contact between North America and Europe at a much earlier date than previously thought. Also, huge stone circles located in Siberia have indicated a possible connection between peoples now divided by the Bering Strait when a land bridge joined the continents. The medicine wheels may yet provide evidence of more prehistoric contact between peoples than previously supposed.

Mauna Kea, Hawaii, USA

The Big Island of Hawaii is the site of some of the world's most spectacular and most active volcanoes. In fact the island is actually the aggregation of five major shield volcanoes: Mauna Loa, Kilauea, Hualalai, Kahala and Mauna Kea. The whole Hawaiian chain of islands stretches some 1,500 miles, and contains eighty-two volcanoes.

Mauna Kea, or White Mountain, rises 4,200 metres above sea level but would be the world's highest mountain if measured from its base beneath the sea. From that perspective it measures about 9,750 metres – taller than Everest. Mauna Loa is the world's most massive mountain: about ten thousand cubic miles. While Mauna Kea is inactive, last having erupted over three millennia ago, Mauna Loa erupted as recently as 25 March 1984.

The legend of the Hawaiian volcanoes is centred around the volcano goddess Pele. Her first home, according to the myth, was on Niihau. She got into conflict with her sister, Na-maka-o-Kahai, the goddess of the sea, who chased Pele from island to island, each time destroying the home that Pele had created for herself there. Eventually she set up home at Halemaumau, at the Kilauea Caldera. Writer Herb Kawainui Kane, in *Pele, Goddess of Hawaii's Volcanoes*, makes the point that: 'As long as the earth is alive with quakes and eruptions, Pele will live in Hawaiian hearts and minds as the personification of the natural phenomena of volcanic activity.'

It is said that Pele makes an appearance before every eruption, in the guise of an old woman. Islanders claim to be able to see her face in the new flowing lava. She is feared and respected by Hawaiians and they offer her gifts of ohela berries and maile leis to appease her temper. Her power is celebrated in chanting and in both ancient and modern hula dancing.

One story of Pele tells of an old man who crossed her. He was walking over the Mauna Kea ridge when he saw a perfect lava rock perched on a hill. He took it for his garden, but as he got into his car he began to feel ill, and worsened as he approached his house in Kona. Once he was home, the man called the doctor as he now had a high fever, and by the time the doctor arrived he was unconscious. The doctor saw the rock, and knew that his patient had been struck down by Pele for taking it. He also knew that there was nothing he could do to save the man, except to stay with him until he died.

While Pele is unquestionably Hawaii's best known and most revered goddess, she had competitors in ancient times who form part of her legend. Her primary enemies were four other goddesses, all deities of the mountains: Lilinoe was both a goddess of Haleakala and Mauna Kea – she was married to Nana-Nu'u who had survived the great floor and who lived in a cave on Mauna Kea; second was a snow maiden of Mauna Kea known as Waiau, who is associated with Waiau Lake on the mountain. The third snow goddess was Kahoupokane, who is associated with Mount Hualalai. The fourth – and the one still well known today – is Poliahu, who also lives on the mountain and who still constantly fights with Pele.

It is said that on one occasion Poliahu and the other goddesses came down from Mauna Kea to go sledding. Pele enjoyed the sport, and on this occasion she turned up in the guise of a beautiful young woman. Poliahu encouraged the woman to join in with them, but as the game progressed she realised that the woman was none other than her arch-rival Pele. Pele brought fire out of the mountain, and chased Poliahu back to the summit; in revenge Poliahu covered the mountain with her white cloak. They fought with fire and ice, and the resultant lava flows and quick cooling created the land forms of Laupahoehoe and Onomea.

The eruptions of the volcanoes are said to be Pele still attempting to use fire to defeat her enemies, but Poliahu always wins in the end. She, and her other snow goddess companions, keep snow on the mountain tops which melts and provides the water to keep the land fertile.

Science and legend meet on Mauna Kea. The rarefied air of the high mountain has encouraged scientists to build several of the world's largest telescopes at the top.

Mitla, nr Oaxaca, Mexico

Mitla is at the upper end of the Tlacolula Valley, one of the three valleys that together form a three-pointed star shape that is the Valley of Oaxaca. While **Monte Alban** (see entry), once a social and political centre, is at the junction of these valleys, Mitla is more remote, perhaps influencing its choice as a religious centre.

There are rock shelters in the hills above Mitla that indicate evidence of human habitation there since several thousand years BC; the village itself was occupied from around AD 100. Its name is derived from Nahuatl Mictlan, meaning 'the place of the dead'. In the Zapotec language it is known as Lyobaa, 'the burial place'.

The seventeenth century Spanish priest Francisco de Burgoa described Mitla as a main centre of the Zapotec religion. It is regarded as second only to the nearby, and better known, Monte Alban.

The buildings are generally low, horizontal structures enclosing plazas. Decoration is elaborate, with wall panels decorated with hard stucco and detailed mosaics. These mosaics are a defining feature of Mitla, with walls often covered in repeated geometric patterns. Constructed of thousands of stones laid one atop the other, some protruding and some recessed, the patterns are similar to Greek designs and are known as grecas. Many believe that the patterns display specific images: for example, some represent the feathered serpent Quetzalcoatl, or a stylised version of Lightning – one of the primary deities of the Zapotecs. Mitla is believed by many to represent the highest expression of Zapotec architectural skills, although alternative theories attribute the mosaics to the Mixtec culture which came to dominate both Mitla and Monte Alban.

Visitors to the site often report feeling something mystical in the surroundings, still powerful after many centuries. One described there being 'something fascinating about repeating geometric patterns . . . when you are among the buildings, it feels appropriate to talk in hushed tones'.

The most characteristic architecture is the Group of the Columns at the Great House of Pezalao. The Great Hall of Columns is rectangular, and includes the Columna de la Vida (the Column of Life). One legend says that you can predict how many years of life you have left by embracing the Column and calculating the space left between your outstretched hands. The group contains two piazzas: the northern one is bordered by platforms on all four sides and contains the main building. The central patio contains the remains of an altar.

Because Mitla was more purely a religious site than Monte Alban, the high priest, or Uija-tao, lived there. The conquering Spaniards, on their arrival, likened him to the Pope. This eminent figure lived in a temple, called a yohopee, meaning 'house of the vital force'. Of this building only the columns and walls remain in the present time.

Zapotec religion was based on two main deities: Sky and Earth. There was also a distinction between those objects which contained life and those that did not. Lightning and Earthquake contained life, Lightning being the most important. The dead of the ruling class would be expected to join Lightning as cloud people (known as 'bed zaa') and from the realm of the divine they would intercede on behalf of the living Zapotecs to ensure their good fortune. Cloud people would be roughly the equivalent of saints in Catholicism.

There are beautiful tombs located in the northern and eastern buildings where the ruling classes were buried, no doubt to gain their good fortune when they met with Lightning in the afterlife. It is probable that only very special people were interred at Mitla; it seems to have been a special burial site, reserved for the ruling classes and with the special purpose of sending them to the gods.

Monte Alban, nr Oaxaca, Mexico

Monte Alban is located on a high spur overlooking the Oaxaca Valley, about seven miles from the city of Oaxaca. It was the capital of the Zapotec culture.

The Zapotecs had no legends of migration, believing themselves to be born directly from rocks, trees, and jaguars. They worshipped many gods, mainly the rain god Cosijo, and also worshipped their ancestors and followed a cult of the dead. They were a highly developed civilisation that flourished over two thousand years ago. In art, architecture, mathematics, and calendar, the Zapotecs had cultural affinities with the Olmec, ancient Maya, and Toltecs.

The artificially levelled hilltop site of Monte Alban has a fifty-five acre central plaza surrounded by several terraces, palaces, and platforms situated to the north and south. Residential structures were located on the hillside terraces which probably also contained gardens. This archaeological site also contains pyramids, temples, a ball court, passages, and an observatory.

Zapotec ball courts differ from those of the Maya; there are no stone rings and the court is shaped like a capital I. The sides of the court were sloping, but it is thought that this was part of the game rather than terraces for spectators. It is not thought likely that the game was used for human sacrifice, as is speculated of the Mayan counterpart.

There are many vaulted and frescoed tombs at Monte Alban – regarded as some of the most elaborate in the Western hemisphere – displaying the power of the Zapotec culture that created this site.

One building, the temple of the Danzantes (the dancers), contains bas-relief figures that were once believed to depict dancers, though more recent thinking suggests that they may show victims of sacrifice or slain enemies. Another theory is that the building was once a hospital and the figures are a 'wall mounted medical text book'. Amongst 150 figures there are images of deformities, and a woman in childbirth.

Another building is the only one not aligned with the cardinal points of the compass, and is thought to have been used for astronomy; hence it was given the name The Observatory. It is composed of about forty carved slabs taken from the Temple of Danzantes. It has alignments with the setting positions of the Southern Cross and Alpha and Beta Centauri, and also aligns with the rising position of the star Capella.

Monte Alban flourished from around 500 BC to AD 500; at its peak it had a population of about twenty-five thousand people living in a strictly stratified society. Their unique social structure included kings, with priests maintaining power in domestic affairs; their government was essentially a theocracy. Monte Alban, one of the first cities in MesoAmerica, began as the regional capital of a state that integrated the peoples of the Valley area, and it developed over time, venturing into military and commercial activities. A later phase of its development involved its connection to the politically powerful city of Teotihuancan. The reasons for

Monte Alban's decline are unknown, but over time the Zapotecs became influenced by the Mixtecs who later used the site for burials.

The city may have been known to the Zapotecs as Dhauya quch o Dauyacach, or the Hill of the Sacred Stone. The Mixtecs called the place Yucucui – the Green Mount. By the time of the Spanish conquest it had been virtually abandoned; its present name comes from that of the Spanish conquistador Diego Lopez de Monte Alban (or Montalban).

There are still Mayan people today who speak Zapotec and keep elements of the culture alive.

Nazca Plains, Peru

On a high plateau some sixty miles long and five miles wide, near the Peruvian coast, is an area of land that has been the subject of much controversy for decades. The area is known as Pampa Colorada (Red Plain), and was inhabited by the Nazca people; what they left behind is the most striking example of ground art anywhere in the world.

There are thousands of carved lines which, from ground level, seem almost random and meaningless, but from the air it becomes apparent that they form huge ground drawings of figures and animals. Investigator William H Isbell categorised the lines as: long straight lines, geometric figures, pictures of plants and animals, rock piles, and hillside decorations. The images include birds, spiders, fish, a monkey, and more. Some lines run for a great distance, some even for miles, but for no obvious reason; the lines vary from fourteen centimetres wide to several hundred metres wide. These ground carvings are at least fifteen hundred years old.

The desert floor in that area consists of dark stones atop a base of creamy pink soil. The images were created by removing the dark surface stones and exposing the lighter soil, and then sometimes using the removed stones to create piles and patterns. The dry, stable climate of the region – it is one of the driest and least wind-affected climates in the world – has contrived to maintain the integrity of the lines over the centuries.

The question that summarises the mystery is: why would people incapable of flight produce carvings that could only be appreciated from the air? Suggestions range from the obscure – for example, that the designers simply did not want them appreciated by the human eye – to the bizarre – that they were carved out as 'runways' for extraterrestrials in their spaceships. The belief that the lines had an extraterrestrial connection probably started when James W Moseley, in the October 1955 issue of *Fate*, suggested that the Nazca people must have 'constructed their huge markings as signals to interplanetary visitors or to some advanced earth race . . . that occasionally visited them.' This idea was taken up by Louis Pauwels and Jacques Bergier in their book *The Morning of the Magicians*, and finally gained popularity as a result of the same idea being promoted in *Chariots of the Gods?* by Swiss writer Erich von Daniken. He suggested the whole plain represented an 'airfield' for aliens.

Others have made the point that perhaps the Nazca people could take to the sky in hot air balloons: but efforts to prove this have remained a controversy. What evidence does exist seems to fall into two categories: firstly, that paintings on pottery found in the area depict what seem to be balloons or kites and, secondly, that wide circular 'burn-pits' containing blackened rocks have been found at the end of many of the lines, from where the balloons could have been launched. Bill Spohrer tested this theory out, by making a balloon using only materials that would have been available to the Nazcans of the time and launching it from a burn-pit. It flew to a height of 120 metres for a few minutes.

Perhaps, however, the question of viewing the lines is being examined through the eyes of 'Western' culture used to the idea of aerial observation. Perhaps the lines can be viewed from the ground very effectively, if lateral thought is given to them. Persis B Clarkson, an archaeologist and expert in geoglyphs at the University of Winnipeg, walked the lines on the ground and mentally created an image of what she was walking, drawing the image she created. When checked with an aerial observation, her drawing was accurate. Perhaps therefore the lines had powerful meaning to the Nazcans in allowing them to visualise their religious symbols, as part of religious observances.

Of course, they could also have been designed so that the gods could appreciate them from their lofty heights. That would be consistent with the beliefs of many early cultures, and the animal shapes could have represented the forms which the Nazcans believed their gods adopted when on earth.

Research in 1984 by volunteers from Earthwatch, an international non-profit organisation that supports scientific research, proved that the design and construction of the lines was quite possible without taking to the air or relying on aliens. They produced a straight line that ended in a spiral thirty-five metres long and one metre wide in just an hour and a half.

The American scholar Paul Koosk believed that the lines represented: 'the largest astronomy book in the world', thinking the lines indicated astronomical alignments. Although Koosk died before being able to research or develop his theories fully, the work was picked up by the German-born astronomer and mathematician, Dr Maria Reiche. Although she suggests that the lines do represent astronomical configurations, her work has not received the acclaim of other scientists who point out that the plethora of lines and the multitude of stars available make apparent matches difficult to prove beyond random chance. Undaunted by her critics, she spent fifty years studying and protecting the lines and drawings – even after being confined to a wheelchair, she still chased people away from the area if they looked like damaging the patterns. Of her death in 1998 at the age of ninety-five, President Alberto Fujimori said: 'This is a really painful and sad loss for Peruvian archaeology . . . Perhaps those "Nazca lines" should even be renamed after her.' It was her efforts which encouraged UNESCO to make the two hundred square miles of the desert a World Heritage site in 1995.

Most favoured theory amongst archaeologists is that the lines are a combination of markings to indicate irrigation systems, and images that have religious significance and mark out parts of pilgrimages. This was first mooted by Peruvian scholar Mejia Xesspe in 1926, when he put forward the idea, based on the traditions of the Incas who followed the Nazcans, that they might be sacred roads. The Incas believed that the natural landscape was imbibed with energy – now a widely favoured belief around the world when discussing sacred sites anywhere. Astronomer and anthropologist Anthony Aveni, at Colgate University in New York, headed up a research team which compared the Nazca lines with the ceque system of the Incan capital of Cuzco (see entry for **Sacsayhuaman**). When Aveni's group compared the Cuzco ceques to the Nazca lines they found that the Nazca lines also radiated outwards, like the spokes of a wheel, from 'ray centres'. This suggested to them that perhaps the ceque system of imaginary lines could have been based on the physical Nazca markings. Surveying eight hundred of the lines they found, according to Aveni, that each of the 'ray centres' of the Nazca lines 'bore an uncanny likeness to one another. Each one consisted of a natural hill or low mound topped by a rock cairn that may have served as an identifying marker'. Up to forty lines radiate out from the hilltops, often connecting to other hills nearby, and many of the lines were oriented along water sources. Aveni believes that: 'All these facts seem to point to at least one absolute certainty: the construction of the lines was connected in some important way with water.'

Archaeologist Johan Reinhard agrees with the basic premise that there is a connection between water and worship reflected in the lines. 'The straight lines are sacred pathways to a place, from which they worshipped the water source. Now that can be symbolic worship towards the ocean, or it can be, as it normally was, invoking the mountain deities.'

Although exceptional because of their extent, such ground art is not unique. Such patterns are a tradition along the Pacific coastal desert areas from central California to northern Chile. Some eight hundred and fifty miles to the south of the Nazca plain is the largest human figure in the world, laid out upon the side of Solitary Mountain. Known as The Giant of Atacama, the figure is 120 metres tall and is surrounded by lines similar to those at Nazca. On the Pacific coast, in the Andes foothills, is a carving shaped like a giant candelabrum or trident. And further to the south, Sierra Pintada (the Painted Mountain) is covered with huge depictions of spirals, circles, warriors and a condor.

Perhaps one use of the lines, for the Nazcans and for us, is to stimulate wonder and thought. As Maria Reiche said: 'We will never know all the answers, that's what a good mystery is all about.'

Ninstints, Queen Charlotte Islands, Canada

The Haida people are North American Indians who originally lived in British Columbia and Southern Alaska, though today they are mainly concentrated on Graham Island.

Ninstints is situated on Anthony Island, part of the Queen Charlotte Islands, and was the original settlement and main village of the Haida Indians during the 1700s. Known as Skungwai'ai by the Haida peoples, Ninstints is the most isolated of their villages.

Most of the Haida lived in villages consisting of a small number of houses. For three decades from 1787 Ninstints was an important destination for those engaged in the fur trade. Such trading greatly increased the wealth and importance of the village and by 1841 Ninstints consisted of an impressive twenty houses and a population of three hundred and eight people.

Unfortunately smallpox was introduced into the village in December 1863 and it virtually decimated the population. Within ten years the site had ceased to be one of permanent habitation. Because of its relative isolation Ninstints has been the least disturbed of the abandoned Haida towns, greatly increasing its value to those studying the ancient sacred sites of the native peoples. It is also a sacred site for the present day Haida peoples.

Many of the original totems and long houses remain there today. Although some of the poles were removed in 1938 and 1957, Ninstints still houses the largest collection of Haida totem poles in their natural state.

The island was proclaimed a Provincial Park in 1958 and declared a UNESCO World Heritage site in 1981.

Ollantaytambo, Cuzco, Peru

The name Ollantaytambo is derived from the Quechua language. Ollanta was the personal name of an Incan captain and Tambo means a city that offered lodgings, food and care for travellers. Ollanta's history comes down to us through oral tradition, and then was written as drama by the priest Antonio Valdez during the eighteenth century. *The Ollantay Drama*, a *Romeo and Juliet* style play, is considered a classical work of Quechua literature. It tells the story of Captain Ollanta, of Inca Pachakuteq's army. He was a much admired soldier, brave and skilful, but had a secret love affair with the monarch's daughter, Kusi Qoyllur. He was unable to marry her as he came from a lower social standing, and in revenge for his disappointment Ollanta incited the population of his town to rebel against the imperial army. War followed for ten years. Eventually Ollanta was captured and taken for execution, but by the time he arrived in Qosqo the Incan Pachakuteq was already dead, succeeded by his son who spared Ollanta and allowed the lovers to marry.

Ollantaytambo was a major Incan fortress, clinging to the side of a rocky outcrop high over a valley. It was the site of several battles, including a defeat of the Spaniards by Manco Inca in 1536. It is a good defensive site; invaders would have had to breach the steep defensive terracing while being attacked. Manco Inca also used the intricate water channels to flood the plain below, a further obstacle for the enemy to overcome.

It was more than a fortress, however; it was an urban centre and, like most Incan constructions, it contained places of worship, in particular the Sun Temple.

The present-day town is located in the same place as the urban sector was in Incan times. It is the only place in Peru where people are still living in the same buildings that were once the homes of the ancient Incan nobility. Indeed, the streets still have their ancient names. Many years ago a meeting of the local Indian peoples was held in Ollantaytambo, and the town was declared the World Capital of the Indians.

Perhaps the most striking feature of the area is a face carved into a nearby steep mountain peak that had to be scaled by the

Incan craftsmen so that the work could be carried out. It must have been no mean achievement without modern climbing equipment. On the winter solstice (21 June in the southern hemisphere) the sun lines up directly with the eye of the profile and, across the valley, streams in through a window at the ruins and on to an altar.

The rock used to build the terracing at Ollantaytambo was quarried from a mountain four miles away over the valley. The massive granite blocks were cut out, shaped and polished, then transported to the fortress-site up the hill on the other side of the valley, and set into place without mortar, so precise was the cutting. The river was diverted so that the stones could be brought across the dry river bank, the water temporarily flowing elsewhere. The Sun Temple was constructed from huge red porphyry (pink granite) stones, also brought from several miles away.

What remains of the Sun Temple are some boundary walls and the classical major wall that most historians believe was part of the High Altar. It consists of six enormous stone blocks each weighing around ninety tons. The construction is unusual for Incan architecture and suggests that the architects were brought from the region of Lake Titicaca.

On the surface of one boulder are three carved symbols representing the three stages of the Andean World: Hanan Pacha (heaven), Kay Pacha (earth surface) and Ukhu Pacha (the underground). There are other carvings which, according to some scholars, represent gods of the Andean mythology.

Towards the north of the religious sector entrance gate is a series of ancient water fountains that, because of their location, are thought by scholars to have been ceremonial and used for worship of the water god; one inside a mud-brick square building still functions.

There are also remains of carvings on the site which were part of a complex solar observatory, used to measure the sun's movements during the year as well as determining solstices and equinoxes.

Palenque, Mexico

At an elevation of just under three thousand metres, situated on the eastern edge of the Rio Usumacinta Basin in the foothills of the Sierra Oriental de Chiapas, are the ancient ruins of Palenque, now in the Palenque National Park. Often hidden in fog and surrounded by dense forests alive to the call of the howler monkey, the ruins are some of the most evocative in South America. The dense forests served as a useful protection for the city. The Spanish conquistador, Cortes, came within a short distance and never saw it, as by then the lush forests had completely overgrown it.

The site was first occupied around 100 BC, but the peak of occupation ran from about AD 600 to 800. The ruins consist of two main parts: the ceremonial area and the settlement bordered by fields where agriculture supported the population.

The ceremonial area contains many important buildings, including: the Pyramid (or Temple) of the Inscriptions, the Palace, the Temple of the Sun, the Temple of the Cross, the Temple of the Foliated Cross, the Temple of the Count, and the Ball Court. The structures were erected by Palenque's rulers. Foremost of these was Pacal (whose name means 'shield') who reigned from AD 615, when he was twelve, until his death in 683 at the age of eighty. Pacal took control from his mother, Lady Zac Kuk, who had reigned for a short time. He claimed his mother was the mother deity of three Mayan gods, and through this he claimed divine heritage.

Pacal is interred in a stone sarcophagus under the Pyramid known as the Temple of Inscriptions. He was buried adorned with jade ornaments and a jade mask. The sarcophagus is covered with an elaborately carved lid. The Temple of the Inscriptions is perhaps the most famous of Palenque's ruins, first examined in detail in 1952. It is the tallest in Palenque at twenty-three metres, constructed on eight levels, and has sixty-nine steep steps.

Palenque was governed by twelve rulers, all priest-kings and military rulers claiming divine descent. Pacal and his children were the most prominent, and responsible for most of the city's construction. On Pacal's death his son, Chan-Balum (whose name means 'snake-jaguar'), assumed control and ruled for eighteen years. In addition to work on the Pyramid of the Inscriptions, Chan-Balum was responsible for building the Temple of the Cross, the Temple of the Foliated Cross (or Temple of the Jaguar), and the Temple of the Sun.

On Chan-Balum's death his brother, Kan-Xul took control, reigning for a further twenty-three years. He redesigned the Palace to more or less the condition in which we find it today. In particular he designed the tower which may have been used as an observatory. The Palace is a maze of rooms, underground chambers and courtyards. Kan-Xul also built the Temple XIV.

Palenque offers much scope for study: only thirty-four of an estimated five hundred ruins have been excavated. It is a site of great mystery; for example the Temple of the Jaguar has carvings similar to Hindu artworks, and has a foliated cross motif similar to one displayed at Angkor Wat in Cambodia.

The lid of Pacal's sarcophagus has been the subject of much speculation, some of it quite wild. It is claimed that it reveals a great deal of astronomical data that some researchers believe should not have been available to ancient peoples. Perhaps the most famous speculation is that made prominent by Erich von Daniken in his book *Chariots of the Gods?*, which was published in 1968. He asserted that the carving of the figure 'clearly depicted' a space traveller, and described him as sitting at the controls of a spaceship, his foot on a pedal, and watching apparatus in front of him. From the rear of the spaceship can be seen flames from the rocket exhaust. However, in 1976 Ronald Story published *The Space Gods Revealed* which, chapter by chapter, took apart von Daniken's speculations. In the chapter 'The Palenque Astronaut', he focused on the artist's drawing of the lid which von Daniken used to demonstrate his theory, and alleged that 'certain details of the drawing have been blacked out' and that, when examined in full detail, it is clear that the figure is dressed in typical Mayan adornment and is depicted 'in a state of suspension between two worlds – the world of the living and the world of the dead'. Far from wearing a spacesuit, as von Daniken claimed, he is naked except for ornaments and jewellery. The image is consistent with other Mayan art of the time.

Petroglyph Provincial Park, Peterborough, Canada

The Peterborough Petroglyphs site is one of the largest known concentrations of prehistoric rock art in Canada and is now a revered sacred place. Around nine hundred images are carved into the limestone outcrops: animal, human, abstract and symbolic. They represent the rich and varied spiritual life of the Anishinabek peoples who created them. The images date from between AD 900 and AD 1400.

Today, members of the Ojibwa Anishinabe Nation honour this location as a sacred site, calling it Kinomagewapkong which means 'the rocks that teach'.

Sacsayhuaman, Cuzco, Peru

Sacsayhuaman is an ancient fortress situated near the Incan capital of Cuzco (Cuzco means 'navel' in the Incan language – a reference to its central position in the empire). The origin of the name Sacsayhuaman is unknown; it has been various translated as Speckled Falcon, Marbled Head or Royal Eagle.

Incan masonry is one of the most astonishing sights in ancient architecture, and is famous for its precision; in many cases it is impossible to slip a sheet of paper between stone blocks placed together centuries ago. The ruins of Sacsayhuaman are prime examples of this. Theories to account for this extraordinary masonry work have been varied, and often bizarre. The explorer Colonel Fawcett wrote in *Exploration* that the Incas had acquired a herb that could dissolve stone. The Spanish invaders claimed the Incas must have used demons. Erich von Daniken in his *Chariots of the Gods?* suggests that extraterrestrial visitors aided the ancients. However, more recent studies around the world have shown that our ancestors were simply more adept than previously believed.

Sacsayhuaman appears to come from the time of the Inca Pachacuti, who is attributed with consolidating the Incan Empire. Although unquestionably a fortress, Sacsayhuaman was more; it was also a significant religious site. The main ramparts consist of three huge parallel walls, zigzagging together for four hundred metres. The inner buildings and towers are made from rock brought from around twenty-two miles distant. It has been suggested that the zigzagging construction of the walls shows that the fortress was also a temple to the god of lightning, an important god to the Incas. It has also been said that the city of Cuzco was designed like a cougar or puma, and that Sacsayhuaman was the head of the beast.

One large stone structure in Sacsayhuaman has carved into it a zigzag shape that may represent lightning, or a serpent. According to the local legends, warriors would insert their fist into the 'head' of the 'serpent' which would give them, according to writer Alan Landsburg, 'strength, courage and magical powers to overcome their enemies'. He felt dismissive of such stories, but became more impressed when he put his compass into the cavity and 'it began spinning as if agitated by some unseen force'. That sacred sites seem to have strange magnetic effects has been noted world-wide, and recent studies of healing and other powers of magnetism may yet offer some confirmation of the Sacsayhuaman legend.

Cuzco itself is famous for its system of ceques. The city has four roads leading out to the extremes of the Incan empire. These roads were contained within forty-one imaginary straight lines called ceques, which radiate out from The Temple of the Sun. The ceques aligned the Incan sacred places (or huacas). Many of the huacas were also positioned at points of underground water sources relating to Cuzco's irrigation system, suggesting that the practicalities of water needs for this agricultural people, and their religious observances, were linked. (See entry for **Nazca**.)

At the centre of Cuzco were the Huacapata and Cusipata regions where the major religious festivals were held, usually under the watchful eyes of the ruling Inca of the day. In 2000 archaeologists discovered sixteen tombs, containing what Octavio Fernandez of Peru's National Cultural Institute believed were the remains of the royal families.

Cuzco was also regarded by the Incas as the capital city of the rain and sea god, Viracocha. Viracocha appeared during the time of the Great Flood (the Incan myth of the great flood parallels many such flood myths around the world), after which he created the sun, moon and stars, and then disappeared into the sea, promising to return one day.

Shiprock, New Mexico, USA

Located in north-west New Mexico, Shiprock is the remnant of a volcanic eruption that happened around thirty to forty million years ago. The main area of the landform is six hundred metres high, five hundred metres in diameter, and stands around 2,300 metres above sea level. It takes its name from its similarity to a clipper ship. Shiprock is also known as Tse Bitai (or The Winged Rock) in the Navajo language. It is a sacred site to the indigenous people of the area.

It was first climbed in 1939 by members of the Sierra Club of California; however, climbing it is an offence to the Navajos, and it is now illegal. There is a good reason for this. According to their legends, the Navajo were once under attack from enemies and they prayed to their gods to deliver them safely. The ground they were standing on rose into the air, took wings, and flew them to safety, depositing them in the desert, and The Winged Rock remained forever at the site. These early Navajo ancestors lived only on Tse Bitai, and came down just to get water and plant their crops. Then one day, while the men were working on the plains, lightning cleft the rock, leaving only a sheer cliff where the slopes used to be. The men could not get back up and the women and children there starved to death. Their bodies are deemed to be there still, and the Navajo would prefer them undisturbed.

The sad truth is that many people do ignore the Navajo beliefs and, disrespectfully, climb the rock. Several people have died doing so, and there is a memorial plaque on the route to remind people of the dangers.

The rock is situated on Highway 666, the Devil's Highway, so named because of the association of the devil with that number. It is also known as Satan's Speedway and The Devil's Dragstrip. The area around Shiprock itself is also where several UFO sightings have been claimed.

Teotihuacan, Mexico

This large urban centre, some twenty-five miles to the north-east of Mexico City, is an archaeological site containing the ruins and remnants of the earliest city in the western hemisphere, and was first occupied as a small settlement during the first century BC. It probably coalesced out of a number of small villages after, as archaeologists believe, a four-chambered lava-tube cave was discovered there. Caves were central in MesoAmerican religion, being places from where the gods and ancestors emerged into the human world, as well as being portals to the underworld. The Teotihuacan cave may have been particularly significant as its four lobes could have represented the four parts of the MesoAmerican cosmos. The Pyramid of the Sun was built directly over the cave in the second century AD. By this time the city had grown into an important centre, and flourished until around 700–750, when it was destroyed. No one knows why the city declined, though many believe some catastrophe befell it, and it is not understood why the inhabitants appear to have tried to burn it and raze it to the ground when they evacuated it. Alternatively, it might have been sacked and destroyed by invaders, possibly from the city of Cacaxtla, 130 miles to the east.

The people of ancient Teotihuacan had affiliation to the Mayan culture of the Yucatan and Guatemala, and they had a significant influence on later Mexican cultures, such as the Aztecs. Although the city was only discovered by the Aztecs long after it was destroyed, they believed it to be part of their own legends. According to Aztec myths, the world had been created and destroyed four times: by jaguars, fire, wind and flood. After the fourth destruction, the gods met at Teotihuacan to decide which of their number should throw himself into the ritual fire to become the fifth creation. Nanahuatzin leaped into the flames and became the fifth sun of creation, a light for all mankind.

Some of the most important sacred sites in the world are found in Teotihuacan, including: the Pyramid of the Sun, one of the largest structures ever built in the western hemisphere; the Pyramid of the Moon; and the Avenue of the Dead, a broad road bordered by the ruins of several temples. The temples contain frescoes that probably depict religious and mythological tales; Teotihuacan was known as the City of the Gods by the Aztecs who discovered its ruins. They were so impressed by its obvious former splendour that they believed it to be the birthplace of the gods.

Most spectacular structure of all is the Pyramid of the Sun, the third largest pyramid in the world. This sacred building was made of rubble, mud, and earth, faced with stone, and topped with a wooden temple. The Sun Pyramid was excavated and examined during the first decade of the twentieth century by Leopordo Batres and since then two tunnels have been cut into it, revealing more information. Another excavation was undertaken by the Instituto Nacional de Antropologia e Historia, directed by Eduardo Matos Moctezuma, in 1992-3.

When built, the Sun Pyramid was approximately 215 metres square at the base, and about sixty-three metres high. It was later enlarged at least twice and is now 225 metres along each side. The pyramid was situated on the east side of the Avenue of the Dead, in the northern half of the city, and central to the area between the Moon Pyramid and the San Juan Canal. It originally consisted of four stepped platforms, a temple, and the Adosada platform, which was built over the original main façade of the pyramid.

The Ciudadela is a massive enclosure located at the centre of the city, each side of which was about four hundred metres long. The interior, which could contain approximately one hundred thousand people, probably half the population of the city, is surrounded by four large pyramids built on platforms. The Pyramid of the Feathered Serpent (Quetzalcoatl) is the central structure. Two residential compounds are adjacent: the North Palace and the South Palace, which probably provided living and working space for the administrative centre. The palaces were excavated by the Proyecto Arqueologico Teotihuacan of the Instituto Nacional de Antropolgia e Historia in Mexico.

The Avenue of the Dead was the main thoroughfare of Teotihuacan. Over one and a half miles long, it ran from the Moon Plaza in the north to the Ciudadela and the Great Compound sites to the south. Possibly it once extended even further, to the mountains. The main area of the Avenue was that between the Moon Pyramid and the Rio San Juan channel, and would have been flanked by platforms. Apart from providing access, there was an efficient water-drainage system running under the Avenue, draining the buildings either side of it.

The Moon Pyramid is located at the northern end of the Avenue of the Dead, and remains the least understood major structure in Teotihuacan. Recent work there, under the direction of Saburo Sugiyama, associate professor at Aichi Prefectural University in Japan, located a tomb which seems to have been created to dedicate the fifth phase of construction of the Pyramid. It contained four human skeletons, animal bones, conch shells, jewellery, obsidian knives and more. There is a similar tomb at the site which seems to relate to the pyramid's fourth phase of building; this earlier tomb holds only one human skeleton, a sacrificial victim, as well as animal remains and offerings. Of the recent find, Sugiyama said: 'As a result of the final discoveries, we find explicit signs of militarism in the culture since its early periods.' The cultural and social changes implied by the differences between phases four and five suggest that a shift in the culture may also be reflected in the Feathered Serpent Pyramid and the Pyramid of the Sun. These two later structures were built together, and much later than the Pyramid of the Moon.

The alignments of buildings in Teotihuacan suggest advanced astronomical beliefs, and certainly long-term planning. The Avenue of the Dead runs 15.5 degrees east of due north, parallel to the front of the Pyramid of the Sun and along a line between the Pyramid of the Moon and the Cerro Gordo. The Pyramid of the Sun and the cave entrance associated with it seem to be aligned with the stars known as the Pleiades, which have more recently, in the West, become a focus of UFO lore and belief. The harmony of buildings with the topography of the area and the celestial bodies suggests an advanced mythology. Archaeoastronomer John Carlson wrote: 'Nowhere is the bond between sky and earth more evident than at Teotihuacan.'

It was a strictly organised city, tightly governed by religious leaders who had complete control over the minds, spirits, and bodies of the people. The priests were also skilful astronomers who monitored and influenced the cycles of public life, and organised the religious ceremonies. The influence of religion delved deeply into every household; domestic altars were normal in even the poorest homes. Teotihuacan's art reflected the religion and mythology of a richly spiritual people, and was centred around the feathered serpent god Quetzalcoatl, as well as a pantheon of other gods. Quetzalcoatl, one of the most important gods in Mexico, had the body of a snake and the feathers of a bird. He was a god of nature for the inhabitants of Teotihuacan, but became a culture god identified with the planet Venus for the Aztecs.

Teotihuacan's civilisation was contemporaneous with that of ancient Rome, and its empire lasted longer. At its peak, the city was the major site of pilgrimage, or early 'tourism', in MesoAmerica. Travellers to the Valley of Mexico would generally include a visit to Teotihuacan, partly to gaze in wonder at the brightly-painted buildings, or to trade, or to worship. Thousands of villages in the Mexican highlands would empty out at certain times of the year, the people heading for Teotihuacan's plazas to take part in the ceremonies designed to ensure the future prosperity of the city and the people of the Valley.

Tiahuanacu, and Lake Titicaca, Bolivia

Tiahuanacu (or Tiwanaku) is a major pre-Incan urban and religious site south-east of Lake Titicaca, near the modern village of Tiahuanacu. At 3,800 metres up in the Andes, it was the highest city in the ancient world. Radiocarbon dating suggests that the city was founded before AD 300. Certain structures were left uncompleted when, for unknown reasons, work in the area ceased in about 900. They city was already in ruins when the Incas arrived in the region.

In the past Tiahuanacu was a flourishing port at the edge of nearby Lake Titicaca, suggesting that the water has receded about twelve miles and the level has dropped 240 metres since then.

Stonework at Tiahuanacu reveals some of the most skilful

craftmanship known in South America, and there is the earliest use of metal for structural purposes yet found in the western hemisphere.

The Akapana pyramid is the largest structure at the site: it was once a terraced pyramid some fifteen metres high and 152 metres in length on each side. Its base is formed of beautifully cut and joined stone blocks. Within the retaining walls are six T-shaped terraces with vertical stone pillars, an architectural technique that is used in most of the other Tiahuanacu monuments. On the summit of the Akapana there was a sunken court serviced by a subterranean drainage system.

Probably the most famous monument at Tiahuanacu is the Gateway of the Sun, a huge sculpture weighing fifteen tons, carved in low relief, with the figure of a god holding two staves topped by eagles' heads; around his head is a halo of shapes and puma heads. These motifs are also found on pottery located at the site. This has led to the speculation that Tiahuanacu was once the centre of a powerful religious cult, probably extending through Bolivia, Chile, and the Pacific Coastal area.

Nearby Lake Titicaca is also regarded as a most sacred site. There were rumours for centuries of stone structures hidden within the lake. In 1968 Jacques Cousteau, an underwater explorer, and his team spent many days searching for these alleged structures, but found nothing. However, in 1980, Hugo Boero Rojo, a Bolivian author and scholar, announced the finding of archaeological ruins beneath the lake on the north-east edge. At a press conference he said: 'We can now say that the existence of pre-Columbian constructions under the waters of Lake Titicaca is no longer a mere supposition or science-fiction, but a real fact. Further, the remnants found show the existence of old civilisations that greatly antecede the Spanish colonisation. We have found temples built of huge blocks of stone, with stone roads leading to unknown places and flights of steps whose bases were lost in the depths of the lake amid a thick vegetation of algae.' This is further confirmed by reports in early 2001 that recent dives in the lake had also located the structures, including a temple. Lorenzo Epis, the Italian scientist leading the work, commented: 'The holy temple measures

660 feet [200 metres] by 160 feet [49 metres].' The BBC reported: 'A terrace for crops, a long road, and a 2,600-foot [790 metres] long wall were also found under the waters of the lake . . . the ruins are pre-Incan.' Bolivia's vice-minister for Culture, Antonio Equino, commented: 'Our civilisations have left more footprints than we had thought.'

There is an apparent contradiction, however, in the lake having receded and there being structures beneath its waters. The reconciliation can only lie in the structures having been built before the lake existed at all. This suggests the area was subject to huge change, which perhaps was a contributory reason for the abandonment of the site by the original local peoples. Peruvian legends include a flood-myth story, similar to those found all around the world, which suggests a genuine event at some time in history.

As Boero Rojo commented: 'The discovery of Aymara structures under the waters of Lake Titicaca could pose entirely new theses on the disappearance of an entire civilisation, which, for some unknown reason, became submerged.' The original peoples of Tiahuanacu may have been the victims of flood, and, because of the geography of the area, the flood waters that became Lake Titicaca could not run off and have only gradually evaporated over the centuries.

Lake Titicaca is the largest lake in South America and the highest navigable lake in the world. It contains forty-one islands, of which Isla de Titicaca is the largest; many are populated. According to Incan mythology, the world was created by the god Viracocha near Lake Titicaca. After the flood Virachocha descended to earth and created plants, animals and men on the empty land; he built the city of Tiahuanacu and appointed four world rulers including Manco Capac. Manco Capac and Mama Huaca emerged from the depths of Lake Titicaca to found the Incan Empire. To this culture, the entire lake was therefore a sacred site.

The religion of Tiahuanacu probably centred around the cult of Viracocha. The chieftain would have been regarded as both king and arch-priest, and was probably considered the incarnation of Viracocha on earth. According to legend, Viracocha is described as a fair-skinned man with a white beard, wearing a long robe and sandals, and carrying a staff. He was kind and peace-loving, but he was challenged by evil people who forced him to leave. On his departure they mocked and taunted him. He left for the Pacific, vowing one day to return.

One theory of the people at Tiahuanacu is that their forebears were the ancestors of the Incas, and that their city was once the capital of an empire that would one day become the Incan empire. These people were forced to leave, and migrated to Cuzco where they set up a new base for their empire.

The Incas regarded Lake Titicaca and the surrounding area as their former home and honoured Viracocha as the god who had instructed them to build the city of Cuzco. Archaeological evidence suggests that Cuzco may have been built around the time Tiahuanacu was in decay, supporting this belief.

MYSTICAL AND SACRED SITES IN AUSTRALASIA

Arta-Wararlpanha, Flinders Range, South Australia

Arta-Wararlpanha (aka Mount Serle), a peak in the northern part of the Flinders Range, is a sacred site for the Adnyamathanha people, who explain the creation of the Range through their mythology.

Once, when the country was flat, is was visited by a kangaroo named Urdlu and a euro (a type of wallaby) named Mandya. Urdlu had plenty to eat but Mandya was hungry and sought food from the kangaroo. Eventually Mandya located Urdlu's source of food by following him, for which the kangaroo was angry and beat the euro. Mandya went off to be on his own and pulled a pebble from a wound. When he blew on it the hills of the Flinders Range rose up from the plain, and the more he blew the more the hills that rose up. Urdlu, being a kangaroo that lives on the plains, saw that eventually he would end up with no home and so he swept his tail, pushing back the Flinders Range to its present location.

The sacred place, Arta-Wararlpanha, was itself created by two snakes in the Dreamtime (see entry for **Kata Tjuta**).

It is one of the last areas where the Adnyamathanha people held out against invaders and their ritual masters, who led the resistance at the turn of the nineteenth century, are buried there. The site is therefore sacred both mythologically and historically to the Adnyamathanha people.

Borobudur, Java, Indonesia

Borobudur is a Hindu-Buddhist temple near Magelang on the island of Java. It is one of the finest, and earliest, shrines in the region; it was built in the ninth century AD, abandoned in the eleventh century – when political power moved from central Java to the east – and excavated by Dutch archaeologists in the early twentieth century. There are a number of eighth century stone shrines to the god Shiva, but it is likely that any earlier temples made of wood have not survived the ravages of the climate. The Borobudur temple consists of eight step-like stone terraces atop one another. The first five terraces are square and surrounded by walls displaying Buddhist sculptures; the upper three are circular, each with a ring of bell-shaped Buddhist stupas. The arrangement is topped by a large stupa at the centre of the highest circle. It is probable that the early Hindu builders constructed the shrine to Shiva and then abandoned it unfinished, and it was completed by Buddhists to create what would then have been the largest Buddhist stupa in the world.

Borobudur symbolises the structure of the universe. Pilgrims ascending the steps are symbolically walking upwards from the material world to nirvana. It influenced temples built at Angkor, Kampuchea, such as the magnificent Angkor Wat (see entry), and it is an Indonesian national monument.

Kata Tjuta, Australia

Also known as The Olgas, and The Place of Many Heads, Kata Tjuta rises some six hundred metres above the plains of Northern Territory, Australia, around thirty miles to the west of Uluru (Ayers Rock). It is part of the Uluru-Kata Tjuta National Park (see entry for **Uluru**), and is situated at virtually the geographical centre of Australia. It is made up of thirty to fifty domes of conglomerate rock, covering eleven square miles; the tallest of the domes is around 546 metres high.

Geologically the domes result from tectonic and geomorphic processes, but equally important are the local myths of their origin. It is a vitally significant traditional Aboriginal area, where Aboriginal peoples still live and work, and where traditional languages are used widely as the 'first language'. In October 1985 the ownership of the location was handed back to Anangu, the indigenous peoples of the Western Desert of Australia.

The rare and important flora and fauna of the area originally justified the Park being included in the World Heritage List in 1987. In 1994 it was relisted for its cultural values, because of the relationship demonstrated between the Aboriginal people and the land; it became only the second cultural site in the world to be recorded as a 'cultural landscape'.

The concept of 'cultural landscapes' is important in the modern world, where reaching back into the mythologies is increasingly significant to people. The conservation of such sites is designed to reflect not just the physical, but also the social, religious, spiritual, and cultural setting. It is therefore a holistic approach to conservation. Such an attitude accommodates the traditions of the indigenous peoples, and their relationship to the land and the environment. Anangu and the Australian Nature Conservation Agency (ANCA) now conserve and manage the Park jointly, in what is seen as a landmark in the progress of the Aboriginal Land Rights Movement. More significantly, the management of the Park is governed by Anangu law and tradition. Anangu culture, social structure, and ethics are explained by Tjukurpa, which is the Anangu word which refers to the beginning of time, to the creation period, also known as the Dreamtime. As stated by Yami Lester, Chair of the Uluru-Kata Tjuta Board of Management: 'We've been always saying the land is important to us for Tjukurpa, now other people from overseas and non-indigenous people recognise that it's of cultural importance – it makes me feel good that it's been recognised at last.'

The Aboriginal mythology of the area insists that part of Kata Tjuta is a sacred female location in which men are forbidden, or at least discouraged. One visitor to the area – an aboriginal man who therefore remained at a distance – described the appearance of Kata Tjuta as 'like the body of a giant female, lying eroded from sunlight and wind since the Dreaming time.' It is said to be a site charged with considerable energy.

The Dreamtime is the aboriginal mythology of creation. It represents the time when everything in existence came into being as one holistic system. In the Dreamtime the ancestors found the Earth a featureless void. Some ancestral spirits, the serpents, pushed up the rocks as they squirmed underground, and formed the hills and ridges. Other spirits came from the sea and from the air. They created the world, its laws, languages and customs.

According to tradition, many of the ancestral beings still inhabit the Anangu lands. Their travels are marked by iwara (paths). Iwara are not visible, and need to be interpreted by the Anangu people. Kata Tjuta is one of the sacred meeting points in a network of such ancestral paths. There is similarity between this belief and that in the existence of leys which are commonly accepted in the West.

The Aboriginal traditions are at present, as in the past, maintained and passed on through inma (ceremony), song, dance and the arts and crafts. Tjukurpa is not written down. The stories told are complex and full of symbolism and metaphor.

By engaging in rituals taught by the tradition, Aboriginal peoples can connect with their ancestors by bringing djang – the ancient spiritual energy – into the present. They believe that each soul is connected to its ancestors, and that the rituals, enhanced by the energies of locations such as Kata Tjuta, activate the soul and make the connection.

Kata Tjuta is associated with many Dreaming ancestors. One of the most important of these is Wanambi, the serpent, who is said to live in a waterhole atop the rocks during the wet season, and in the dry season travels to one of the gorges in the area. Part of the site is therefore sacred to the Rainbow Snake – the most powerful deity in the Aboriginal pantheon – and it is taboo to light fires in that area, or to drink at the waterhole, in case the Rainbow Snake becomes angry and aggressive.

The caves on the southern side of Walpa Gorge in Kata Tjuta are typical of parts of the site which are associated with women. It is said that during the Dreamtime the Corkwood Sisters piled high the corkwood tree blossom which later became the caves. To the east are the camps of the Mice Women and the Curlew Man who form the basis of a fertility ceremony. The Curlew Man is one of the guardians of the departed.

A particularly impressive rock pillar is said to be the body of Malu the Kangaroo Man, dying in the arms of his sister Mulumura, the Lizard Woman. In mythology, he died, killed by dogs, after journeying from the west. Erosion in the rock represents his wounds, and a rock mound at the base of the monolith is said to be his intestines which spilled out of his injury.

The site is also associated with the Pungalunga Men and the god Yuedum who gives plant foods to humanity. The Pungalunga Men were the cannibal giants who lived in the Dreamtime and who hunted humans for food.

Laura District, Queensland, Australia

Some of the most spectacular rock art in Australia is found in northern Queensland in the Laura District, north of Cairns. The art has been dated to approximately fifteen thousand years ago, and depicts figures and schematic images relating to Aboriginal mythology. The art on the wall of the Emu Gallery is particularly evocative. Animals, birds, spirit creatures and shamans feature amongst the designs, and it seems that some of the figures were drawn as magical defenders against invaders.

It is a place of sacred pilgrimage for aborigines due to its Dreamtime associations (see entry for **Kata Tjuta**).

Laura is the home of the spirit beings known as Quinkin. The Quinkin are spiritual depictions of lust, symbolised by images of the male sexual organ. According to legend, during the Dreamtime, Tul-Tul the Plover left his wife and son to go hunting. One of the Quinkin, Ungarr, was aroused by the sight of the woman and raped her. During this act the woman died, and Ungarr hid in his home in a tall dead tree. Tul-Tul found his wife dead, but was able to bring her back to life and heal her. As a vengeance on the Quinkin, Tul-Tul set light to grasses at the bottom of the tree, burning Ungarr to ashes. All that remained of him was his penis which would not burn and which Tul-Tul chopped into pieces, scattering it round the country. This is the mythological explanation of how men and women received their penises and clitorises.

Melville Island, Northern Australia

Melville Island, and neighbouring Bathurst Island, are home to the Tiwi people. The treacherous channel separating the islands from the mainland prevented any serious contact with outsiders until 1900, the people therefore being largely left to their own customs until that time.

In their Dreamings the Tiwi people describe the emergence of their own ancestors' social structures, religion and the Islands themselves, beginning with the emergence of a blind woman Mudungkala, who rose out of the ground at Murupianga in south-eastern Melville Island. She crawled across the bare land and created the island, separating it from the mainland. With her she carried her three children: two daughters and her son Purukuparli. She then crawled southwards and disappeared, leaving the children behind. They became the ancestors of the Tiwi people. At Yipanari on the eastern side of Melville Island, Purukuparli married Bima, great-granddaughter of his sister. They had a son, Jinani, who was neglected and died. Purukuparli was enraged by his son's death and carried his body into the sea off Yipanari, crying that death would become the fate of all Tiwi. He drowned and a strong whirlpool formed.

Bima's father, Tokwampini, the Honey Bird Man, organised the Pukumani ceremony – a mortuary rite – for Purukuparli, directing the creation of grave poles, bark baskets, spears and other artefacts. After the ceremony was performed, Tokwampini instructed the ancestors in the laws of marriage and social behaviour, and they dispersed to metamorphose into the flora, fauna and objects of the island, thus ending the period of creation.

Mount Agung, Bali

The Peak of Bali volcano, known in Indonesian as Gunung Agung (the Great Mountain), is the highest point in Bali at 3,014 metres. It is the object of religious veneration and has been compared to Mount Olympus in the myths of the Greeks. It is the centre of the world for the Balinese, who believe it to be the home of the god Siwa and therefore a place of eternal holiness.

It is said that the gods rest above the summit and, when they are displeased, Agung showers the land with stone and ruin. After a dormant period of 120 years, the volcano erupted in 1963, killing sixteen hundred people and making some eighty-six thousand homeless. This eruption began during the greatest Balinese ceremony and exorcism of evil, Eka Dasa Rudra, that takes place only once every one hundred years. Many Balinese believe that the eruption was a sign of the gods' disapproval of the Sukarno regime; certainly it marked the beginning of crop failures, forced re-settlement of thousands, anti-communist purges and, ultimately, the end of the regime which fell in March 1966.

Of an early eruption it is said that Hyang Putra Jaya, an incarnation of Siwa, descended to the Earth to reside on the summit of Gunung Agung. After the following eruption, a spring is said to have emerged on the slopes of the mountain, water from which now forms an important part of religious ceremonies held at the Besakih temple.

Balinese myths about the mountain are many. One insists that the gods made the mountains as their thrones, and that they made the highest on Bali: Mount Agung. Another myth has it that the gods found the island of Bali insecure and wobbly, and to stabilise it they placed on it the heavy, holy, Mount Agung. Other stories claim that the mountain was raised to provide the gods with a place from where they could view all of Balinese life, and that when the gods come down from the heavens they use the mountain as a stepping stone on their way to reside in Bali's holiest temple complex, Besakih. Still another says that Siwa made the mountains to ensure the stability of the whole Indonesian archipelago, and achieved this by slicing three peaks from the Himalayas, and depositing them in Java, Bali and Lombok.

Every Balinese temple contains a shrine dedicated to the mountain's spirit. Other religious artefacts on the island, including temple offerings and cremation mounds, are shaped in the form of mountains to show reverence for Mount Agung. The Balinese always sleep with their heads pointed towards Mount Agung, and all temples and shrines on Bali point towards it. Life on the island centres around the religion which is a blend of Hinduism, Buddhism, Malay ancestor worship, and animism.

Bali is known as the 'island of a thousand temples', though there are somewhere between ten thousand and twenty thousand temples, not including the private shrines in individual dwelling houses – and virtually every dwelling has one.

In every village there are three main temples, collectively called Kahyangan Tiga. The temple Pura Desa, dedicated to Brahma (the power of creation), also functions as a village hall and as a centre for local politics. The second temple, called Pura Puseh, is dedicated to Wisnu (preservation). The third temple, called Pura Dalem, is dedicated to Siwa (annihilation), and is located near the cemetery as it is the temple of the dead.

The most important Balinese Hindu temple, known as the Mother temple, or Pura Besakih, is situated on the slopes of Mount Agung. It was supposed to have been erected there to appease the anger of Siwa, and prevent further volcanic eruptions. Besakih comprises over eighty temples within twenty-two temple complexes on seven terraces, with steps so numerous that it is said they cannot be counted. It houses the ancestral shrines of all Hindu Balinese.

To the Balinese, temples are regarded as merely pleasant resting places for the gods during their times on the island, and are usually empty except during ceremonies.

Nimbin Rocks, New South Wales, Australia

Although only a small town in northern New South Wales, Nimbin is one of the most important places in Australian mythology. It is named after the mythical figure Nyimbunji, a most powerful shaman gifted with supernatural powers, and is famed for its healing qualities.

The scared place of energy is actually located nearby at Nimbin Rocks, where those who seek to be shamans visit. At that site, they would undergo tests to draw out and attain shamanistic power, and learn to communicate with the spirit world so that they could become leaders of their communities.

Nyimbunji also features in a myth of giant dogs – a theme found in various forms all over Australia. According to the story, Nyimbunji and a colleague Balugaan had two dogs, who chased a kangaroo to a place called Ilbogan where it turned into a water snake. The dogs were later caught by locals who cooked them.

Nyimbunji and Balugaan caught the killers of their dogs, took up the dogs' corpses and carried them home to a waterfall at Mount Widgee, where the dogs turned to stone. At night, however, the dogs turn into huge dingoes and prowl around. Mount Widgee is also a sacred place for the Bundjalung people who live in the area.

Pea Hill, nr Noonkanbah, Western Australia

Peak Hill, or Umpampurru, is a most significant sacred site to the Noonkanbah aborigine population. The mythical hero Unyupu fought two snakes here, the fight creating the Fitzroy River. The battlefield was crossed by Nangala, pregnant wife of the Jangalajarra snake, as she travelled. Also, Looma the blue-tongued lizard-woman stopped at the site as she journeyed to her final resting place. Because of such a powerful association with mythical figures, the site became highly charged; it is a powerful djang (spiritual energy) site, particularly for women, guarded as it is by a female spirit. It is also a djang place for snakes, frogs and lizards.

Pea Hill is a site where a number of scared objects are stored, including inma boards. These are the sacred soul-boards of the desert people, which connect an individual to his of her ancestors, and to the Dreaming lines of the country. They can also be magical weapons.

Uluru, Australia

Uluru, also known as Ayers Rock, is near Kata Tjuta, and is embraced by the same National Park. It is a place of spiritual potency, and many go there seeking a mystical experience; reportedly many achieve it. It is the most sacred place in Australia for Aboriginal peoples, where many songlines and Dreaming tracks come together.

The sandstone monolith rises some four hundred metres above the general ground level; it is the largest single lithic outcropping in the world. According to Aboriginal myth, it was built in the Dreamtime by two boys who played in the mud after a rainfall.

(After their play they travelled south to the Musgrave Range, then turned north to the table-topped Mount Connor, where their bodies can still be seen today as boulders.) The rock is in the custodianship of the Pitjantjatjara and Yankuntjatjara people, and represents the end of the Dreamtime Age and the beginning of the Modern Age.

The rock has a sunny side and a shady side, a reference to the myth cycles. The shady side, in legend, concerns the Rock Python people. One of them carried her eggs on her head and buried them at the eastern end of Uluru. While the Rock Python people were camped there, they were attacked by a party of Liru, the poisonous snake warriors. The south-west face of the rock is said to display the scars left by the battle. A Rock Python woman who fought in the battle is represented, her features preserved on the eastern face of a gorge; and the face of an attacking Liru warrior can be seen on the western face. These are not carvings; they are the Aboriginal interpretations of natural rock formations.

This is the Aboriginal worldview: that the consciousness of humans is the reverie of the Earth's ecology, and the monuments such as Uluru represent the activities of mighty beings who lived on the Earth during the Dreamtime.

Winbaraku, Northern Territory, Australia

Just west of Haast's Bluff in the Macdonnell mountain range in the Northern Territory is the sacred site of Winbaraku. In Aboriginal mythology, this is the birthplace of Jarapiri, the Great Snake ancestor who created the Earth. The site consists of two jutting peaks: the taller is Jarapuri, and the lesser is the Nabanunga women who sought to take him to their home. In the mythology, he refused to leave and remains in the mountains. It is a very sacred site because there are many important Dreamtime ancestors associated with it: the Hare-Wallaby; the Melatji Law Dogs; Mamu-Boijunda; the Barking Spider; and Jarapira Bomba, another snake. The site is particularly important to the Walbiri Elders, who believe that many of their ancestors visit the site on their travels.

For the Walbiri people creation began at Winbaraku. The

shaping of the world took place through the workings of Mamu-Boijunda and Jarapiri, who emerged from the Earth at that site. Jealousy and desire were also created there, and this resulted in the first ancestors leaving their home and travelling across the land, while the Barking Spider remained in a cave beneath the hill.

Wullunggnari, Kimberley Plateau, Western Australia

Wullunggnari in the Kimberley Plateau is one of the most sacred places of the Kimberley people. Three stones there represent the Great Flood, which to the Kimberley Aborigines represents a Dreamtime flood which wiped out most of the population of the world, except for one boy and one girl who grabbed hold of the tail of a kangaroo and were carried to higher ground. These two children became the ancestors of all humans. (The parallels to flood myths all around the world are obvious). Wandjina, the spirit ancestors of the Kimberley Aborigines, were held to have rested at Wullunggnari during the time they created the world. The site is represented by a stone altar in front of a cave, and nearby is a tree, Walguna, the tree of wisdom, knowledge and law, which is used for ceremonies when it is hung with sacred objects.

Aborigines would travel to the site to be symbolically born, arriving naked and without weapons and tools. Sacrifices would be made with small pieces of meat, and people would bathe in sacred waters. The area is used for the initiation ceremonies of boys coming of age, and is a powerful djang site – that is, a site of great natural Earth energy, also known as a thalu place.

SELECTED GLOSSARY OF SPECIALIST TERMS USED IN THE TEXT

Acropolis
A natural outcrop of rock around which a community develops; usually housing the most important and sacred sites at the highest point.

Animism
The doctrine that all objects have a spiritual, or inner, being. A development of animatism which early peoples followed, believing that the inanimate objects they held sacred were endowed with spiritual 'life'.

Avenue (as related to stone circles)
Avenues run to or from henges, and are usually marked by embankments or lines of standing stones. Most are thought to have been ceremonial walkways.

Barrow
The earlier form of burial mound in northern Europe; often flanked or surrounded by ditches.

Cairn
A burial mound of any shape of size. (Also used to describe a pile of stones marking a grave, or other special point.)

Cenote
Mexican word for a steep-sided sink-hole, as at Chichen-Itza (see

entry). A source of water, but sometimes used for sacrificial purposes.

Ceques
'Imaginary' lines, similar to British 'leys', that are part of the Incan tradition. Ceques were indicated by sacred places (huacas) arranged on each line.

Chaitya-hall
A vaulted preaching hall.

Djang
Aboriginal concept of ancient spiritual energy.

Dolmen
A megalithic tomb with a small chamber, or standing stones, topped by a large capping stone.

Dreamtime/Dreaming
The aboriginal time of Creation; the basis of aboriginal mythology.

Equinox
The times during the year when day and night are of equal length.

Gopuram
Stylised gateway, usually an entrance to a temple.

Henge
An earthen rampart circle, often enclosing a wooden or stone circle, though the latter were usually constructed at later dates within the original henge.

Huacas
Incan term for their sacred places and mystical sites.

Kalacakra
The highest form of Tibetan mysticism.

Karma

In Hindu and Buddhist traditions: the sum of actions during a lifetime which must be balanced by the next incarnation or existence.

Ley

A straight line connecting sacred or prehistoric sites; thought by some to represent lines of natural earth energy.

Linga

Phallic symbol of the Hindu god/goddess Shiva.

Mandapam

A large open hall in a Hindu temple complex, usually pillared and often containing carvings depicting religious scenes.

Mastaba

A low rectangular structure covering a rock tomb, connected by a vertical shaft.

Megalith

Simply means 'large stone'. May be used to refer to any single such stone, or sometimes to a group of stones.

Menhir

A single standing stone.

Monolith

A single block of stone, often shaped into a monument.

Omphalus

A conical stone, in Greek antiquity representing the navel of the Earth.

Outlier

A single standing stone, positioned some way from a group or circle with which it is associated.

Pagoda
Hindu or Buddhist temple or sacred building.

Prakaaras
Passages which surround the Sanctum Sanctorum of a temple.

Pueblo
A Spanish-based name used in the Americas for a communal village or settlement.

Ramayana
The story of Rama; a Hindu epic that is the basis of much mythology.

Saddhu
A wise or holy man, a sage.

Samkalpa
A vow of worship.

Shakti
In Hindu represents the power of the supreme goddess.

Shaman
Wise people, healers and spiritual leaders of early, native, cultures. Said to have access to the spiritual world of the deities.

Solstice
The two times during the year when the sun reaches the highest, or lowest, point in the sky at noon.

Stupa
A stupa is not a building in the strict sense of the word; traditionally it is a burial or reliquary mound, and today is more often a symbolic object. To be more precise; a stupa is a symbol of the final release from the cycle of birth and re-birth: the Parinirvana or the Final Dying.

Thalu

Aboriginal word for a sacred place or site.

Thirtha

Indian word for a bathing place, but used to describe also a crossing place from the material world to the divine realm.

Tirthankaras

The enlightened sages who guided the development of Jainism.

Trilithon

Three stones in a particular formation: two standing and capped by one other. Not unlike cricket stumps in appearance, and most famously displayed at Stonehenge.

Tumulus

Ancient burial mound (plural: tumuli).

UNESCO

United Nations Educational, Scientific and Cultural Organisation. An agency of the United Nations created in 1946. One of its briefs is to protect and maintain sites of important cultural heritage.

Wat

Place of worship or religious education.

REFERENCES AND RECOMMENDED READING

In addition to specific books and articles mentioned within the text, the following sources of reference are likely to be of interest to those seeking to follow up reading on mystical and sacred sites.

Bishop, Peter and Darton, Michael, *Encyclopaedia of World Faiths*, MacDonald Orbis, 1987

Bond, Frederick Bligh, *The Company of Avalon*, Blackwell, 1924

Bord, Janet and Colin, *Mysterious Britain*, Grafton Books, 1972

Brooksmith, Peter (ed.), *The Unexplained*, Orbis Publishing

Caruana, Wally, *Aboriginal Art*, Thames and Hudson, 1993

Coe, Michael D, *Mexico*, Thames and Hudson, 1988

Courtauld, Caroline, *In Search of Burma*, Frederick Muller, 1984

Forbes, Robert, *An Account of the Chapel of Roslin 1778*, Edinburgh, 2000 (originally James Murray, 1778)

Grant, Will, *Rosslyn*, Dysart & Rosslyn Estates (undated)

Harpur, James, *Atlas of Sacred Places*, Cassell, 1994

Heyerdahl, Thor, *The Kon-Tiki Expedition*, Allen & Unwin, 1950

Landsburg, A and S, *In Search of Ancient Mysteries*, Corgi, 1974

Langley, Myrtle, *World Religions*, Lion, 1993

Le Quintrec, Charles, *The Stones of Carnac*, Ouest France, 1980

Lilliu, Giovanni, 'Sardinia's Origins' (in: *Sardinia – The Future Has Ancient Roots*), Italia Turistica, 2000

Lincoln, Henry, *The Holy Place*, Jonathan Cape, 1991

Maltwood, Katherine, *A Guide to Glastonbury's Temple of the Stars*, James Clarke, 1929

Mudrooroo, *Aboriginal Mythology*, Aquarian, 1994

Palmer, Martin and Palmer, Nigel, *Sacred Britain*, Piatkus, 1997

Queally, Jackie, *The Lothians Unveiled*, Celtic Trails Scotland, 2000

Roberts, Anthony, *Glastonbury: Ancient Avalon, New Jerusalem*, Ryder, 1978

Robins, Joyce, *The World's Greatest Mysteries*, Chancellor, 1989

Robinson, Roland, *Aboriginal Myths and Legends*, Hamlyn, 1969

Rosslyn, Earl of, *Rosslyn Chapel*, Rosslyn Chapel Trust, 1997

Scarre, Chris, (ed), *Times Archaeology of the World*, Times Books, 1999

Smart, Ninian, *The World's Religions*, Cambridge University Press, 1989

Story, Ronald, *The Space Gods Revealed*, New English Library, 1978

Stowe, Judith A, *Siam becomes Thailand*, Honolulu: University of Hawaii Press, 1991

Sykes, Homer, *Mysterious Britain*, Weidenfeld & Nicolson, 1993

Tettoni, Luca, (photo), *Myanmar Style*, Thames & Hudson, 1998

Tournavitou, Iphiyenia, *The Ivory Houses at Mycenae*, British School at Athens, 1995

Tull, George F, *Traces of the Templars*, King's England Press, 2000

Vaughan-Thomas, Wynford and Hales, Michael, *Secret Landscapes*, Webb & Bower, 1980

Westwood, Jennifer, *Albion*, Granada, 1985

Wilson, Colin and Grant, John, *Mysteries*, Chancellor, 1994

Wilson, Colin, *Atlas of Holy Places & Sacred Sites*, Dorling Kindersley, 1996

Wilson, Colin, *From Atlantis to the Sphinx*, Virgin, 1997

Wilson, Damon, (ed), *The Giant Book of Lost Worlds*, Parragon, 1998

INDEX OF PLACE NAMES

CONTACT US

by letter to:
The Leys
2C Leyton Road
Harpenden
Herts
England
AL5 2TL

or by fax:
01582 461979

or by e-mail:
johnandanne@paranormalworldwide.com

The authors' website can be accessed:
www.paranormalworldwide.com